Managing the primary school

Joan Dean

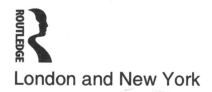

London and New York

First published 1987 by Croom Helm
Reprinted by Routledge 1989, 1990
11 New Fetter Lane, London EC4P 4EE

This edition published 1995
by Routledge

Simultaneously published in the USA and Canada
by Routledge
29 West 35th Street, New York, NY 10001

Typeset in Palatino by LaserScript, Mitcham, Surrey
Printed and bound in Great Britain by
Mackays of Chatham PLC, Chatham, Kent

British Library Cataloguing in Publication Data
A catalogue record for this book is available from the British Library

Library of Congress Cataloging in Publication Data
A catalogue record for this book has been requested

ISBN 0–415–11293–1

Managing the primary school

This new edition of *Managing the Primary School* brings up-to-date the discussion of the tasks and skills which are central to the role of the headteacher. Like the first edition, this book deals with all aspects of that role, taking into account the implications of the Education Reform Act and the National Curriculum.

Each chapter considers a particular area of running a school with chapters covering children's development, the curriculum, staff selection, development and appraisal, and interpersonal skills and communication. The book also examines the changing relationships with parents and governors and the headteacher's involvement with marketing the school and managing the budget. Throughout, Joan Dean reviews recent research into the relevant areas, paying particular attention to studies of effective schools.

This book will be invaluable to all headteachers in primary schools and also to other members of management teams, advisers, inspectors and consultants working with primary schools.

Joan Dean has worked as a teacher, lecturer and headteacher and has been senior primary adv'   for Berkshire and chief inspector for Surrey. She now works   a free   consultant and was awarded the OBE in 1980 for he.   She has written many books including *Managing the Secondary School* (Routledge 1993), *Inspecting and Advising* (Routledge 1992) and *Organising Learning in the Primary Classroom* (Routledge 1992).

Educational management series

Series editor: Cyril Poster

Managing the Primary School
Joan Dean

Schools, Parents and Governors: A New Approach to Accountability
Joan Sallis

Partnership in Education Management
Edited by Cyril Poster and Christopher Day

Management Skills in Primary Schools
Les Bell

Special Needs in the Secondary Schools: The Whole School Approach
Joan Dean

The Management of Special Needs in Ordinary Schools
Edited by Neville Jones and Tim Southgate

Creating An Excellent School: Some New Management Techniques
Hedley Beare, Brian Caldwell and Ross Millikan

Teacher Appraisal: A Guide to Training
Cyril and Doreen Poster

Time-Constrained Evaluation
Brian Wilcox

Performance-related Pay in Education
Edited by Harry Tomlinson

Evaluation in Schools: Getting Started on Training and Implementation
Glyn Rogers and Linda Badham

Managing Change in Schools
Colin Newton and Tony Tarrant

Managing Teams in Secondary Schools
Les Bell

Managing Evaluation in Education
Kath Aspinwall, Tim Simkins, John F. Wilkinson and M. John McAuley

Education for the Twenty-First Century
Hedley Beare and Richard Slaughter

Education 16–19: In Transition
Eric MacFarlane

Parents and Schools: Customers, Managers or Partners?
Edited by Pamela Munn

Opting for Self-Management
Brent Davies and Lesley Anderson

Managing External Relations in Schools
Edited by Nick Foskett

School-based Management and School Effectiveness
Edited by Clive Dimmock

Effective Schooling for the Community
Tony Townsend

Contents

List of illustrations   vi
Foreword   vii

1 Leadership and management   1

2 The school development plan   20

3 The children   36

4 The curriculum   53

5 Organisation   73

6 Managing change   89

7 Marketing the school   98

8 School administration   105

9 Managing children's behaviour and social education   120

10 Managing people   130

11 Skills with people   146

12 Communication   162

13 Staff selection and professional development   178

14 School and community   200

15 Evaluation   220

16 Personal organisation   231

References   241
Index   246

Illustrations

FIGURES

1.1	The tasks and skills of management	14–17
2.1	School analysis	26–9
2.2	Network analysis	31
4.1	The curriculum	54
4.2	Planning the curriculum	60
4.3	Year planner	63
4.4	Unit planner	64–5
6.1	Preconditions for change	93
8.1	Major administrative tasks	107–8
12.1	Information needed by adults in the school	166
12.2	Information needed by teachers	166
12.3	Information needed by teachers with additional responsibilities	167
12.4	Information needed by the headteacher	167
12.5	Information needed by ancillary staff	168
12.6	Information needed by children	169
12.7	Curriculum information needed by children	169
12.8	General information needed by children	170
12.9	Information needed by governors	170
12.10	Information needed by parents	172
15.1	Assessments and performance indicators	224–6

TABLES

4.1	A guide for planning the time allocated for each subject in each year	61

Foreword

The usefulness of Joan Dean's books to teachers and all involved in education is attested by their popularity. This volume, although described as a second edition of a work previously published by Routledge in 1987, is virtually a new work since it covers the changing circumstances of so many of our schools. If it was helpful then, it is doubly so now. The pressure headteachers and their senior staff are under to manage a vastly increased range of skills and tasks needs support of a high order. Local education authority staff are being pared to the bone, and much of the support that they once gave must now come from elsewhere. The practical nature of the contents of this book recognises that need, but also understands the constraints under which schools now operate. It therefore provides much in the way of advice and self-help check lists that enable schools to monitor and evaluate their work effectively without the need for complex and time-consuming processes. This is a book that should be in every staff library.

Cyril Poster

Chapter 1

Leadership and management

There is now a good deal of evidence to confirm the view that in any school the leadership determines the quality of what happens (e.g. Fullan and Stiegelbauer 1991, Mortimore *et al.* 1988). It is, of course, possible to find excellent teachers in indifferent schools, but unusual to find work of quality taking place throughout the school unless the headteacher and others in larger schools are offering appropriate leadership.

In a small school the headteacher's leadership may be sufficient to influence the whole school, but as the school grows larger there is a need for good leadership at other levels and the overall quality depends upon the ability of the headteacher to delegate and the ability of other teachers to lead their colleagues. There is a sense in which all teachers have some managerial responsibilities. Teachers manage children in the classroom. They also take part in management activities if the school works on the basis of involving the whole staff in making major decisions.

The small size of primary schools in comparison with secondary schools makes it possible for good headteachers to lead by example. They are very much members of the staff team and are in daily contact with all the staff in a way which is impossible in the average secondary school. They are able to influence incidentally throughout the day and draw the staff together as a team, which if they are skilled and fortunate, will help to create a common vision of where the school is going which inspires everyone's work and gives it coherence. It is this opportunity to work as a team which has created some of the most excellent primary schools.

Alexander defined successful primary headteachers as 'those who remained in close touch with classroom realities and teachers' everyday concerns, who valued and developed individual staff potential and encouraged collective decision making' (Alexander 1992 149).

Some outstanding primary headteachers can almost instinctively create a team and help it to function, just as a few outstanding teachers work instinctively and need little training. However, most people are less gifted and need to learn some of the skills involved in leadership and management if they are to fulfil their potential as headteachers or as leaders at other levels in the school.

It is also easy when a school is small to feel that there is no need for systems for managing its affairs. The Department for Education (DFE) paper *Good management in small schools* makes the point that:

> Planning is no less important in a primary school of 30 pupils than in a secondary school of 1,300. Indeed in some ways the smaller the school, the more important it is to stand back and ensure that there is a clear line of vision of direction, responsibilities and priorities.
>
> (DFE 1993: 4)

Leadership and management in schools today are not easy. The legislation of the past few years has increased the load of headteachers and senior staff very significantly and they are under pressure from many sources. There are unending demands upon time and energy and there are times when the load is very heavy. Fortunately there are other times when things seem to go well and a headteacher can begin to feel that his or her work has actually made a difference to the way staff develop children's learning.

Being a leader means knowing where one is going and working to achieve a shared vision with colleagues. Beare *et al.* describe this as:

> A mental picture of a preferred future – which is shared with all the school community and which shapes the programme for learning and teaching as well as policies, plans and procedures pervading the day to day life of the school.
>
> (Beare *et al.* 1989: 100)

Fullan and Hargreaves make the point that:

> Vision building should be a two way street where heads learn as much as they contribute to others . . . . The head's visions should be provisional and open to change. They should be part of the collaborative mix. The authority of the head's views should not be presumed because of whose views they are but because of their quality and richness . . . . Collaboration means creating the vision together, not complying with the head's own.
>
> (Fullan and Hargreaves 1991: 119–20, 123)

The vision must be about children learning. This is the first and most important aim for all schools. All other aspects of the school are subsidiary to this. The appearance of the school and the classrooms, the structure of the staffing, the way the money is spent are all means to this end and this needs to be kept clearly in everyone's mind.

A headteacher and some senior members of staff in larger primary schools are also managers. Being a manager means getting things done which lead to the realisation of the vision through and with other people. One criterion by which managers might be judged is their effectiveness in delegating tasks and enabling others to carry them to a successful conclusion. Alexander (1992) describing the the Leeds Primary Needs Programme noted that in a number of schools the head's vision of education was very different from the reality within the school. This suggests that it is important for staff to work together to achieve the overall vision of the school and to consider together how it is to be achieved.

The word 'manager' used in the context of education is comparatively new. Yet it is in many ways descriptive of what is involved. Good management means accepting people and resources as they are and helping them to develop and work together to agreed ends. The skilled manager looks for ways in which the interests and abilities of each individual can contribute to the good of the whole and he or she tries to create an organisation and a climate in which this can happen.

There is a good deal known about management which has relevance for schools. Fayol (1949), a mining engineer, suggested that management had five elements – forecasting and planning, organisation, command, coordination and control. He also pointed out that there are two kinds of authority: that which derives from the office held and that which derives from personal ability and experience; both are needed for successful management. Authority is the power to issues instructions and obtain compliance with them. Responsibility automatically rests where authority is exercised.

This is evident and relevant in schools. As headteacher you have authority in the simple sense (defined above) because of the office you hold, but your effectiveness depends a good deal on your personal experience and abilities.

There is a built-in responsibility for others in any management role, which in schools is not only a supervisory responsibility, but essentially a responsibility for supporting the people for whom one is responsible.

The DFE paper quoted above suggests that schools need a management framework:

> A management framework is a defined set of relationships and responsibilities within an organisation. It establishes accountability and provides clarity for individuals within the organisation by answering the basic questions of 'who does what?' and 'who is responsible for what?'
>
> (DFE 1993: 7)

WHAT IS EFFECTIVE LEADERSHIP?

Headteachers of primary schools are very often appointed because they have been successful classroom teachers. Those appointing headteachers generally look for good thinking about primary education along with appropriate skill and experience as a teacher and some experience of leading adults.

Being a good leader and manager in school or elsewhere is more than being good at the job being managed. You may be an excellent classroom teacher but this does not automatically mean that you will be a good headteacher. Skill in the classroom may at first win the respect of other staff but unless you acquire skill in leading a group of adults, this respect will be dissipated all too rapidly.

Caldwell and Spinks (1988: 31) list the following qualities of leadership in a headteacher who:

- enables the sharing of duties and resources to occur in an efficient manner
- ensures that resources are allocated in a manner consistent with educational needs
- is responsive to and supportive of the needs of teachers
- encourages staff involvement in professional development programmes and makes use of the skills teachers acquire in these programmes
- has a high level of awareness of what is happening in the school
- establishes effective relationships with the Education Department [the Local Education Authority], the community, teachers and students
- has a flexible administrative style
- is willing to take risks
- provides a high level of feedback to teachers
- ensures that a continual review of the school programme occurs and that progress towards goals is evaluated.

(Caldwell and Spinks 1988: 31)

All leaders have to live with other people's view of their role. Everyone connected with the school will have ideas about what you ought to do and they will exert pressure on you to conform to their expectations. You have to reconcile these views with your own view of your role, re-membering that initially confidence is engendered when a person behaves in expected ways.

You need to select carefully the issues over which you are prepared to take unusual and sometimes unpopular steps. It is not a sign of strength to insist when everyone is passionately opposed to what is being suggested. It often means that those concerned spend a great deal of time grumbling when they might be doing something more positive. The art is to select the time when there is enough going for an innovation to allow it to succeed. This is discussed in more detail in the chapter on managing change.

The ability to lead is not just a quality of personality which you either do or do not possess, although some people have achieved a great deal because of personal charisma and the vision they set before their followers. Leadership involves performing specific tasks. You may find it easier to perform these tasks if you have certain personal qualities and these qualities may be cultivated to some extent, but it may be more profitable to consider the skills and knowledge needed to perform specific leadership tasks effectively and to concentrate on these. You may well develop appropriate personality traits for the job by cultivating the skills needed to perform the tasks involved.

The style of leadership in primary schools has changed considerably in recent years. The headteacher is no longer expected to carry out the leadership task alone and it is usual for other teachers and very often governors also to be involved in the process of setting goals and creating policies as well as considering how these will be achieved. The size of most primary schools makes it possible to involve most teachers in this kind of discussion and this makes the task of leadership of a primary school rather different from that of a secondary school. This still leaves you as the overall leader but if you involve others in the tasks of management you will be supported by your colleagues who will see many of the decisions as their own. This reduces the pressure on you, and in sharing the tasks of leadership, you are preparing others for the task of leadership in their turn. It is also worth noting that since the human brain can hold only a limited number of ideas at one time, the decision taken by a group is likely to be the result of having considered a larger number of possibilities than the decision taken by an individual.

What do we know about effective leadership in school? The Department of Education and Science paper on school development plans (DES 1991a) notes that the headteacher plays the most important role in getting management right. It suggests that this is likely to be most effective when the headteacher:

- has a mission for the school
- inspires commitment to the school's mission, and so gives direction and purpose to its work
- coordinates the work of the school by allocating roles and delegating responsibilities
- is actively and visibly involved in planning and implementing change, but . . .
- is ready to delegate and to value the contribution of colleagues
- is a skilled communicator, keeping everyone informed about important decisions and events
- has the capacity to stand back from daily life in order to challenge what is taken for granted, to anticipate problems and spot opportunities
- is committed to the school, its members and its reputation, but . . .

- objectively appraises strengths and weaknesses so as to build upon the best of current practices in remedying deficiencies
- emphasises the quality of teaching and learning, lesson by lesson and day by day
- has high expectations of all staff and all students
- recognises that support and encouragement are needed for everyone to give of their best.

There are a number of ways you can view the tasks of management and leadership. The DES booklets on development planning (1989, 1991) stress the need for evaluation or audit, then planning, then action with these three repeated in a cycle each year or more frequently if necessary.

The successful leader supports individuals and makes them feel of value. This involves discussion with members of a team and a policy of encouragement which may be critical in a supportive way. Your encouragement is important to all teachers and other staff as well as to children and it is important to see that everyone who works in the school is encouraged from time to time.

A team is formed of individuals and will be successful only if the individuals learn to work together. Your task is to encourage the feeling of belonging to a team, of mutual trust, support and cooperation.

The support of individuals and of the team is undertaken in order to perform tasks. This gives purpose to the activity and provides criteria for judging success. The overall task for the school is the learning and development of the children.

Charles Handy (1976: 96) suggests that there are four sets of influencing factors which a leader must take into consideration:

- The leader's own preferred style and personal characteristics
- The preferred style of leadership by the subordinates in the light of circumstances
- The task, its objectives and technology
- The environment, the organisational setting, the group and the importance of the task.

He suggests a 'best fit' approach with the view that leadership will be most effective when the requirements of the leader, the subordinates and the task fit together.

All researches about effectiveness must start by considering how to define what is effective. The basic criteria are what happens to the children in the school and how well they perform. A great deal is involved in this. As headteacher or senior member of staff you have to work through other people, so effectiveness in this case will also be concerned with ability to manage and motivate people and to organise the work of the school, so that the children achieve as well as possible.

Effective leadership is strongly linked to what is known about effective schools. A good deal of research has been done in this field and most of it stresses the importance of the quality of the leadership. Fullan and Stiegelbauer (1991), for example, identify four factors underlying successful improvement processes in schools. The leadership has a feel for the improvement process and there is a guiding value system, together with a great deal of interaction and collaborative planning and implementation. They suggest that the effective school is one that is ready for change,

Reid *et al.* (1987: 18) describing a school improvement project thought the following eight factors to be characteristic of the effective school:

- curriculum focussed leadership
- supportive climate in the school
- emphasis on curriculum and instruction
- clear goals and high expectation for children
- a system for monitoring performance and achievement
- on-going staff development and in-service
- parental involvement and support
- LEA support

Mortimore *et al.* (1988) in a study of London junior schools found that the length of time a headteacher had been in post was significant in relation to the effectiveness of the school. Headteachers were at their most effective in their influence on children's progress when they had been in the school between three and eleven years. Mortimore *et al.* (1988: 248) also found eleven factors associated with a school which is effective not only in terms of children's achievement but also in terms of their overall development. These were as follows:

1 Purposeful leadership of the staff by the headteacher
2 The involvement of the deputy head [and the extent to which the deputy head enjoys delegated responsibilities]
3 The involvement of the teachers [in the curriculum planning and the overall life of the school]
4 Consistency among teachers [in their approaches]
5 Structured sessions [where there is a framework within which children can work]
6 Intellectually challenging teaching
7 A work-centred environment [in which teachers spent time discussing work with children]
8 A limited focus within sessions
9 Maximum communication between teachers and pupils
10 Record keeping [in which teachers keep written records of each child's work and progress]
11 Positive climate

Overall the researches seem to suggest that the effective school has an effective headteacher who works collaboratively with the staff, sharing with them a vision of where the school is going and placing emphasis on achievement. Many studies seem to show that the school 'culture' is important for effectiveness.

Beare *et al.* (1989) suggest that the culture of the school can be enhanced in various ways. It is essentially a matter of shared values. They also suggest that a school needs heroes in the life of the school or in society who exemplify the shared values. Shared values may also be experienced in the form of repeated rituals and ceremonies.

Deal describes the culture of an organisation as follows:

> Culture is an expression that tries to capture the informal, implicit – often unconscious – side of business or any human enterprise. Although there are many definitions of the term, culture in everyday usage is typically described as 'the way we do things here'. It consists of patterns of thought, behaviour and artefacts that symbolise and give meaning to the workplace. Meaning derives from the elements of culture; shared values and beliefs, heroes and heroines, ritual and ceremony, stories, and an informal network of cultural players. Effective businesses show a remarkable consistency across these cultural elements.

He goes on to develop this further in relation to schools:

> In school [where] diverse expectations, political vulnerability, and the lack of tangible products make values, beliefs and faith crucial in determining success, the development of a solid culture is even more important than it might be in business.
>
> (Deal 1985: 608)

A paper by Hallinger and Murphy (1986) suggests that effective North American schools operate differently according to the social background of their children. Schools with children whose background is of high socio-economic status are supported in their expectations of children by the expectations of parents. Where the background of children is of low socio-economic status this is not so and the school has to set its own expectations. In this context the effective principal was forceful in establishing high expectations and standards and there was much use of rewards for children using devices like exhibitions of 'children of the month' and frequent use of assemblies and honour rolls and public lists which recognised academic achievement, improvement, citizenship, attendance and behaviour. This was not needed in the schools with high socio-economic background.

As headteacher, you also work on the boundary of the school, interacting with those outside it and relating to what happens within to the outside. Your effectiveness as headteacher must therefore also be concerned with your ability to manage the boundary. This has become much more important with the changed role of governors stemming from the Education Reform Act (1988). Managing the boundary means learning to work with governors so that they really contribute to the school and feel part of it. Managing the boundary from other points of view may mean controlling it so that the school benefits from the good effects of what is outside and is protected from the adverse effects.

Effectiveness as a leader might be defined more broadly in terms of the ability to draw together a community of people in pursuit of common goals. It involves inspiring, stimulating, motivating, directing and influencing as well as providing an organisation which supports the work in hand. The effective leader draws together the parts of the organisation and ensures that they all contribute to shared aims.

When you first take on a managerial role it is not easy to assess and come to terms with the positional power of the new post. Sometimes people under-estimate the effect of their new authority and may be surprised that suddenly, since promotion, their words and actions have an added weight. Conversely, some people over-estimate what the new role allows them to do in over-riding the views and ideas of others. In fact any position allows a person to do some things but the trust and confidence of colleagues must be won in order to do others. New leaders would be wise to fulfil people's expectations of someone holding their post before attempting to do much which is new and unusual.

The power vested in those in leadership roles is bound up to some extent with their ability to provide sticks and carrots as a result of the executive power vested in the office. Headteachers now have greater influence over salaries and promotion than formerly, but there are many other forms of reward which are important to people, including praise and encouragement, the offer of additional responsibilities, the chance to shine, additional resources, together with disapproval and withdrawal of opportunities. The evidence generally suggests that reward is more effective than punishment for adults as well as children.

The National Association of Secondary School Principals paper (NASSP 1982: 4) looks at studies concerned with leadership behaviour which identify six important leadership functions:

1 develop goals, policies and directions
2 organise the school and design programmes to accomplish the goals
3 monitor progress, solve problems and maintain order
4 procure, manage and allocate resources
5 create a climate for personal and professional growth and development
6 represent the school to the district office and the outside world.

The same paper also stressed the value of a high level of expectation on the part of the principal:

In high achieving schools, principals did not let teachers 'write off' children as non-learners particularly because of their race or social class. In low achieving schools the principal helped to depress the teachers' expectations of their children by saying, for example, that they weren't doing too badly for children of their background. Furthermore, the principal's lack of 'push' towards the teacher was carried over into the classroom by teachers who, in turn, expected little of their children.

(NASSP 1982: 23)

They also found that a recurrent characteristic of successful schools was the amount of respect shown to teachers and children. Here the principal set the tone. They found too that where the principal took a strong interest in the quality of teaching this encouraged change and development in teaching methods. Principals also set the tone for discipline in school.

This was confirmed by Rutter *et al.* (1979) who found that in the higher achieving schools the headteacher helped to set the general discipline standards for the whole school. Headteachers set standards by what they singled out for comment, whether praise or criticism, and by their own behaviour.

The NASSP study also found that successful principals evaluated the work of the school against its agreed goals. In Britain the Education Reform Act (1988) has ensured that evaluation plays a much larger part in the work of teachers and headteachers than it did formerly. The school development plan requires evaluation and there has for some time been a stress on the value of self-evaluation. The DES booklets *Planning for school development* (1989a) and *Development planning – A practical guide* (1991a) both suggest auditing the current state of a school as a preliminary to building the development plan.

Marshall and Mitchell (1989) found that women were more attuned to curriculum issues, instructional leadership, teachers' concerns, parental involvement, staff development, collaborative planning strategies, community building and the like. They concluded that women were more likely to possess characteristics associated with effective leadership in schools than men. This would seem to be an argument for the appointment of more women to leadership positions in this country too!

MANAGEMENT STYLE

When people move into leadership and management roles in school, their experience of possible styles of management is usually limited. Most people have seen only a small number of headteachers or senior staff at work and these may represent a limited range of models. As leader you have to apply to the performance of leadership and management tasks;

your abilities, personal qualities, views of the role and the circumstances in which you are working. The particular mixture of approaches and behaviour you choose becomes a style of management which develops slowly as you become more experienced.

When people first take on management roles, they draw on the models they have known, however unsuitable these may be, because this is all the information they have. A person may copy behaviour observed in others or react against it. As time goes by, each person discovers what works for him or her, and becoming more confident in the leadership role, gradually develops a style which enables other people to predict his or her reactions. This makes for trusting relationships and makes everyone's work easier, because they do not need to find out what the leader thinks every time they take action.

An aspiring manager needs to study a variety of models, looking for ways of dealing with situations and people, and for aspects of management and leadership style which may be appropriate for him or her. You need to study deliberately how other people do the job and select from what you observe a way in which you feel it is possible to work. Within the school this kind of opportunity should be part of staff development for middle managers.

One way you can set about the process of working out your own style is to take a hard look at your strengths and limitations, perhaps involving someone else with close knowledge of your work, in the process. There are many successful ways of leading and managing and how people actually behave in practice is a mixture of their ideas and personality.

A headteacher has to decide how far to be democratic and how far autocratic. The democratic process can be slow and people may become impatient, particularly if they have been used to an autocratic style of leadership. It may, in some circumstances, be better to be more autocratic at the beginning of headship than you may wish to be later, if this is what people expect and are used to.

Most schools are gradually moving towards a more collegiate mode of operation and few headteachers now work in isolation. The leadership of schools is usually in the hands of a senior management team rather than a single person. In the case of the small school, this may be a matter of the whole staff working together. Democratic forms of leadership offer good staff development opportunities because in order to make a sensible decision a group needs to study the situation carefully. It is also valuable to involve children in some decision making, since part of the school's task is to train young people for life in a democratic society. Some involvement of parents and governors may also be valuable.

It is also necessary to consider those matters which can be decided by the headteacher or headteacher and senior staff or governors, and those which require the full involvement of the rest of the staff.

People differ in the extent to which they like to work out why they should follow a particular course of action. Many leaders make very good decisions by hunch or intuition which is perhaps another name for sensitivity to others and to the situation. It is the kind of sensitivity which leads a person to sense the best thing to do at a level below that of conscious thought. There is, nevertheless, a need today for a clear rationale both for what the school as a whole is doing and for different parts of its work. Too much is questioned by children, parents, governors and the community to make it possible to arrive at decisions without clear reasoning behind them. People holding senior posts in a school should be able to support practice with theoretical explanations or reasoned argument. They also need to have some kind of theoretical frame of reference in order to be able to judge new developments. On the other hand, it is all too easy, if your mind works that way, to spend a lot of time theorising and yet be unable to put the theory into practice. A balance is needed.

A person whose vision is strong needs to be careful to pay enough attention to the ideas of others. If you find that no one else seems to have ideas you should be suspicious about whether you are welcoming the ideas that are offered. When you first take up a new appointment people may be slow to offer ideas, but if they go on being slow, it is probably your fault. One of your tasks is to help everyone to be more fluent in having ideas and carrying them through.

A slightly different problem is when you have lots of very good ideas. If you do not limit those offered at any one time or limit them to those people who can take them, others will start to take the view that 'it isn't any use the rest of us thinking of things because he/she is sure to have a much better idea'.

This isn't an easy situation for a leader. Sometimes it will be necessary to stand back and watch people struggling through to the idea you started off with. Sometimes you will realise that by speaking instead of keeping quiet, you have stifled a possible idea before it came to birth.

THE TASKS AND SKILLS OF MANAGEMENT

The Project on the Selection of Secondary Headteachers POST Project, the study of the appointment of secondary school headteachers (Morgan *et al.* 1983), found that most appointing committees were inclined to consider the personality of candidates rather than their skills and experience of the tasks involved in headship. This is familiar to many people who have been involved in the appointment of headteachers and others. Adjectives like 'hard-working' and 'enthusiastic' are likely to be used in discussing candidates along with phrases like 'intellectually able', 'makes good relationships', 'strong personality' and so on. Interviewing panels will also be considering the appropriateness of an individual's experience, knowledge and competence. However, when the decision is being made, qualities of personality are well to the fore as criteria. This has changed a little in some areas as a result of the POST Project, but governing bodies are now responsible for the appointment of headteachers and unless they contain people used to industrial methods of appointment, may still place most emphasis on personality.

This is, of course, a very proper concern in making an appointment. The personality of a headteacher is crucial to his or her success but it should not be the only criterion. Appointing committees need to remember that any managerial post involves the ability to undertake specific tasks and the appointing committee needs to ensure that the successful candidate has experience of a number of them, and has the kind of approach and skill which will enable him or her to learn where the tasks are new.

When a teacher is appointed to a post of responsibility the appointing committee has to judge whether a candidate possesses or will be able to learn the skills to perform successfully in the new role The judgement for middle management posts may have to be based on the teacher's performance in the classroom which may or may not be a good predictor of ability to manage adults. In more senior posts candidates will have experience of managing adults and the selection procedure should find out how successfully each candidate was able to do this.

It is perhaps easier to make judgements about this if one starts from the tasks involved in a given post and considers the skill and knowledge likely to be required for their successful performance. This kind of analysis is also useful in training people for posts of responsibility and may provide an opportunity for self-assessment for those aspiring to senior posts.

The precise nature and the distribution of management tasks may vary from one school to another and different people will undertake them in different ways, but the broad outline of the tasks at each level is roughly similar.

The list which follows outlines some of the tasks of leadership and management. These are not all tasks for the headteacher but tasks for the senior management of the school as well. Similar lists could be given for teachers with other levels of responsibility. Management also involves specific skills and those are listed in the last column of the table.

Many of these skills and much of the knowledge required has its counterpart in the classroom. When you first come to a senior post in school you have to learn to adapt your knowledge of managing children to managing adults. By the time you reach headship you should have had experience in other senior posts and possess many of the skills required to undertake the tasks listed (see p. 14–17). The process is ideally a continuous one from being a manager in the classroom to managing a

	TASKS	SKILLS
The school development plan	Articulate aims for the school Ensure that aims are considered and reviewed Draw up the school development plan Articulate and implement policies	Presentation Communication Negotiation Leading discussion Decision making Planning Evaluation
The children	Ensure that the developmental needs of children are considered Ensure that there is intellectual challenge Ensure that there is provision for the most and least able Monitor the development of each child See that there are equal opportunities for all Ensure that there is provision for social, moral and spiritual development	Observation Communication Planning Evaluation
The curriculum	Articulate the curriculum philosophy of the school Ensure that the National Curriculum is implemented and that religious education is provided See that cross curricular themes and dimensions are provided Maintain oversight of continuity and coherence Encourage curriculum development	Presentation Communication Planning Negotiation Decision making Evaluation

Figure 1.1 The tasks and skills of management

	TASKS	SKILLS
Organisation	Organise the school effectively for teaching and learning Develop an effective management structure Deploy staff effectively Ensure the effective use of time, space and resources	Presentation Communication Negotiation Discussion leadership Problem solving Decision making Planning Delegation Evaluation
Managing change	Identify the changes needed Assess the situation Plan and implement changes Evaluate the effectiveness of changes	
Marketing the school	Make regular surveys of parental views Analyse strengths, weaknesses, opportunities and threats Set public relations objectives Plan and implement a public relations programme Evaluate the success of the public relations programme	Communication Making surveys Analysing situations Planning Delegation Evaluation
School administration	Oversee the administrative work of the school Manage the school finances Take responsibility for the school building and environment Ensure conformity with health and safety regulations	Administration Financial management Negotiation Planning Evaluation

Figure 1.1 continued

	TASKS	SKILLS
Managing children's behaviour	Establish a philosophy of care Establish and maintain acceptable behaviour patterns Ensure provision for personal and social education Establish and maintain a record-keeping system	Observation Negotiation Discussion leadership Delegation
Managing people	Lead and motivate staff Delegate effectively Agree staff salary policy with the governors and implement Deal with staff problems Have knowledge of relevant legislation	Consultation Communication Negotiation Presentation Decision making Problem solving Interviewing Administration Appraisal
Communication	Ensure appropriate communication for everyone Create and maintain a communication system Ensure that information travels in all directions Seek information and feedback from all levels Evaluate the effectiveness of communication	

Figure 1.1 continued

	TASKS	SKILLS
Staff selection & development	Organise and assist with staff appointments Evaluate appointments procedure Establish policy for staff development and appraisal Create a development programme for all staff Evaluate the staff development programme Maintain staff records and provide any necessary reports	Interviewing Observation Appraisal Planning Organising Reporting Evaluating Communication
School and community	Represent the school to the outside world Work effectively with governors Involve parents in the work of the school Create and maintain links with contributory and transfer schools Encourage the use of the community and neighbourhood for learning	Communication Planning Organising Negotiating
Evaluation	Assess the current state of the school Establish a policy for assessment and evaluation Organise an evaluation system	Evaluation Communication Negotiation Planning

Figure 1.1 continued

school. Management ability is best acquired by practising it within the school through a gradual increase in the responsibility a teacher undertakes, and where possible working with expert and experienced colleagues and talking over performance and progress. It is the responsibility of every headteacher to see that colleagues are gradually developing their management skills so that they are ready for greater responsibility when the time comes. Opportunities for management courses should also be provided so that teachers have the chance to look more broadly at management issues and individuals can do much to improve their own performance by observing others at work and by trying out ideas.

CONCLUSION

As soon as you analyse something into its component parts it loses something of its wholeness. Being a headteacher is more than undertaking a series of tasks, however skilfully you work. You are never dealing with one thing at a time, never working to achieve only one goal. You are at the centre of a very complex series of activities in which each situation and each action contains growth possibilities for a number of goals. You have to become skilled at recognising and using situations as they arise and at recognising potential in your staff.

Analysis also suggests that activities are finite, whereas in practice the development of a school or a person is a slowly evolving process which is continuous. You plan developments and start to carry them out, and, as you work, the goals to which you thought you were working change as growth takes place and the original pattern becomes something more and new goals emerge. People change and develop and create new possibilities. And as teams develop they enlarge the experience and possibilities of their members. This happens even when there are no government interventions to change patterns of working and at the present time the changes are even more frequent and far reaching than usual.

Growth involves both assimilating new experience and the ability to see past experience in a new way. It is your task as a leader to enlarge the experience of those you lead.

Among the most important characteristics of a leader is a belief in yourself and in those you lead – a belief that everyone is in the process of growing and developing.

Behind all the thinking and research about effectiveness and leadership lies the questions 'What do we mean by effective?' What we mean by effectiveness in education depends upon what we think education is for and our definition of educated people. The National Curriculum and all that we do in addition is a means to an end, the end of creating an educated population. Our views of what constitutes an educated person should help us to evaluate what we do in school. The following is an attempt at a definition:

Educated people are those who have achieved sufficient maturity and balance as individuals and as members of society to enable them to cope with major change as well as the stresses and conflicts of daily living. They will have developed a framework of meaning for life which informs and governs their behaviour and makes it possible for them to choose and act with wisdom. They will have developed self-images which are realistic but confident, based on good knowledge of their own strengths and limitations. They will be independent in many aspects of living.

They will enjoy learning and will have developed in their initial education a sufficient understanding of the underlying ideas in the major areas of human knowledge, sufficient of the skills they require and sufficient interest in them to enable them to go on learning.

Alongside this, they will have developed more general skills of study. They will be able to think things out and will be good at solving problems, whether these are practical problems or academic ones. They will have the ability to learn from observation at first hand and by questioning other people as well as learning from books and computers. They will be able to sort out ideas and information so that they can use them to tackle problems and meet demands. They will have ideas and will know how to use them as well as being receptive to ideas from other people.

They will have developed the skills of communication to a high level in a number of modes and be able not only to speak and write fluently and appropriately but also to be skilled at communicating through computers, graphically, mathematically and through movement.

They will enjoy and practise the arts and take pleasure in fine craftsmanship. They will enjoy and care for the environment and feel responsibility towards it.

They will have learned to live with others, sensitive to them, skilled in understanding and responsible and caring in attitudes. They will have ability to cooperate and work in various roles within a group and and will have learned democratic modes of behaviour. They will have knowledge of how individuals and societies function.

Everything that happens to children, in and out of school, contributes to their development and learning. Everyone has a responsibility for the education of the young.

Chapter 2

The school development plan

AIMS

Schools are now obliged by law to state their aims. The effectiveness of the headteacher might be judged by how far the school is achieving its stated aims.

The aims of any school are complex. They are first of all concerned with the children's academic achievement. The school is not only attempting to enable children to acquire knowledge and skills but is also concerned with their socialisation, their moral behaviour, their spiritual development, their attitudes and much else besides. In addition it is concerned with the adults in the school community. A school is a learning place for everyone who works there.

Schools also need to think through their own practice and re-think and question it from time to time. The advent of the National Curriculum has created new sets of pressures for teachers which need to be taken into account. Alexander makes the following point:

> The only proper way to arrive at sustainable definitions of good educational practice is by sharing and analysing ideas and values, marshalling and examining evidence and applying both processes to the task of formulating principles.
>
> (Alexander 1992: 122)

The management tasks involved in developing aims, objectives and policies and making them reality through the school development plan are as follows:

Articulate the aims for the school
Ensure that aims are considered and reviewed
Draw up the school development plan
Articulate and implement policies

ARTICULATE THE AIMS FOR THE SCHOOL

Every school now has to make a statement about its aims and publish them for the benefit of parents and other interested members of the public. If the aims are to be to part of the thinking of governors and staff and to some extent that of parents and children, then there is a need to involve as many people as possible in arriving at the school's statement of aims. They will then need to be revised on a regular basis which means further discussion. Only new schools will be concerned about articulating aims for the first time. For most schools it will be a matter of reviewing aims annually in relation to the school development plan and various policies and documents.

At the primary stage schools are naturally very much concerned with the developing child and with the way in which the school can influence that development. Schools also prepare children for the future however, both the future of later education and for adult life. Today's children will become adults in a world we can only speculate about. We know that tomorrow's world will in many ways be different from the world as we know it today and that people will probably need different skills, some of which we cannot foresee. There are many skills, qualities and much knowledge, nevertheless, which we know that tomorrow's adults will need, some because they are part of being a human being and some because of their general applicability.

In this context it may be helpful to consider a number of criteria in relation to the school aims.

Curriculum

It is suggested that as part of the curriculum the school should be concerned with children:

- learning within the National Curriculum
- preparing for life in a multi-cultural, multi-lingual world and for closer links with Europe
- developing the skills of communication, numeracy, study, problem solving, personal and social behaviour and information technology
- having economic and industrial understanding
- developing concern for their own health through health education
- preparing for adult life through education in citizenship
- acquiring knowledge of religious education

Personal and social development

In addition schools need to be concerned with children:

- acquiring self-knowledge and developing as people
- learning to live and work with others
- having concern for equal opportunities for all
- preparing for adult life by learning about the world of work
- preparing for parenthood
- developing concern for the environment
- acquiring a framework of meaning for life and a value system
- developing positive attitudes and self-esteem

Staff development and community relationships

A school also needs to have aims for the adults and for its relationship with parents and with the community. The following areas need to be developed:

- the work of teachers and other adults
- the school's public image
- relationships with parents
- relationships with contributory schools
- relationships with schools to which children transfer
- relationships with the local community

The school building and environment

In addition the school will need a programme of improvement to the school building and environment and for the purchase of equipment. This will also be part of the school development plan.

ENSURE THAT AIMS ARE CONSIDERED AND REVIEWED

If these aims are to be part of everyone's thinking about the school there will be a need to consider how they can be achieved. When aims are initially arrived at, everyone can be involved in considering them, but as time goes on those who were initially involved may forget the experience and new people will have joined who were not part of the original discussion. You need to have ways of building consideration of aims into the work of the school so that they are kept before people.

One way of doing this is to ask that plans each year from each teacher show how the work is related to the school aims. The school development plan itself must show this, and this will help people to keep aware of the aims. It may be a good idea to put them in the governors' report to parents each year so that parents are kept aware of what the school is setting out to do. In short, every opportunity for reminding people of the school's aims needs to be taken.

Aims need to be turned into practical objectives which can be seen to be achieved and in turn become plans for work. These will be part of the school development plan and part of the plans of each teacher within the school and for each subject within the curriculum.

While the school's aims should inform the school development plan and it should be clear that the development plan fulfils the aims, it needs to be stated much more in terms of objectives. For example, a school aiming at good relations with its local secondary school might include in its objectives statements such as the following:

1 All teachers of the final primary year should know the work of the first year of the secondary school in the major curriculum areas. Curriculum coordinators should also know this in their subject areas.
2 There should be at least three occasions in the year when the teachers of the final year of the primary school and the appropriate curriculum coordinators meet the teachers of the first year of the secondary school to discuss the curriculum and individual children.
3 All curriculum coordinators should be familiar with the thinking of the heads of the appropriate departments in the secondary school.
4 All teachers of the final year of the primary school should have visited the secondary school and seen teaching in action. If possible the reverse should happen also (This would, of course, be more difficult where there are a number of secondary schools to which children transfer).

These statements can be turned into direct action and the action can be seen to be achieved. These are the terms in which the school development plan needs to be written. If objectives have success criteria written at the same time there will be no danger that they are stated in too loose a form and the success criteria will provide for evaluation at a later stage.

Aims and objectives need to be accepted by those whom they concern. Those who have taken part in formulating aims or who have been involved in turning aims into objectives are more likely to accept them and make them part of their work and this is particularly important where teachers are concerned.

The statement of aims must also recognise that parents and children have expectations of the school. It is helpful to involve some parents and governors in a number of your discussions and explain some of what you are doing to the children; but you will still need to explain aims to the large majority of parents and this will need doing each year as new children come into the school. Teachers often assume that parents and children are aware of what the school is trying to do when in fact the parents assume that the school's aims are much the same as those of the school which they themselves attended.

Teachers may take the view that children do not need to know why the school works in a particular way, yet the view of school that the children take home is the one that parents most frequently meet and if you do not make it clear to children what the school is about, as far as this is possible, it is not surprising that parents misunderstand what is happening. Children often have a valuable perspective on their experience in school if we can find a way of tapping it.

The ancillary staff too are able to make a better contribution if they understand what the school is about and what is being attempted. They may also be better ambassadors for the school.

DRAW UP THE SCHOOL DEVELOPMENT PLAN

All schools are now required to produce a development plan. This has made a standard procedure of something which good schools have been doing for a long time and most LEAs have provided documents to help schools with this process. The DES published two useful papers on the school development plan (DES 1989a, 1991a) and there is much useful information in the Audit Commission paper *Managing within primary schools* (Audit Commission 1991).

There is a great deal of evidence from research into effectiveness in school which shows that effective schools work collaboratively (Little 1982, Reynolds 1985, Reid *et al.* 1987, Mortimore *et al.* 1988, Beare *et al.* 1989, Handy and Aitken 1986). The school development plan offers a particular opportunity for everyone to work together to contribute. It is worth setting aside at least one in-service education and training (INSET) day for thinking through the various parts of the plan.

Most writing about school development plans suggests that there is a cycle of reviewing the situation, planning, implementing and evaluating and then going through the same process again the following year building on the work already done. Plans also need to be both long-term and short-term, planning some activities for the coming year and others on a three or four year prediction. While the massive changes which have been coming into education do not encourage headteachers and governors to plan for the long term, there is nevertheless value in planning broadly and adapting plans as developments take place.

Reviewing the situation

Most schools will have worked through several development plans and will probably have undertaken a number of annual reviews. It is worth thinking about the best way to review annually without making this too large a task. If the school has undergone inspection since the last development plan was drawn up, this will provide material for the revised plan.

The Surrey paper on the school development plan makes the following point:

> Whatever the aspects reviewed, it is important to use a variety of ways of assessing and to look from the points of view of different groups and individuals concerned, including parents and pupils as well as the head and staff. It should also be remembered that the leader of any group tends to get information that has already been carefully filtered. It is therefore important to devise ways of getting information at first hand.
>
> (Surrey LEA 1990: 6)

A good way forward would seem to be first to identify from the previous year those areas which have shown themselves to be clearly in need of review and then to consider whether there are new areas which should also be considered. The list which follows may help in determining areas which should be investigated. One useful way of using this list would be to ask each member of staff to complete it, perhaps working with colleagues teaching the same year group or on some other basis.

The DES publication (1989a) on school development plans stressed that it is important to set the audit of the school in the context of its aims and values. A basic question is 'Have we achieved our aims?' You also need to consider whether the school is meeting the policies and initiatives of central and local government.

The second DES publication (1991a) suggested that selecting areas for audit is done by the governors on the advice of the headteacher and that carrying out the audit is the responsibility of one teacher or a team working with the headteacher. In a small primary school this is a matter for the whole staff with the headteacher coordinating. In a larger school it may well be possible to have a team led by a senior member of staff. The intention of the team is not that it does all the work. Everyone needs to have some involvement, but the team is responsible for organising the review.

The areas chosen for review should be fairly limited, with the idea that the school looks at everything over a period of several years. The plan can then be adapted year by year. There will always be areas which suggest themselves as being particularly in need of attention.

Your next task is to consider priorities among the areas selected. You may feel that some may not be urgent and could be put into the plan for a future year. Other priorities may be treated together where there is common ground among them.

Once the areas for review have been selected the team is then responsible for organising the next stage. Responsibility for different parts of the review could be given to different members of staff so that everyone is involved in some way. This needs to be drawn together and the DES

SCHOOL ANALYSIS	++	+	av	−	− −

Core and foundation subjects and RE
  Reading
  Writing
  Speaking and listening
  Mathematics
  Science
  Technology
  History
  Geography
  Art
  Music
  Physical education
  Religious education					

Skills
  communication
  numeracy
  study
  problem solving
  personal and social
  information technology					

Themes
  Economic and industrial understanding
  Personal, social and health education
  Education for citizenship
  Environmental education					

Dimensions
  Equal opportunities for boys and girls
    children of different races
    children of different ability
    children of different social background
    children with disabilities
  Multicultural education
  European education
  World education					

Curriculum continuity
  home to school
  playgroup/nursery to school
  infant/first school to junior/middle
  year to year
  teacher to teacher
  primary to secondary school					

Figure 2.1 School analysis

SCHOOL ANALYSIS	++	+	av	–	– –

Overall organisation
   teacher deployment
   grouping for learning
   provision for most able children
   provision for least able children					

Use of time
   timetable arrangements
   use of time by teachers
   use of time by children
   use of time by office staff
   use of time by other staff
   time spent on different activities					

Resources
   provision and use of:
     books
     equipment
     information technology
     space					

Arrangements for planning
and decision making
   effectiveness
   involvement of staff
   involvement of children
   involvement of governors
   involvement of parents					

Effectiveness of pastoral care Role of class teacher Children's attitudes and behaviour					
Effectiveness of record keeping Involvement of children in their records Maintenance of records Use of records					

Effectiveness of day to day
running of school
   arrangements for lunch
   arrangements for assembly
   arrangements for break times
   arrangements for wet breaks
   staff duties					

Figure 2.1 continued

SCHOOL ANALYSIS	++	+	av	−	− −

Effectiveness of administration
    work of office staff
    financial planning
    accounting
    arrangements for ordering goods and
    equipment
    correspondence					

Environment
    quality of environment
    cleanliness
    state of repair
    arrangements for dealing with
    maintenance
    state of grounds
    arrangements for grounds maintenance
    children's care of the environment
    use of environment for learning					

Communication of head and deputy with
    teaching staff
    other staff
    children
    governors
    parents
    contributory schools/playgroups
    transfer schools
    local community
    LEA
Communication among staff
Communication with children
Communication from parents
Communication of staff with governors
Communication of staff with parents					

Staff performance
    headteacher
    deputy
    curriculum coordinators
    classroom teachers
    office staff
    caretaking staff
    dining room and kitchen staff					

Figure 2.1 continued

SCHOOL ANALYSIS	++	+	av	–	– –

Staff selection and development
   arrangements for staff selection
   arrangements for needs assessment
   induction of new staff
   support for newly qualified teachers
   staff development programme for trs
   development opps for other staff
   INSET days
   arrangements for appraisal
   staff records					

Relationships with
   parents
   governors
   LEA
   contributory schools/playgroups
   transfer schools
   neighbourhood and community
Public image of the school
Arrangements for public relations					

Arrangements for evaluating
   overall curriculum
   curriculum materials
   teaching approaches
   match of curriculum to individuals
   individual progress
   record keeping
   outcome of SATs					

Arrangements for evaluating
   organisation for learning
   day-to-day organisation
   general administration
   financial administration
   pastoral care
   discipline
   planning
   communication
   staff selection
   staff development
   appraisal
   evaluation systems					

Figure 2.1 continued

paper (1991a) suggests that it is a task for the headteacher. The same paper also stresses the value of getting an external view. This will, in the first place, come from the governors, but you could get a view from external advisers.

Making the plan

Your next task is to make plans for each of the areas identified. Here again parts of the plan can be delegated to individuals and groups. For example, curriculum coordinators may be responsible for planning within their own areas and other tasks may be shared around.

You need to create a school framework for planning so that each contribution fits the overall plan. This should give the way the plan should be set out. It might include statements about the following:

- aims and objectives
- performance criteria
- plans for achieving the objectives
- implications for staff development
- the implementation plan
- responsibilities for parts of the programme
- cost in time and money
- arrangements for evaluation of the programme

Each stage of the implementation plan needs to be worked out. One useful way of doing this is to use network analysis. This involves writing down the major 'events' in the plan. These are activities which happen at a point in time, such as the following:

- the publication of a discussion paper outlining problems which need to be tackled
- a meeting to discuss the paper with a group of staff
- agreement about some action.

This will provide material to start the analysis.

The next task is to set out on paper a number of circles divided across the centre. An event is written in the top half of each circle and the bottom part gives the earliest and latest date by which each event might take place.

Between the events there will be action, sometimes several different actions running concurrently. Actions are represented by lines joining the events. These should be entered before the dates are set because the amount of time needed will depend upon how much there is to be done between events.

Lastly the dates should be entered. The finalising of dates may need to be left until the whole development plan is brought together so that

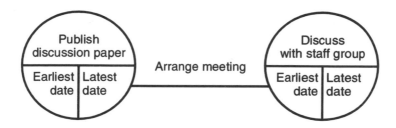

Figure 2.2 Network analysis

different parts of it can be planned in sequence, but proposed dates should be entered on the network. Dates may then need to be modified so that not too much is taking place at the same time with the same people.

Network planning is very useful as a group method of working, using a flipchart to set out the steps which need to be taken. It has the additional advantage that networks for different programmes can be placed side by side to see how they relate to each other.

Each part of the programme needs to be the responsibility of individuals or groups. It should be quite clear what each person is expected to do.

It is essential to know what the plans suggested will cost and to re-draw them until they are within the budget. It may be helpful to groups to be given a target sum for their planning with the possibility of negotiating for more if it seems necessary. This will help all teachers to be aware of the school's finances.

Thought should also be given to the time involved in any plan. Teachers' time is not elastic and there are already enormous demands upon it. If time is considered in planning there is some hope that plans will be realistic. It may also be a matter of planning so that time is made for some people to undertake development work. It may be worth spending some money on supply teaching in order to provide time for planning. You may also like to substitute for a teacher yourself in order to give that teacher time to plan. The more involved the staff become in the development plan the more likely it is that they will implement it well.

Evaluation should always be considered at the planning stage. The following should be decided:

- how the evaluation will be done
- when it will be done, including ways in which information about the success of the programme can be collected as the work takes place
- who will be responsible for it
- what kind of reporting will be needed.

Once all the sections of the plans have been set out, they need to be drawn together to make the overall plan. You then need to check to see that time is sensibly planned, that not too much is expected to happen at the same time and that costs are realistic. You may need to postpone some plans or parts of plans until a later year.

Implementing the plan

Once the plans have been agreed by the staff and by the governors they can be implemented. If each group involved has allocated responsibilities adequately this should simply be a matter of starting work on what has been planned. The Surrey paper (1990: 24) suggests a number of key questions which might be considered at this stage:

1 are individuals clear about their responsibilities in implementing the plan?
2 are the deadlines, time scales and budgetary implications clearly understood by all?
3 are success criteria (performance indicators) set for each person and each task?
4 who will monitor the outcome?

Evaluating the outcomes

Each group and individual involved in the planning needs to consider evaluation so that this can go forward alongside the work planned. There should be provision for monitoring the programme as it proceeds and each part of the plan should be the specific responsibility of one individual. Monitoring might involve discussing the progress of the plan regularly with individuals, observing work in progress, checking on children's work, looking at records and so on. Decisions need to be made at the planning stage about the frequency of the monitoring and its cost in terms of time. More detailed information about methods of evaluation is given in chapter sixteen.

There is also a need to evaluate the overall success of the plan. It will be important to consider whether the work planned was too much or too little; whether the devolution of responsibilities worked effectively; whether the monitoring and evaluation were effective; how far objectives have been achieved; whether the staff development programme was adequate to support the developments planned; whether the work done has affected children's performance.

ARTICULATE AND IMPLEMENT POLICIES

Aims and objectives are closely linked with policies. A policy might be described as a statement of the behaviour expected in a given context. Schools need to make policies explicit, setting them down as a statement of guidance for staff or children and attempting to establish a normal way of working in given circumstances. Policy statements need to be part of the staff handbook so that all staff are aware of them and some will be part of the school prospectus.

Just as aims and the school development plan need to be discussed with everyone concerned when they are being formed, so in making policies you need to involve all staff and governors and sometimes parents.

Policy statements will vary according to the subject in question but are likely to contain statements such as the following:

- the overall philosophy and principles operating in the area in question
- the attitudes expected
- the roles of those concerned
- specific arrangements needed
- the organisation of any material resources or equipment
- methods of reviewing progress and recording where appropriate
- the support available to teachers
- relevant staff development
- the place of any links with contributory schools or transfer schools.

Policies will be needed in each major area of school life. The following are suggested:

Curriculum

- what is to be taught at each level, taking the National Curriculum into account
- how the most and least able are to be dealt with
- teaching methods
- the way work is to be presented and marked

There will also be a need for policy statements for each aspect of curriculum. These should be the responsibility of the appropriate coordinator.

Organisation

- the way children are grouped for learning, the use of time and space and the reasoning behind the organisation
- staff responsibilities and relationships
- the communication system
- the organisation of the school office.

Planning and decision making

- the way the school development plan is built up
- the role of teaching and other staff in overall planning
- the decision making patterns
- the way finance is dealt with.

Pastoral care and discipline

- what is expected of teachers by way of pastoral care
- the behaviour expected from children
- how problems are to be dealt with
- children's records.

Assessment and evaluation

- what is to be assessed and how
- the part that assessment and evaluation play in the life of the school
- the way children's work and behaviour are assessed
- the way teachers and other staff are assessed and the appraisal system
- the way the headteacher's work is appraised.

Community relationships

- relationships with the governing body
- relationships with parents
- relationships with the local community
- relationships with other schools
- public relations.

Equal opportunities

- for boys and girls
- for children of different ethnic groups
- for children of different abilities
- for children with disabilities
- for children of different social backgrounds.

Staff development

- overall philosophy
- organisation for staff development
- needs assessment
- induction of new staff

- provision for supporting newly qualified teachers
- the way the staff development programme is built up
- evaluation of the staff development programme
- development opportunities in the daily life of the school.

Staff selection

- the system used to select staff.

Policies have to be implemented by the whole staff and they represent the values and vision of the school. It is therefore important that staff are involved in their development. This can provide a valuable form of in-service work for many teachers. The extent to which a headteacher devolves the writing of policies depends a good deal on the stage a school has reached in its development. There will be situations for a headteacher newly in post where the staff find the headteacher's vision very foreign and they will therefore be hesitant about spending time writing policies. In this situation it may be best for the headteacher to produce basic policies in essential areas to stand until the staff are ready to go further.

There are also other groups which may need to be consulted about policies. For example, parents will have views about the school's communication and you may find it useful to gather a small group of parents to discuss what they would like by way of communication about their children's progress and about the work of the school generally. Similarly you have to decide what it is important to discuss with governors.

Parents may also have valuable contributions to make about the pastoral care and discipline. If home and school act together on discipline, both are likely to be more effective.

Before you start on making any particular policy, you need to consider your own stance and where you would wish to stand on principle. If you know you are very much at odds with groups whose views you need to consider, it may be better to leave the policy for the time being if you can, or leave the most controversial parts of it, if you can get by for a while without making a decision. You then need to work with those people who are able to change in the direction you are seeking until there are enough people ready for a more general change.

Usually it is easier than this. There are generally sufficient people to move on many policies and you may simply need to spell out areas where you feel very strongly and make it clear which solutions you would find unacceptable, while welcoming other ideas until agreement is reached.

Chapter 3

The children

The management tasks in relation to children are as follows:

> Ensure that the developmental needs of all children are considered
> Ensure that there is intellectual challenge
> Ensure that there is provision for the most and least able
> Monitor the development of each child
> See that there are equal opportunities for all
> Ensure that there is provision for spiritual, social and moral development

ENSURE THAT THE DEVELOPMENTAL NEEDS OF ALL CHILDREN ARE CONSIDERED

It is your task as headteacher to see that all teachers consider children's needs, abilities, experiences and interests and match their teaching to the stages of development which individual children have reached.

During the primary school years children experience considerable development. They come into school at five with very varied experiences. Some will find the language of school and the behaviour expected of them comparatively familiar although there will be many new words, new behaviours and ideas for them to learn. Others will find that the teacher speaks differently from their parents and that behaviour which is accepted at home is not considered acceptable at school. Some will be ready to settle down to learning straight away. Others will need to learn to concentrate. Boys may be less ready to settle to learning than girls and demand more teacher attention because of their behaviour.

At five many children are egocentric and need to learn how to get on with other children. Those who have experienced nursery school or playgroup are at an advantage here. Gradually, as they grow older, the peer group becomes more important and they learn the social skills needed for getting on with other people. An increasing number of children have reached puberty by the time they leave the primary school.

During the primary school years children are developing as people. They are trying out different forms of behaviour and ways of relating to other people and discovering which ones produce good reactions. Children learn from the experiences that come their way and these begin to make up their view of the world. The values of those around are made evident in the reactions of others to their behaviour, as well as in conversation, and children begin to develop their own sets of values – a process which will continue for many years.

The school affects the way children develop. This is a positive task for the school. The thinking behind ideas of readiness for particular learning is not that the school simply waits for children to be ready. The teacher's task is to prepare children so that they *become* ready for the next stage in their learning. Everything that happens to children contributes to the picture of themselves that they are forming. These self-images will in turn affect later development because children begin to see themselves as people who are good at some activities and not so good at others and this encourages them to persist with those things where they feel competent and abandon those where they feel they may do badly. It is therefore important that the school encourages each child to be as successful as possible over a wide range of activities. A person's self-image and self-esteem will affect learning and behaviour throughout life.

Children are not only affected by their peer group in school. They also use older children and teachers as models. Eckholm (1976) and many others suggest that situations in which older children are invited to teach younger children have considerable benefit in providing models for the younger children and developing responsibility and reinforcing learning in the older children. One school which tried this, undertook a project with a Year Six class who then had to produce material to help the seven-year-olds to undertake the same project. The teachers of the two classes commented on the fact that they had a one-to-one teaching situation from which both groups gained a great deal.

The way children are treated demonstrates the value that teachers and other children place upon them. The expectations of teachers and parents affect performance. A teacher may quite properly make remarks such as 'I expect you to do better work than that,' demonstrating the teacher's expectations. Teachers also sometimes make comments like 'If that's the best that you can do' or 'That's not bad for you' which demonstrate that the teacher has low expectations for the child or group of children and this in turn affects their self-image. The 'Three wise men' report comments 'The mounting evidence about teacher under expectation and pupil under-achievement . . . means that teachers must avoid the pitfall of assuming that pupils' ability is fixed' (Alexander *et al.* 1992: 27).

The overall organisation of school and classroom help to form children's self-images. One of the reasons why most primary schools have moved away from streaming by ability, for example, is the effect that this had on the expectations of the least able and the way in which the self-images of children in low streams affected their view of their ability to learn. While there is a case for ability grouping for some activities within the class, it is very important that children in low ability groups are able to succeed so that their presence in the group adds to rather than subtracts from their confidence in their ability to learn. It is also important that they are not in these groups permanently and for all work, since this would have a similar effect to streaming. It is better to have mixed groups for much of the work and to group by ability only where it appears necessary for the work in hand. Galton (1992) notes that where groups are interactive children learn more in mixed groups than in more homogeneous ones.

Bennett reminds us that children come to school with

> ideas or schemata', which they use to make sense of everyday experience. These schemata are partial and incomplete. Learning in classrooms thus involves the extension, elaboration or modification of these schemata. This is achieved by the learners making sense of new knowledge in the light of what they already know.
>
> (Bennett 1992: 6)

He goes on to make the point that teachers must spend time finding out what these ideas are like if they are to be able to teach children effectively. Both Bennett (1992) and Galton (1992) suggest that in addition children need the opportunity to discuss what they are learning and this suggests that much more work needs to be done in collaborative or cooperative groups than is currently the case.

The learning process also depends upon experience. Words, whether spoken or written, mean only as much as the experience children bring to their interpretation. Thus primary education depends a good deal on the experiences which children bring to school as well as on the experiences it is possible to offer them as part of their learning. These experiences are the raw material of the ideas that children have developed. This creates an important observation task for the teacher, who, whenever a new piece of work is started, needs to talk with the children to discover their experiences and the language they have for discussing them. It is a very useful device in preparing for new work to list the language which will be needed and consider the experience which will be necessary to understand the language.

Alexander writing of the Leeds Primary Needs Programme identified four features essential to a properly founded needs policy or programme:

a clear *definition* of the categories of needs in question; procedures for the *identification* of children within each category; means for the *diagnosis* of the precise needs of each child so identified; and appropriate educational and curricular *provision* to meet these needs.

(Alexander 1992: 137)

He is making the point that children with social disadvantage, ethnic minority children, children with learning difficulties and to some extent all children have specific needs which should be carefully considered and met.

The primary school also has a responsibility for starting children on the process of learning how to learn. This involves developing the ability to observe, to find out in different ways including from other people and from books, to sort out and organise what one has found out and present it to others in a variety of forms. Children at the primary school stage need to learn how to settle down to work and concentrate on a task. They also need to learn to listen and take in what is said.

ENSURE THAT THERE IS INTELLECTUAL CHALLENGE

Numbers of Her Majesty's Inspectorate (HMI) reports have commented that schools which teach the middle range of children comparatively well, fail to extend the learning of the most able children. This is generally because there is too little work which is intellectually demanding and this applies to all the children in the school and not only to the most able.

It is interesting to assess the questions teachers ask their classes. At the primary stage and to some extent at the secondary stage, the questions tend to be a matter of recall rather than questions which are intellectually demanding. Brown and Wragg (1993) found that of a thousand questions asked by teachers, only 8 per cent were intellectually demanding. Most teachers need to ask more questions which require children to imagine, to speculate, to reason, to provide arguments and think outside the terms of the question. It would be valuable for a staff to spend some time on an in-service day thinking about the kinds of questions they ask and considering how they could ask more challenging questions.

Montgomery (1984), in describing classroom observation for appraisal, suggests that one of the teacher activities an observer might look for is what she calls 'positive cognitive intervention' or PCI for short. This is where a teacher makes a comment or asks a question or intervenes in a child's learning in some way which develops his or her thinking. This would be a very useful form of observation for a headteacher spending time in classrooms. Teachers might also spend time observing each other if this can be arranged, looking out for this kind of intellectual challenge or extension of children's thinking. Looking for such activity in the work of others will tend to make observers more likely to include it in their own work.

ENSURE THAT THERE IS PROVISION FOR THE MOST AND LEAST ABLE

It is a very difficult task for teachers to ensure that all their children are learning. It is very easy for teachers to provide for the middle ability group within the class, dealing with the less able as and when they can and assuming that the most able will get on because of their ability. It is the responsibility of the headteacher to see that there is provision for all children. This may mean making additional provision available for individuals and small groups of children especially for children whose mother tongue is not English and children with serious problems which require individual attention. It certainly means seeing that provision is made within normal classes.

The school needs a policy which makes it clear that it is the responsibility of all teachers to provide for all the children in their care. It is also important to have a member of staff coordinating this work and supporting colleagues in making provision both for the most and the least able.

Provision for these groups may mean providing work which is open ended which can be tackled at a variety of levels. It will also be necessary to provide work which matches the needs of individuals.

Children with learning difficulties

Children with difficulties cannot afford to waste any time in the classroom. It is essential to analyse children's problems so that the work provided matches their needs closely. For example, there should be a careful analysis of a child's phonic knowledge, if there are reading difficulties and of particular problems in mathematics and work should then be designed to match these particular problems. The analysis of these problems may be a task for the special needs teacher if there is one, who then suggests work to the class teacher. If teachers work together to provide material for such children the school can build up a stock of work which matches common problems.

Teachers will also need to consider making provision for small steps leading up to levels within the National Curriculum and much may be learned from contact with special schools on this. The process of doing is well described by Lewis (1991) in *Primary special needs and the National Curriculum*.

The school may also like to consider the kind of help which could be given to children with learning difficulties by their parents who are often keen to do something to help and also by volunteer parents within the school. They may hear reading and take part in paired reading, play learning games with children. Such work needs careful supervision by the teacher but can be very valuable.

Roberts makes the following point about the role of the teacher:

> There is every reason to suppose that teachers who minimise the disadvantages or handicaps that their children may experience, who keep a watchful eye on their own prejudices and who concern themselves with future possibilities, rather than past failures, may help children to achieve higher standards of work and behaviour than would normally be thought possible.
>
> (Roberts 1983: 11)

The National Curriculum Council publication on special needs *A curriculum for all* (1989b) stresses the need for positive attitudes from school staff who are determined to ensure their fullest participation in the National Curriculum. The leadership of the headteacher in establishing these attitudes is very important.

Able children

It is very tempting for busy teachers to take the view that very able children will make progress anyway and that it is not necessary to do anything very special for them. HMI reports suggest that much more needs to be done to extend such children's abilities. It is part of the task of the classroom teacher to see that this happens and the task of management to see that such children are identified and monitored and given work which makes demands upon them.

Meeting the needs of the most able may include three kinds of activity. In the first instance they are likely to cover the work of the class with greater speed than the majority and provision should be made for this. They may need material which covers the ground rather more quickly or they may perhaps miss out steps which seem unnecessary. This is mainly a matter of the school building up material which allows for this.

In topic work very able children need to be encouraged to pursue aspects of the topic which make greater demands on their thinking. For example, the supplementary study units at 'Key Stage 2' (NCC 1993a) in history include a study of land transport. A very able child should be able to work on a theme like 'The effect of different forms of transport on the lives people lived'.

Yet another way of making work sufficiently demanding for the very able is to take real life problems and ask them to find solutions. For example, an older child or a pair of children might be asked to produce a school handbook which could actually be given to parents whose children are entering the school. This would involve discovering what information was actually wanted by parents and children and attempting to put it together in a form which would interest them. It involves writing for an audience, speaking with people and asking questions, all of which are part of the National Curriculum requirements for English. It lends reality to the task if it is intended to use the booklet for the planned purpose.

A local guidebook is another possibility. Making teaching material for younger children may also be a useful activity. This might be a booklet or a game but it involves studying the level of performance of the younger child as well as the material to be learned.

Schools often withdraw groups of children who have learning difficulties. There is also a case for withdrawing children who are very able for more demanding work. Lunch time clubs may also help to cater for their interests.

MONITOR THE DEVELOPMENT OF EACH CHILD

Your task as headteacher here is to see that each child is considered as a developing individual and to be sure that all teachers are aware of the crucial part their own expectations and behaviour play in the development of their children. You may do this mainly by talking with teachers and children in an informal way; but there is much to be said for sitting down with each teacher in turn to talk through the development of the children for whom he or she is responsible, particularly those who pose any kind of problem. In a large primary school, the deputy head and the teacher in charge of the infant or first school department should undertake some of this activity.

The other way in which you can monitor the progress of each child is by looking at records and reports and at teachers' notes and at the work of children. These will enable you to identify children whose progress it is important you discuss with teachers, although it will be unusual in most primary schools if you are not very quickly aware of some of the children whose progress needs careful monitoring. There are children who pose problems but are quiet and are less likely to stand out, however, and records and reports may be useful in identifying them. Documentary evidence may also be valuable in identifying the very able.

SEE THAT THERE ARE EQUAL OPPORTUNITIES FOR ALL

Every school needs to have a whole school policy on equal opportunities for all children. This is not only a matter of equal opportunities for girls and boys and children of different races, important as these issues are. Schools may also discriminate without realising it against children of working class background, against children with handicaps and against children of different abilities – sometimes the most as well as the least able. Many local authorities have policies and documents about equal opportunities and offer schools guidance on these issues. A whole school policy is needed which grows out of staff discussion in which everyone has been involved. Your involvement as the headteacher and your support of the policy will be crucial. It will also be important to make the policy clear to parents. The whole issue of equal opportunities needs to be looked at regularly with particular reference to the hidden curriculum. Staff, ancillary as well as teaching, need opportunities to talk about their own prejudices and attitudes if they are to support a whole school policy.

Alexander makes a point about teachers:

> For schools to take seriously their responsibilities in this regard, attitudes and perceptions at the levels of individual teachers have to change, sometimes radically, and for this to happen the teachers concerned need to become more knowledgeable about societal and cultural matters and about the nature and the causes of prejudice.
>
> (Alexander 1992: 15)

Work on equal opportunities applies not only to work in the classroom but to the way the school runs from day to day. It will be important to see that no aspect of school life poses problems for any particular children because of their race, gender, class, ability or disability. The school's task is to educate all children to take their place in a plural society and to try to produce people who value this pluralism and enjoy its richness.

It is perhaps worth remembering that adults generally, and children to some extent, have fundamental attitudes towards people who are different from them. These attitudes in young children tend to be brought from home and may be at a subconscious level, influencing behaviour without the person concerned being aware of it. Teachers need to be conscious that they may hold and be influenced subconsciously by such attitudes themselves. Very often the attitudes children hold towards those who are different from themselves have little to do with their experience and much to do with the attitudes their parents hold. These deep seated attitudes are difficult to change and the most that schools can hope to do is to change conscious attitudes so that they help to govern behaviour.

Gender

The last decade has seen considerable changes in the position of women in society and much greater consciousness of the need for girls to be encouraged to aim for careers which were not previously open to them. However, girls still do more chores at home than boys and it should not be forgotten that children's earliest experience in most cases is of mother in the home. It is probably also the case that, for many children, the example given at home is still of mother dealing with domestic issues, even if she is also in employment.

It is therefore important for the school to do everything possible to raise the sights of girls and increase their aspirations and encourage broader choices of courses and careers. This might be thought of as simply a matter for secondary schools, but foundations of attitudes are laid in the primary school and teachers need to be aware that they can influence the way both boys and girls think about gender. Ideas about what is a suitable activity for boys and for girls are often very firmly held by primary school children and there should be opportunities for discussing this. It may also be a matter of attempting to change attitudes on the part of boys, since some of the attitudes of girls are conditioned by the way boys regard and treat them. The way teachers deal with each other and the way they talk about each other may also influence the way children relate to each other. It is also useful to discuss these issues with parents. Alexander notes that there is a tendency for teachers to be dismissive about gender issues. 'Gender related ways of thinking, seeing and acting are so deeply embedded in the consciousness of individual groups' (Alexander 1922: 17).

He also makes the point that in many schools mathematics and computer technology are the province of men, usually at a senior level, whereas language and art are the province of women usually at a less senior level. Subjects like art and music tend to be coordinated by teachers on the main professional grade. These arrangements have implications from which children make inferences.

There is a tendency to regard gender issues as something concerning girls in particular. Boys have their own problems in accepting their gender, particularly where the local idea of masculinity is macho. They may need to be given confidence that it is possible for boys to enjoy the arts, to be gentle, to show emotion and have some of the characteristics which tend to be regarded as feminine as well as more masculine characteristics.

Race

A school needs to consider both multicultural education and anti-racist education. Multicultural education will stem naturally from some aspects of the National Curriculum and schools today should be concerned not only with the European dimension of education but with world dimensions for children who are growing up in a world where what happens far away now affects what is happening close to us. The celebration of holidays and festivals from different cultures, study of countries from which children of other races come, literature from other cultures and much else may all contribute. Teachers should be constantly looking at the curriculum with the multicultural approach in mind. Schools need to celebrate the diversity of their children and teachers need to show that they value having children of different cultures. This is just as important in schools which are not racially mixed as it is in schools which are.

It is much more difficult to tackle the question of race more directly. There should be opportunities for discussing human rights issues, items in the news, racial stereotype issues such as anti-semitism and much else. Drama offers a particular opportunity for exploring the feelings of others. History and geography both have contributions to make in discussion of situations in which racism has been evident. There are also opportunities to tackle the issues of racism arising out of incidents where there has been conflict between children of different races. There is the possibility that discussion and work on racism may reinforce rather than counteract prejudice but this is no reason to ignore the problems that exist. We need to be constantly learning about the best way to live in a plural society.

Issues of race are particularly important in all-white schools where it is easy to assume that there is no problem. Children growing up in communities where they seldom meet people of other races have a particular need to consider the effects of racism and to have a multicultural dimension to their curriculum. Schools in such areas may profitably make links with schools which have a more mixed population. Schools in all areas might also make links with schools in third world countries.

Social class

It is very easy to underestimate working-class children, particularly if their speech is strongly regional. Our low expectations for such children probably have something to do with our poor showing internationally at the lower end of the ability range. This is compounded by the fact that such children often have low expectations for themselves, partly the result of low teacher expectation and partly of parental expectation. There is a cycle of expectation whereby parents, because of their own experience, have written off school learning as something not worth having, and then pass this view on to their children whom they do not expect to do well at school. This is in contrast to some other cultures where a much wider range of parents expect success in school from their children.

The task of the school is to try to raise expectations so that such children break the cycle. This again is something which you as headteacher can influence by not accepting low expectations from teachers but constantly encouraging both teachers and children to aim high. Praise for teachers who do well with children of working-class background is important. It is also valuable to get across to working-class parents that the school has high expectations of their children.

Ability

Discrimination by ability is closely related to discrimination by social class. There is evidence from research that we underestimate children of both low and high ability (e.g. Bennett *et al.* 1984). The National Curriculum demands that we make the curriculum accessible to all children and this may mean developing steps towards attainment targets for some children rather than aiming at them directly.

There is also a danger that able children will be underestimated because they have chosen the easy path and do just enough to get by. It is, for this reason, important to see that teachers are both aware of those children known to have exceptional ability and vigilant for others who may not have been identified. In a sense equal opportunities for such children means giving them different and more demanding opportunities than those given to other children.

Children with disabilities

It is also easy to assume that a child with a serious physical handicap also has learning difficulties, particularly in cases where the handicap limits speech. A child may have good intelligence but have been unable to develop it because of deafness or a speech problem. He or she may therefore be unable to show the ability which is there. Children with serious physical disabilities may also have difficulties in writing and using tools which may lead to an under-estimation of their abilities.

The equal opportunities policy

A whole school policy on equal opportunities would include the following:

- a statement about the attitudes expected from staff towards all children, together with some comment about the kinds of children to whom it may apply in particular
- information about what teachers should actually do to support the equal opportunities policy
- statements about specific responsibilities for seeing that the policy is implemented
- information about the way the implementation of the policy will be assessed

Assessing the equal opportunities programme

It is not enough to have an equal opportunities policy. There must be regular assessment of how well it is working. The people best placed to make this assessment in a school with juniors on role are the children although there must also be assessment and discussion about what has happened by the staff. Questionnaires to older children may reveal aspects which are not otherwise evident and these can be followed up with discussion with small groups of children and then with staff. Parents may also have something to say about this.

ENSURE THAT THERE IS PROVISION FOR SPIRITUAL, SOCIAL AND MORAL DEVELOPMENT

Spiritual development

The Office for Standards in Education (OFSTED) handbook (1993: 21) for the inspection of schools states that:

Spiritual development is to be judged by the extent to which pupils display:

- a system of personal beliefs, which may include religious beliefs
- an ability to communicate their beliefs in discussion and through their behaviour
- willingness to reflect on experience and and to search for meaning in that experience
- a sense of awe and wonder as they become more conscious of deeper meanings in the apparently familiar features of the natural world or in their experience

The National Curriculum Council (paper NCC) on spiritual and moral development makes the following statement:

The potential for spiritual development is open to everyone and is not confined to the development of religious beliefs or conversion to a particular faith . . . . The term needs to be seen as applying to something fundamental in the human condition which is not necessarily experienced through the physical senses and/or expressed through everyday language. It has to do with relationships with other people and, for believers, with God. It has to do with the universal search for individual identity – with our responses to challenging experiences, such as death, suffering, beauty, and encounters with good and evil. It is to do with the search for meaning and purpose in life and for values by which to live.

(NCC 1993b: 2)

The paper goes on to suggest that aspects of spiritual development include beliefs, a sense of awe, wonder and mystery, experiencing feelings of transcendence, a search for meaning and purpose, self-knowledge, relationships, creativity and feelings and emotions.

A good deal of this development comes properly under the heading of religious education but there will be many opportunities in other aspects of curriculum. In reading poetry, for example, in science, in history, in art, opportunities may arise which give rise to issues which lead to spiritual development. There should also be opportunities for discussion both with children and among staff as to what constitutes spiritual development and where and how it is developed.

Social development

The primary school has an important role in socialising children, in helping them to learn the general rules by which we behave in our society. Some may come from homes where different rules apply. For example, most schools, but not all parents, discourage children from physical aggression. Children from other cultures may also have learnt different rules at home and teachers are usually sympathetic to young children who find it difficult to come to terms with the rules of behaviour which school imposes upon them. By the time children leave the primary school, however, they should be well aware of what is expected of them.

The OFSTED handbook states that social development is to be judged by:

- the quality of relationships in the school
- pupils' ability to exercise a degree of responsibility and initiative
- pupils' ability to work successfully in groups and to participate co-operatively and productively in the school community
- pupils' growing understanding of society through the family, the school and the local and wider community, leading to an understanding of the structures and processes of society.

Schools are also responsible for the social development of children. Young children starting school see the world from their own point of view and have difficulty in seeing it from the point of view of others. They gradually become less egocentric as they grow older and teachers help with this process by reflecting for them how other people react to their behaviour. They learn to form relationships with others and to appreciate that this may mean making one's own interests subordinate to the interests of others.

Eckholm writing of social development in schools in Sweden, describes it as follows:

> In Sweden, the direction of the social development which the school is to inculcate in the young has been set with the idea of attaining a society that will function closer to democratic ideals than present society. Social development of the kind the school envisages demands another type of consciousness than the type we get today from the

socialisation process. Through socialisation, the individual becomes conscious of the rules now existing in society. But social development aims to make the individual conscious, not only of existing rules, but also of rules that *ought* to exist. Social development thus aims to make the individual capable of standing up for the 'ought' by his very way of being.

(Eckholm 1976: 4)

He goes on the describe work in a secondary school on 'joy' where pupils discussed this with other people and listed things that gave them and other people pleasure. They then went out to put this knowledge into practice in their families and with other people in school. Although this was done with secondary school children it could equally well be done with older children in the primary school.

Primary school children are gradually learning how to live and work with other people and the school can do much to help them with this process. There should be frequent discussion at most stages about how other people feel when faced with different kinds of behaviour. Drama may be useful here in helping children to learn to stand where someone else stands and see with his or her eyes. It is sometimes helpful in dealing with children's misdemeanours to paint a picture of how someone on the receiving end felt about the behaviour which is unacceptable.

One aspect of social development is the ability to take responsibility. Yet very often teachers give the responsible tasks to the children who have shown that they *can* take responsibility, rather than providing practice for those who need to learn how to be responsible.

It is also interesting to note that the OFSTED handbook speaks of working in groups. Several studies (Galton and Simon 1980, Dunne and Bennett 1990, Alexander 1992), have shown that although children in primary classes sit in groups they do not actually do much work in groups. All of the authors above stress the value of group work for children's learning.

Social development should be a positive process in which teachers actively set out to foster attitudes and behaviour towards other people as well as teaching the rules of behaviour which make people acceptable in society at large.

Bullying

A good deal of concern has been expressed recently about bullying in schools and there is evidence (Boulton and Underwood 1992), admittedly in this case from a small number of schools, that a considerable proportion of children are bullied at some stage of their schooling. This may not necessarily be physical. Children find name calling and verbal bullying distressing also. News programmes have also spoken of children being bullied because they have not the clothing which is currently fashionable and in other cases of having such clothing stolen. An analysis by Jean La Fontaine (1990) of calls received on Esther Rantzen's Childline suggests that children are intimidated by a far wider range of harassment than adults are aware of.

Young children are not inhibited about telling the teacher when someone attacks them in some way. The problem here is to decide whether the complaint is a genuine one. On the other hand, children at the top of the primary school are well acquainted with the peer group rule that one does not tell tales. Bullying at this stage may go unrecognized by staff until someone is injured or made ill by the treatment he or she is receiving from the peer group. Some bullying of younger children may also go unrecognised because the child is too frightened to tell the teacher. The ability to recognise the symptoms and incidence of bullying therefore needs to be included in the school care policy. Continual vigilance needs to be exercised by staff and encouragement given to children to report incidents of it they may observe and to help staff to deal with it when it arises. All children in the school need to know that bullying is considered unacceptable and that they will be supported if they help to stop it.

Work in drama may be valuable here in encouraging children to look at bullying from the victim's point of view. Incidents of bullying should also be recorded so that individuals who are inclined to bully and those who tend to be victims can be watched and supported. There should also be a system for dealing with complaints from parents about bullying and with other cases as they come to light. This problem needs continual vigilance on the part of staff, including those with responsibility for supervision at lunch time and other non-teaching staff as well as teachers. All cases reported must be taken very seriously and regarded not only as an infringement of the rules of the school, but as an infringement of its ethos.

Truancy

Although truancy tends to be much more a problem in the secondary than the primary school there is evidence that primary schools do have some truants. A recent survey by the National Foundation for Educational Research (NFER) showed that 9 per cent of 11 year olds were truanting occasionally.

Children who truant at the primary stage are starting a habit which is likely to become worse as they grow older and everything possible needs to be done to deal with with problem. They are often children who are not doing well in school and since disenchantment grows with continued failure it is important for the school to see that as many children as possible succeed in as many areas as possible. Once children start taking days off, they are likely to fail further because of missing lessons. It is important that any incident of truancy is followed up with both the child and his or her parents.

Truancy is likely to be less prevalent where there are shared goals which are clear, commitment to purpose, dedicated teachers, high expectations and collaborative work, active leadership and support, good school organisation and clear policies leading to academic achievement, a rigorous and focused approach to curriculum, a positive and orderly school culture and community relationships. Good schools have fewer truants.

Moral development

Very young children are conditioned to behave in certain ways by the reaction of adults. They learn that certain types of behaviour please adults and other kinds of behaviour displease them. They gradually take as their own the rules that adults lay down.This is the basis on which action is evaluated for a considerable time. Piaget's (1932) work on moral development shows us many fascinating aspects of children's thinking on moral questions. For the young child any action showing obedience to rules or to an adult is good. Rules are given and not to be judged or interpreted; the letter rather than the spirit of the law is important and actions are judged according to their degree of conformity to the rules rather than by the intention behind them. It is naughtier to break fifteen cups by accident than one by intention.

Gradually, as children learn to see from another person's point of view, morality becomes a matter of behaving in certain ways because of one's obligations to others.

The OFSTED handbook states that moral development is to be judged by the following:

- an understanding of the difference between right and wrong
- respect for persons, truth and property
- a concern for how their actions may affect others
- the ability to make responsible and reasoned judgements on moral issues
- moral behaviour.

Moral behaviour must be intentional behaviour and it must be rational, the result of thought about the particular situation. It should be the outcome of a framework of values established in the mind of the individual which furnishes criteria for behaviour. This framework of values forms gradually during the years of schooling and is contributed to by parents and neighbourhood as well as school. School plays a very important part however, and staff need to discuss the values they stand for and the way these are conveyed to children. With young children it will be a matter of establishing that certain kinds of behaviour are acceptable and other kinds unacceptable. As they grow older moral behaviour needs to be discussed with children, helping them gradually to reason through to conclusions about the way they should behave towards others so that they begin to acquire the skill of reasoning out how they should behave in a moral situation. Drama may be valuable here in showing something from different points of view.

Chapter 4

The curriculum

The major purpose of the school is children's learning. Therefore one of the most important sets of management tasks for the headteacher is the management of the curriculum. They are as follows:

Articulate the curriculum philosophy of the school
Ensure that the National Curriculum is implemented and that religious education is provided
See that cross-curricular themes and dimensions are provided
Maintain oversight of continuity and coherence
Encourage curriculum development

ARTICULATE THE CURRICULUM PHILOSOPHY OF THE SCHOOL

As headteacher it is your responsibility to see that there is a curriculum philosophy and a curriculum which is more than the sum of the subjects taught or of the National Curriculum.

Curriculum can be seen in many ways. There is a sense in which all societies educate their young in some way, although it is only relatively recently that this has become a task to be undertaken by people specially trained to do it. Education in every society is concerned with teaching children and young people how to live in that society, whether this is a matter of bare survival or how to have a good life. There will always be some education in the skills the society needs and how to relate to other people. This may be to do with how to show respect to others, how to work within a group or with the rituals of human relationships. There will also be concern about passing on the culture, including such things as the history of the society, its religion, its systems for living together and its values, attitudes and way of life.

You can view the curriculum from three points of view; that of the child, of the content and of the society.

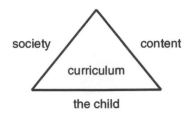

Figure 4.1 The curriculum

These aspects will be stressed differently at different times and in different places and there is pressure at the present time to move from stress on the child to stress on content and society. Kelly states that 'The needs of society are being held to take precedence over the needs of pupils so that a totally different philosophy is being foisted upon the primary school' (Kelly 1983: 18). If this was the case in 1983 it is even more so now.

In a society where education is not a specialist task entrusted to teachers but a matter of adults teaching children to undertake the tasks of everyday living, the curriculum content will be concerned with food, clothing and shelter, hunting or farming skills and the skills and knowledge needed to defend the community, and possibly to increase its goods and territory by fighting its neighbours. There will also be stories, legends and myths to be passed on, religious beliefs and rites and ceremonies to be learned. The curriculum is about the needs of society as perceived by the adults.

When life becomes less pressing and some people within a society have some leisure, they start to develop arts and skills for pleasure and to explore knowledge in its own right. They then want a curriculum for the children which is knowledge-based and which gradually becomes more concerned with the passing on of the culture. Thus we see the curriculum as concerned more with content than with society's needs and it may become divorced from them, even to the point of thinking that it is morally superior to be concerned with knowledge for its own sake rather than knowledge for use.

The third side of the triangle starts with the child. This view was summed up in the first sentence of the Plowden Report (1967). 'At the heart of the educational process lies the child' (Plowden Report 1967: 1). It was present in the work of Rousseau and Froebel and in Piaget and many others, all of whom suggested that to be effective, education must take into account the way children naturally develop and learn. One image which reflects this view is that of the gardener, who takes account of the nature of the plant and treats it accordingly, in order to get it to grow and develop as well as possible. The good teacher works in this way with the child.

These patterns can be seen at many times in history and currently there is a struggle among proponents of all three views of curriculum.

Any aspect of curriculum can be seen from these three viewpoints. If we look at science from the point of view of society, our questions are about how adults use science and the science people need in the adult world.

If we consider science from the point of view of the subject itself, we use different criteria. We ask questions about such matters as the nature of scientific knowledge. What forms of language does it use? How do parts of the subject relate to other parts? The answers to questions of this kind help to identify how the subject can best be taught by considering how the structure of the subject can be built up. The National Curriculum does a good deal of this thinking for teachers but it is still necessary to think out how to teach each aspect of the subject.

Finally we consider the children's view. We must then be concerned with the ideas and the experience children bring to their understanding of the material, the development of thinking skills, the use the children see for what they are learning and the actual way they learn. These considerations enable us to select material for different children, place it in sequence and help them to apply what they are learning. All three of these aspects should be present in the curriculum offered to children and it is a good characteristic of the National Curriculum that for the most part all three aspects can be represented, although the pressure on teachers means that the needs of the child tend to be subservient to the needs of society and the structure of knowledge.

The National Curriculum is stated largely in terms of content. It is equally important to think of it in terms of process. This is the way in which individuals structure and store knowledge to enable them to draw on it when it is needed. The process by which learning takes place determines how the knowledge is stored and structured and although a teacher can offer children a structure, this is less valuable than the process of actually making the structure oneself. For example, a great deal of work in science in the past has given children hypotheses and dictated the experiments which might be done to confirm them. Modern thinking includes involving children developing hypotheses and working out how to test them. This helps children to structure their thinking in a way which the more formal method could never do.

Curriculum can also be defined in different ways which affect how we see it. It has been described as 'all the intended outcomes' of the school. This limits the idea mainly to what happens in classrooms and in classroom-associated activity. But differences between schools are more subtle than this. Some important experiences that children take away from school are not part of the intended outcomes in the same sense as the National Curriculum. Hargreaves (1984) speaks of the hidden curriculum of values and attitudes conveyed by the way the school operates and the way that adults within it behave. But the hidden curriculum is also divided. There is what might be described as the inferential curriculum: the learning inferred by the children from the way the school is run, the things seen to be valued by staff, the way teachers treat children and the examples given. This is not entirely hidden and some of it is intended.

There is also the true hidden curriculum which by definition is learning which is neither intended nor recognised. As soon as this learning becomes recognised it becomes part of the inferential curriculum, but much will still remain hidden. A school may thus be giving messages which its headteacher and staff would not wish to give and it is a good idea to look at this area occasionally to discover if possible what hidden messages are being transmitted. For example, what sort of messages do visitors receive if it is not clear where they should go and what they should do if they come into the school? What sort of messages do girls receive if any task which requires strength is allocated to boys?

The stated curriculum philosophy of the school therefore needs to have reference not only to the intended curriculum, but also to the inferred and the hidden curriculum. The statement about the inferred curriculum is particularly important because it is about values and attitudes and is likely to have a more lasting effect than much else learned at school. Staff need to spend time discussing it and thinking about how values and forms of behaviour are inculcated. Much is conveyed by the way teachers and other adults behave towards each other and towards the children.

Some of these aims will be the subject of direct teaching. Others will be acquired as part of work in different areas of the curriculum. Yet others will be learned as part of the daily life of the school. Children's learning goes on all the time and the way children are treated in school and the expectations of their behaviour affect their attitudes and are part of the learning process. The staff of every school needs to spend time thinking about what children can infer from their treatment and from the daily life of the school.

ENSURE THAT THE NATIONAL CURRICULUM IS IMPLEMENTED AND THAT RELIGIOUS EDUCATION IS PROVIDED

The curriculum a school adopts must firstly provide opportunity for the relevant learning within the National Curriculum and meet any demands made by the local authority, if the school is a maintained school. This is a major task of management which needs leadership from the headteacher but which should involve all members of staff.

Planning needs to start with some decisions about approaches to learning. The staff must decide how far they want a subject–based curriculum and how far they would prefer to use cross curricular topics.

Most schools will expect to work with a mixture of both approaches and schools that opt for a mainly subject-based approach may still wish to make links between subjects and work through subject-based topics. Alexander *et al.* state that 'The introduction of the National Curriculum means . . . that a substantial amount of separate subject teaching will be necessary if every aspect of each programme of study is to be covered effectively' (Alexander *et al.* 1922: 23).

This view is confirmed in the advice of the NCC (1993c) to the Secretary of State on the National Curriculum, 'Key Stages 1, 2'.

The argument against separate subject teaching is that this is not the way in which young children learn. They learn from everything that happens to them. However, primary school learning should gradually lead them towards the idea that knowledge is structured and that some kinds of knowledge are called history and other kinds called mathematics. The argument is really about the point when this division has meaning rather than whether it should be introduced at all. Alexander *et al.* comment as follows:

> To resist subjects on the ground that they are inconsistent with children's views of the world is to confine them within their existing modes of thought and deny them access to some of the most powerful tools for making sense of the world which human beings have ever devised.
>
> (Alexander *et al.* 1992: 21)

The extent of subject teaching is a matter that schools can decide individually, depending on the rate of development of their children. In any case most schools separate mathematics, physical education and music and the initial learning of reading and writing.

The NCC paper (1993a) suggests that learning might be divided into what is calls 'continuing units' and 'blocked units'. It defines continuing units as follows:

> A continuing unit of work is a planned sequence of lessons or activities which relates to a single subject. It is usually associated across a number of levels through which children progress at different rates. It is often concerned with the development of skills which are taught and learned in a progressive and cumulative fashion, for example, aspects of mathematics and reading.
>
> (NCC Planning the National Curriculum at 'Key Stage 2' 1993a)

Blocked units of work may be topics or may be a series of lessons on a particular aspect of curriculum taking place over a comparatively short period. For example, a class may work on a project on living things or may experience a series of lessons on the Romans. The idea of the blocked unit is that it should be something more like a topic which is undertaken in a fairly concentrated way rather than as a series of weekly sessions.

The second major decision for a staff member is one of teaching method. How far is there to be direct whole class teaching, how far group or individual teaching and how far is the work going to be exploratory? This is a matter of thinking through the most efficient and effective ways of teaching. Whole class work is usually the most effective way of introducing something and of drawing together the work of the class at the end of a piece of learning. Research also suggests that whole class discussion gives opportunities for questions which extend children's thinking. (Galton, 1989, Mortimore *et al*, 1988).

It is also important to consider the amount of teacher contact each child experiences. If too much teaching is individual, children experience very small amounts of teacher contact. Group work in which children are genuinely working together offers a half-way house between whole class and individual teaching. Galton (1992) reviewing research into work in groups found that a number of studies showed that children learned more effectively in many areas when they worked collaboratively. Bennett (1992) makes the point that talking is one of the ways in which a child constructs knowledge and that collaborative learning has therefore an important contribution to make. Dunne and Bennett (1990) give many examples of ways in which teachers can plan work in groups. Schools should certainly consider group work as an efficient way of teaching for some work, allowing for children at various stages of learning.

The ORACLE study (*Observational Research and Classroom Learning Evaluation:* Galton *et al*. 1980) found that the most successful teachers in terms of children's progress in English and mathematics interacted with the whole class for 39 per cent of the time and adapted their strategies to the needs of the particular situation. Teachers who worked mainly with individuals did not have time to ask challenging questions, give feedback or discuss work with children at a more than superficial level. Those who worked with groups did better than those who worked with individuals. The research did not find that there were any significant compensating gains for individual work, although these children made good progress in reading.

Alexander *et al*. (1992) also suggest that teachers should adapt their teaching strategy to the situation and plan so that they have time for challenging questions and giving feedback.

Galton (1989), having reviewed the studies by Bennett (1976), Galton *et al*. (1980), Galton *et al*. (1987), Mortimore *et al*. (1988) and Tizard *et al*. (1988) states the situation as follows:

> Whatever the style of teaching adopted, it would appear that the greater the emphasis the teacher gives to organising and directing the curriculum, the greater the progress pupils make in the areas of mathematics, language and reading when these are assessed in terms of

traditional tests. In order to obtain this success teachers tend to make more use of whole class or group instruction; inevitably this means that they restrict the proportion of time when children work on integrated tasks.

(Galton 1989: 60)

He also makes the point that certain effects such as providing feedback, raising questions and minimising routine instructions seem important determinants of pupils' progress.

Galton *et al* (1980) also suggest that children adapt their behaviour to the teacher they are with, changing it when they change teachers. Teachers need to discuss the whole question of classroom strategy and ask themselves questions about the extent to which they are able to provide intellectual challenge and develop children's thinking.

The diagram below gives the stages of planning the curriculum. Each is discussed in the pages that follow.

Consider time available

The first task for the headteacher is to work out the time available for teaching during the school year, allowing for events such as visits and plays and concerts and any other event likely to take time from the teaching programme. This is the time which is available for planned teaching. This does not mean that it should be planned like a secondary school timetable, but that thought needs to be given as to the time available for each aspect of curriculum.

Agree time allocation for each subject

The next task is to work with teachers to agree the amount of time which should be allowed for each subject in each year group. This is intended as a broad guide to planning only. The NCC paper gives the following examples (see p. 61).

Agree continuing and blocked units

The next task is to discuss with teachers which areas of curriculum need to be taught in each of these forms. Subjects where knowledge is built up step by step, as in much work in mathematics and in reading, require continuing units. Subjects which lend themselves to a topic approach may be better as blocked units which can take a good deal of time for a period and then be left for another blocked unit. It should also be remembered that this approach means that not every subject needs to be taught all the time. It may be better to do concentrated work on one area and then move

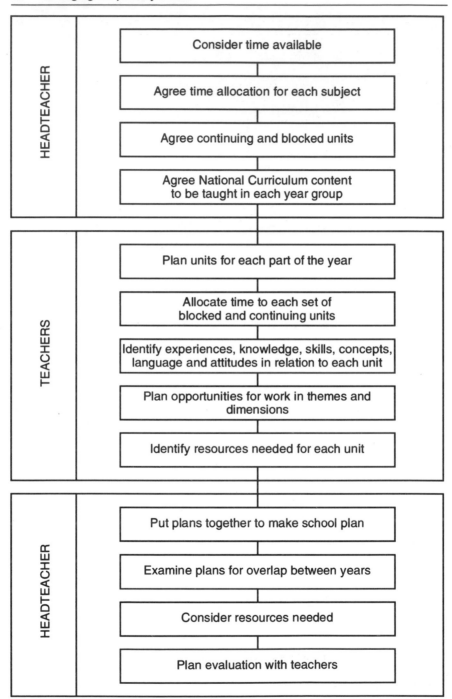

Figure 4.2 Planning the curriculum

Table 4.1 A guide for planning the time allocated for each subject in each year

School A (using a total of 846 hours a year)
For year 5

Subject	En	Ma	Sc	Te	Gg	Hi	Ar	Mu	PE	RE
% of curriculum time	20	17.5	15	7.5	7.5	7.5	7.5	5	7.5	5
Hours per year	170	146	126	64	64	64	64	42	64	42

B (using a total of 823 hours a year)
For year 3

Subject	En	Ma	Sc	Te	Gg	Hi	Ar	Mu	PE	RE
% of curriculum time	28	19	12	7	6	6	6	5	7	4
Hours per year	230	156	100	58	49	49	49	41	58	33

School C (using a total of 823 hours a year)
For year 6

Subject	En	Ma	Sc	Te	Gg	Hi	Ar	Mu	PE	RE
% of curriculum time	26	15	15	8	6	6	6	6	6	6
Hours per year	217	123	123	66	49	49	49	49	49	49

Source: NCC 1993a

to another than to offer a little of a subject every week. Schools can certainly experiment with this pattern and see how it works.

Agree National Curriculum and religious education content to be taught in each year group

The National Curriculum and religious education content needs to be spread over the year groups and it needs to be clear to all staff which Statements of Attainment are being taught in each year group. There will, of course, be a need to revise work in the process of moving on to new topics.

Plan units for each part of the year

Each teacher needs to make long-term plans within the time available to meet the demands of the Statements of Attainment and the Programme of Study. This means allocating continuing and blocked units to each part of each term.

The next tasks are also tasks for teachers. It may be helpful to set these out on a planning form so that each teacher sets about planning in the same way and each then contributes to the school plan. Plans should show how the work contributes to the achievement of the school aims. Suggested planning forms for the year and for each unit are given on pages 63–5.

Allocate time to each set of blocked and continuing units

Once the plan has been made for the year the next task is to plan how much time each unit can be allocated. This must add up to the time available for the year.

Identify experiences, knowledge, skills, concepts, language and attitudes in relation to each unit

In planning each unit it is important to identify exactly what children should have gained by the end of it. One way of doing this is first to list the experiences which children need in order to understand the work and to decide which of those experiences they already have and which must be provided for them. In listing the experiences it is helpful also to list the language which will be needed in order to talk about the work. The next task is to list what children should know, be able to do and understand at the end of the each unit. It is also helpful to think about the attitudes which they should have. This analysis gives teachers performance indicators by which to judge their work.

Plan opportunities for work in themes and dimensions

The themes and dimensions are discussed on pages 66–9. They come into many aspects of the work and it should be possible to include some work on most of them in the process of working with the National Curriculum.

Identify resources needed for each unit

This is particularly important from the financial point of view. Planning may involve material which has to be purchased. It may also involve visits which require thought about financing. It is also helpful to assess how much of the material need for a particular unit is available and whether some materials have to be made. Materials made in this context are likely to be of use in subsequent years.

Put plans together to make school plan

The headteacher then has the task of assembling the plans from the teachers. The school curriculum plan can then be made available to

	Blocked units	Time allowed	Continuing units	Time allowed
Autumn term				
Spring term				
Summer term				
	Total time		Total time	

. . . . .School

School Year 19. . . . . . to 19. . . . . .   Class. . . . .

Figure 4.3 Year planner

School. . . . .

School year 19. . . . . . to 19. . . . . .   Term. . . . .   Class. . . . .

Unit title. . . . . Time allowed. . . . .

Subject area(s) to be covered. . . . .

Statements of attainment to be covered

What experiences do children need? (include those children may already have and those you will provide)

What new language will you need to introduce?

What will children know and understand as a result of this work?

Figure 4.4 Unit planner

What will children be able to do as a result of this work?

What links will there be with themes and dimensions?

What provision will there be for the most and least able?

What resources will be needed, including visits	Approx. cost
Total	

How will you evaluate success?

How does this work help to fulfil the school aims?

Figure 4.4 continued

governors and it may be possible to provide a brief summary for parents. Certainly it should be possible to let parents know what their children will be studying in each year group and to encourage their cooperation in any aspect of the curriculum where they could help.

Examine plans for overlap between years

In putting together the school plan it is important to see that the plans for each year group add up and are not repeating work except by way of revision.

Consider resources needed

The plans will have some implications for the school budget. This needs to be examined carefully at an early stage so that teachers know whether money will be available for any purchases which they need to make.

Plan evaluation with teachers

Evaluation is made easier by the development of performance indicators but they need to be planned from the beginning. Evaluation involves deciding what should be done by way of evaluating the work that has been done and who should do it. It is discussed in detail in chapter fifteen.

SEE THAT CROSS CURRICULAR THEMES AND DIMENSIONS ARE IMPLEMENTED

Curriculum planning must also provide for some learning outside as well as within the National Curriculum and religious education. This is partly described in the NCC publication *The whole curriculum* (1990) which suggests that there are themes and dimensions which should run through the National Curriculum work and be part of the total curriculum experienced by children. The dimensions include:

Having concern for equal opportunities

It is essential in the first place that the staff are concerned with providing equal opportunities for everyone in the school to develop his or her potential, regardless of gender, race, social class or disability. There should be many occasions for discussing this both as a member of staff and with children. (It was discussed in greater detail in the last chapter.)

Developing skills in the following areas

Communication

The National Curriculum lays stress on communication skills and it is particularly important to develop oral communication. However, it should not be forgotten that much communication involves movement and work in drama can be particularly helpful here. Technology also involves communication through drawings and diagrams as well as problem solving.

Numeracy

Being numerate means having the ability to apply mathematical knowledge. Many children can perform the necessary operations in class but are unable to translate them into useful material in other contexts. Teachers need to look for applications of mathematics in all aspects of curriculum so that children gradually become truly numerate.

Study

This is an area which should be taken very seriously by schools. Children should become increasingly independent in study as they grow older and this means that all teachers need to consider the contribution they make to the development of study skills. This is not only a matter of skill in using books and recording but also skill in asking questions, observing, interviewing for information, sorting out findings and organising them into a coherent form. The school needs to define the skills which children should acquire and decide where they are going to be acquired and practised. There should be a policy for study skill development.

Problem solving

Problem solving is a set of skills which can be found in almost every area of curriculum, but particularly in technology and science. It involves defining the problem, setting objectives, reviewing its context and then generating ideas and considering them before deciding which to use. Finally it involves selecting a solution and evaluating the result.

Thinking skills are closely allied with problem solving and involve many of the same processes. Many schools have found it helpful to use some of the ideas put forward by de Bono (1976) which involve a series of activities to be carried out in thinking through a problem or a piece of work. These skills can be applied in almost any situation and children can be encouraged to apply them across the curriculum.

Personal and social education

Personal and social skills involve self-knowledge and the development of a positive self-image. This was discussed in detail in the last chapter. As many children as possible need to experience success but at the same time individuals need to come to terms with their weaknesses and regard them as areas for further development. Failure needs to be seen as part of learning. Building self-confidence is partly a matter of matching learning to individual children and partly a matter of seeing that everyone receives genuine praise for something.

Social learning involves developing competence in dealing with social situations and developing acceptable social behaviour; the ability to work with others to an agreed end, sensitivity to others and the ability to imagine what it is like to be someone else – a skill which can be developed thorough the study of literature as well as in the way some misde- meanours are dealt with. Children also need the ability to make moral choices, thinking through situations and considering how others may feel.

Information technology

This should be part of the work in many subject areas and all children should become competent in its use, able to use word processing not merely as a means of producing good-looking work but as a way of developing a piece of writing. They also need to be able to use spread sheets and databases for a wide variety of purposes.

Preparing for life in a multi-cultural, multi-lingual world and for closer links with Europe.

The need for the development of appropriate attitudes is evident when we consider the way the world is becoming closer. We can no longer live and act in national isolation. We are part of a world where what one nation does affects others. Children need to be made aware of the problems and achievements of other parts of the world.

The NCC publication *The Whole Curriculum* (NCC 1990) also speaks of themes which include the following:

Having economic and industrial understanding

This will develop in the secondary school with work experience and careers education but much can be done at the primary stage to foster interest in the world of work and to develop understanding of some of the issues in manufacturing and selling. Visits to work places and subsequent study based on observation during the visit are a valuable part of primary education.

Preparing for adult life through education in citizenship

Preparation for adult life should involve such things as preparation for life in a democratic society, knowledge of public services, ideas for leisure and appreciation of the fact that ours is a plural society.

Developing concern for their own health through health education

The NCC paper (*ibid.* 1990) suggests that this area should include work on the misuse of drugs, tobacco and alcohol; on sex education, family life education, safety, health-related exercise, nutrition, personal hygiene, environmental aspects of health education and psychological aspects of health education. Many of these topics are part of the science curriculum.

Environmental education

Education about the environment will naturally be part of work in geography, history and science. The school needs to have a positive view of what is involved in education about the environment. This needs to include knowledge of the way environments are shaped by natural forces and then by man. It should also consider the vulnerability of environments and the need for planning to ensure that we do not continue to destroy our environment.

MAINTAIN OVERSIGHT OF CONTINUITY AND COHERENCE

Continuity and progression

The total experience of education should have coherence for each child. This means not only that we should see each stage of education as a continuous process, but that there should be genuine continuity between stages and awareness of the points where discontinuity can occur.

Continuity is related to progression and development. Progression should be evident in the work of the individual child and it is valuable for teachers to discuss what they mean by progression in different areas of work, particular areas such as personal writing and thinking what they want children to be able to do in a particular area of curriculum, in terms of learning skills alongside what they want them to know and understand.

The first discontinuity occurs for children when they leave home and enter school. They move from being one or at most one of a small number with one or more adults to being one of a much larger number with only one adult. Much of the language of school is new, even to children from middle-class homes. Words like classroom and cloakroom are unfamiliar. The teacher may talk about letters and the children will have to discover that this is something different from those the postman brings. Certain kinds of behaviour are expected of them and this too will be unfamiliar. And all this happens without the person or persons who have often been with the child all the time for first five years. Children who have been to nursery school or playgroup have an advantage here. Schools need to do all they can to bridge the move from home to school. Many schools arrange opportunities for new entrants to visit with their parents before entry and spend some time with their new teacher. Some schools also stagger entry so that each new child can be welcomed and looked after. Much depends on the size of entry.

Discontinuity may occur when children move from one teacher to the next even when the teachers are in neighbouring classrooms. Teachers make rules for behaviour in their classes and children have to adapt when they change teachers. Sometimes the teacher may make the rules explicit but sometimes children have to work out what is allowed and this can lead to insecurity.

Records should help to ensure continuity and they are now becoming more useful as teaching tools because they are records in terms of progress in the National Curriculum. There is now no excuse for teachers taking the view that they want to make up their own minds about each child rather than looking at what the previous teacher has recorded. Headteachers need to make sure that teachers really do study the records of the previous year in planning for a new class.

It may also be helpful to arrange for teachers to spend some time before the summer holidays with the classes they will be taking over so that they can get to know what the children have been doing.

Part of the task of management is to monitor continuity. This might be done by checking on the work of a group before and after a change of teacher, looking not only at the work they are doing but also at the demands the teacher is making on them.

Another useful piece of monitoring is to look for evidence of continuity in the work of a small sample of individual children before and after transfer to a new class. It can be very valuable if you can find time to follow what happens to a particular child in the course of a day. Following teachers' records and the records of individual children is also valuable in monitoring what is happening.

There is discontinuity for most children when they leave the primary school for the secondary school in spite of much work to link the two stages. There can also be discontinuity between infant and junior school or between first and middle school. The National Curriculum should help to make the step from one school to the next somewhat easier but transfer to secondary school in particular can still be traumatic for some children, because there may be a need to adjust to a considerable difference in teaching styles, and to being part of a very much larger and more complex organisation. The secondary school teacher may see younger children as much more dependent than the primary school teacher has done and expects them to be dependent even though they have developed good study skills and been accustomed to doing a good deal for themselves.

A school needs a policy for continuity which might contain the following points:

- The need to make education a continuous and coherent process for children
- A statement about the points at which discontinuity can occur, for example, home to school, moving from one teacher to the next and moving from one school to the next
- A statement about the school's policy on helping children to settle into school whether this be directly from home or from another school
- A statement of what is required from teachers taking on a new class. For example, making themselves familiar with the children's records, helping children to know the rules for classroom behaviour
- The arrangements for helping children prepare for transfer to secondary school

Another important task for the headteacher is to look at the coherence of the curriculum. The school curriculum plan will help to create coherence but there is also a need to check what is actually happening on the ground. Are there areas where one aspect of work should be informing another where connections are not being made? Are racial and equal opportunities issues being tackled? What is being learned about industry? Is information technology being sufficiently used? Are teachers making sure that children encounter problem solving and develop study skills? Is there adequate social and personal learning? Are children developing positive self-images? Are teachers providing for the most and least able in their classes? What is happening about gaps in knowledge and skill of individual teachers? If you as headteacher do not concern yourself with these issues, no one else will.

Adults in today's world not only need to give thought to where they stand on such matters as sexual behaviour, but also need to have the ability to make judgements about new issues as they occur. Children in school learning about the important issues of our time are forming their own frameworks of understanding of the world which will help to determine their views about issues of the future. They are also learning strategies for making judgements which can be applied to new situations. Many of the issues which concern the adult world are likely to be part of learning in the secondary school, but there is increasing evidence that younger children are becoming involved in drugs and alcohol and many are already starting to smoke in the primary school years. Prejudice is already taking hold in the nursery school.

This means that primary schools also need to be concerned about these issues. To some extent this will be a matter of teaching the facts of the situation – learning, for example, what smoking or drugs can do to you. In other cases, gender equality, for example, it is not possible to escape making judgements and teachers need to put all sides of the problems and encourage children to see from different points of view. It means discussing with them the ways in which prejudice prevents our seeing other viewpoints. It means attempting to help them to form judgements. The ability to think through controversial issues is one of the most important aspects of learning. Children have the reasoning power to do this at an early age. It is easy to underestimate their reasoning power simply because they lack experience of life.

The school must also be concerned with the formation of attitudes. The way children are treated in school, the respect shown by teachers for each other and for the children, the attitudes to race and gender shown by the staff, all help to shape attitudes. Teachers need to discuss such issues and consider how to handle them. There will never be consensus about many of these issues but there should be understanding among the staff of how different people feel and perhaps an attempt to balance views in what is put over to children. Parents should also know what the school is attempting and where possible their aid should be enlisted.

ENCOURAGE CURRICULUM DEVELOPMENT

It might be thought that with the advent of the National Curriculum there is no further need to consider curriculum development. What is now needed, however, is exploration of the best way to teach the National Curriculum and as headteacher you need to give a lead on this. It may be helpful for a group of teachers to take a particular Statement of Attainment and discuss the various ways in which they could help children to acquire the knowledge, concepts and skills involved.

There is also a need to discover how best to link together different parts of the National Curriculum so that time is used efficiently. There needs to be discussion too about where work on the themes and dimensions can be brought in and how study skills are best acquired. The staff need to be in agreement about ways of developing social skills and the demands for social behaviour which are expected.

Work on the National Curriculum is still comparatively new and this gives it life. It could gradually become dulled as the years go on if teachers do the same thing each year. It is only where a school is constantly looking for ways of developing the work that it will remain fresh and valuable.

Chapter 5

Organisation

Organising learning in the school involves bringing together the statement of aims and objectives, the curriculum and the teachers with the children in the school, who bring to school a unique set of experiences and interests and needs, which affect their ability to take from what the school offers.

Learning starts from experience. Children understand the words of the teacher or the words of a book only to the extent that they can bring experience to their interpretation. We have already seen that a teacher starting on new work needs to discover and build on the experience and ideas which the children already have. The teacher may then present new experiences, helping children to focus on what is significant and to sort, order and classify what they encounter, so that they are able to generalise from their experiences and apply the learning to new situations. In the process of doing this the teacher will aim to extend the children's use of language and so enable them to store and recall what is important in the experience. The children will at the same time be acquiring and practising skills. If learning has been effective they will be able use what they have learned and transfer it to new situations.

Bennett (1992) makes the point that if children are to develop their ideas they need to talk about them. Some of this talk will be with the teacher but they also need opportunities to discuss their ideas with their peers. Group work within the classroom is also an important way of learning. Handy and Aitken (1986) point out that working in groups is part of work in the world outside for many and that school should foster this ability. It is also something required by the National Curriculum

This view of learning presupposes an emphasis on first-hand experience and group work and on the importance of the learning process. It has implications for the way a school is organised and for the part that teachers play.

The management tasks of organisation are as follows:

> Organise the school effectively for teaching and learning
> Develop an effective management structure
> Deploy staff effectively
> Ensure an effective use of time, space and resources

ORGANISE THE SCHOOL EFFECTIVELY FOR TEACHING AND LEARNING

It is your responsibility as headteacher to see that there is an organisation which provides the optimum opportunity for children's learning; deploying people, time and space to the best advantage. This means grouping children in various ways. Within classes too children will need to be grouped for some work. Sometimes this will mean grouping according to ability or stage of learning. On other occasions groups will be formed on other criteria. There should also be both class teaching and individual work selected on the basis of suitability for the particular learning planned. Children may also learn as individuals from computer-assisted or other resource-based materials.

The following principles might be applied to the organisation:

- The overall organisation of the school should enable it to achieve its aims as fully as possible
- All children in the school are entitled to an equal share of expertise and resources
- Staff skills and abilities should be used as fully as possible

Every school starts with certain aspects of organisation decided for it and other aspects where the headteacher and staff can make decisions. The age range of the school and the social backgrounds of the children are given and although the school can work to increase the numbers of children, this is two-edged since increased numbers may result in imbalance in different year groups. In any case many rural schools are the only maintained school provision in the area and can do little to increase their numbers.

There is increasing evidence that the school where the staff work as a team taking decisions together is more successful than the school where all decisions are made by the headteacher. For example, Mortimore *et al.* found that, 'The involvement of teachers in drawing up school guidelines was associated with exciting and stimulating teaching in classrooms and greater pupil involvement with work' (Mortimore *et al.* 1988: 247).

They also found that teacher involvement in decisions about curriculum planning, which classes they were going to teach, decisions on spending and consultation about issues affecting school policy were associated with effectiveness. Decisions about the organisation of the school affect every member of staff and there is much to be said for such decisions being taken collectively.

Fullan and Hargreaves (1991: 3) make the following points about what they call 'interactive professionalism'. It occurs when:

- teachers as a group are allowed greater powers of discretion in making decisions with or on behalf of the children they know best
- teachers make these decisions with their colleagues
- joint decisions extend beyond the sharing of resources, ideas and other immediate practicalities to critical reflection on the purpose and value of what teachers teach and how
- teachers are committed to norms of continuous improvement in the school
- teachers are more fundamentally accountable as they open their classroom doors and engage in dialogue, action and assessment of their work with other adults inside and outside their schools.

The implication of these and other findings is that schools are most effective when there is a strong culture which involves working together.

Critchley and Casey (1986: 27) list the following characteristics of a properly functioning team:

- People care for each other
- People are open and truthful
- There is a high level of trust
- Decisions are made by consensus
- There is a strong team commitment
- Conflict is faced up to and worked through
- People really listen to ideas and to feelings
- Feelings are expressed freely
- Process issues (tasks and feelings) are reviewed.

There would be much to be said for reviewing the work of the staff team in the light of these criteria.

There are certain decisions of principle to be made before you get to the task of grouping children. The first is the extent to which you wish, if you can, to keep children within their year groups. For many schools this is an unreal question because their numbers do not allow this. In other schools uneven numbers in years make it difficult to maintain separate year groups and yet others may wish to mix age groups as a matter of principle. In general research does not support this. Mortimore *et al.* (1988), for example, found that even in single age group classes, teachers tended to be unaware of age differences and to expect the youngest to do as well as the oldest children in the class. The HMI primary survey states that in the mixed age classes which resulted from falling numbers 'there is clear evidence from the survey that the performance of children in these circumstances can suffer' (HMI 1978: 109). Alexander *et al.* also quote evidence from HMI that 'the considerable ability spread in the mixed age class leads to poor match of task to pupil in a third of the classes and a general failure to challenge the most able pupils' (Alexander *et al.* 1922: 26). The HMI survey of first schools also found that teachers found it difficult to cope with a wide range of age but noted that there were some advantages of mixed age classes for the youngest children since they 'may make it possible for new entrants to school to stay and settle in a class for a year or more' (HMI 1982: 59).

Against this is the problem that where age groups are very uneven some way must be found to compensate for the differences between years. Children in any class get a share of the teacher's attention which is affected by the size of the class. Children in a large class get a smaller share than those in a small class although the skill of the teacher makes a difference. A school may decide that mixed age classes are less damaging and difficult to manage than some very large classes. Alternatively the staffing of a large class may be supplemented by some part-time help or by a teaching assistant. Part-time teaching help may make it possible to group children for some work, perhaps by introducing a form of setting in subject like mathematics where the stage children have reached can be very different. Whatever the organisation chosen, teachers need to be constantly aware of the differences in age and development and the effect these have on children's performance.

They also need to be aware of the most able children in their classes and to try to ensure that they are extended as much as possible. Bennett *et al.* (1984) found that while teachers were aware that they sometimes over estimated some children they tended not to be aware that they underestimated others. They found that teachers had underestimated children in 22 per cent of new learning tasks in language and 28 per cent of practice tasks. In mathematics their figures were 14 per cent of new learning tasks and 34 per cent of practice tasks.

The next decision of principle is how far to introduce specialist teaching and how far to rely on the support of coordinators to enable all teachers to teach the whole curriculum. Much depends upon the particular teachers you have and their knowledge and skills. There is certainly an increasing expectation that work at the top end of the primary school should become more specialised because of the demands that the National Curriculum is making on the knowledge and skill of teachers. The advantages of having some specialist teaching is that subject work may be taught at a more demanding level and the children may achieve more within the subject. They are also being prepared for the specialist curriculum of the secondary school. Alexander makes the point that where the class teacher has limited knowledge, he or she may not recognise a child's potential. 'Without appropriate opportunity the child's potential may remain undiscovered and without appropriate curriculum knowledge, providing such opportunities will be beyond the teacher's competence' (Alexander 1992: 24). The disadvantage is that the links between subjects may be lost. Most schools will probably have to make some compromise about this depending upon the skills of the staff. In the same book Alexander suggests that it is valuable for groups of teachers to work together to teach the whole curriculum. This enables children to have the benefit of specialist knowledge and also allows links between subject areas.

There is also a need to consider the actual staffing of the school. It may be possible to appoint teaching assistants if teachers are prepared to have rather more children in their classes. It is possible to have two teaching assistants for the price of one teacher and perhaps by making these half-time appointments it is possible for a number of classes to benefit from their presence. This may make the teachers' work much more efficient because they will not waste time on matters which have nothing to do with actual teaching.

Patterns of organisation

The choices available to the school in grouping children are as follows:

- Age-grouped classes for all work
  This has the advantage that children's learning can be considered as a whole and that time can be used flexibly. It has the disadvantage that individual teachers may not be able to manage the whole curriculum equally well.
- Classes grouped by age and ability: streaming
  This has not been considered good practice in primary schools for many years but there seems likely to be increasing pressure towards forms of streaming where the school is large enough. The advantage is that teachers have a smaller range of ability to teach though this is still likely to be large and could be underestimated. The major disadvantage is that streaming is known to be a self-fulfilling prophecy. If children are placed in a low stream both they and the teachers lower their expectations and in any case the placing of children in one stream rather than another is dependent on keeping groups at a similar size or of a size which fits the rooms available. Children also often have very varied abilities with some children being quite good on one aspect of curriculum and having problems in another. This makes it difficult to decide how to place them. It is generally not a very satisfactory way of organising.
- Classes grouped by age but with some setting

If the school is large enough the problem of the range of ability in some subjects can be met by setting across a year group. This may also be a solution where groups are of unequal size. This has the advantages of streaming but teachers still need to guard against underestimating those in the lower sets and against these children developing low personal self-esteem.

- Mixed age classes

This was discussed above. Here it might be said that it has the advantage that the teacher gets to know the children and their parents really well. Children entering the group have models provided by the children already there and it therefore becomes easier to establish standards of work and behaviour. Able children may be able to work with an older group without difficulty and older children can help younger children.

Against this, vertical grouping can lead to under-performance because teachers expect too little from the older children. Younger children can use older children not only as models for good standards of work and behaviour but as unsatisfactory models. The researches all suggest that the demands on teachers in this context are too great.

- Classes grouped by age with class teachers but supported by specialist coordinators who have been given some time to work with colleagues. The specialist coordinators are still likely to be class teachers so this will require some part-time help which may mean planning staffing so that not every teacher is in charge of a class. This pattern has a good deal to commend it since it will help to increase everyone's skill and knowledge and provides for coordination of work throughout the school.

- Classes grouped by age with class teachers but with some specialist teaching

This seems likely to be the pattern emerging as work in the National Curriculum develops. If you have staff with very marked skills in a particular direction, there is much to be said for letting them do some work in a specialist capacity as well as providing opportunity for them to work with colleagues. The areas in which a school chooses to have specialist teaching may also be a matter of those areas where teachers feel least secure. Specialist teaching may be achieved by exchanging classes, by using part-time staff or by organising so that not every teacher is in charge of a class.

- Team teaching

If the physical provision in the school allows it the school may decide to use some form of team teaching. This may involve two or more teachers coming together for some work so that there is a wider range of expertise available to the children or it may be a way of dealing with all the work.

Team teaching is very difficult in a building where the classrooms are very separate. It is easiest in a building where rooms open into each other and teachers can easily work together.

Team teaching may start with joint work on a project. Here two or more classes may come together for some part of the week. The work may start with a common stimulus, perhaps a visit, and the work developed may be shared by both teachers. This can be done formally by arranging that each teacher is responsible for certain groups or some of the follow-up work can be undertaken by each teacher with children who choose particular topics to pursue. The work may include opportunities for both teachers to draw together small groups or the whole group to feed additional thinking into the project or to talk about what is happening, and the work may end with a common exhibition. An additional part-time teacher or the headteacher may join the group for some of the time so that more teacher expertise is available. Parents with particular skill or knowledge may also contribute.

This kind of activity gives teachers the opportunity to get the feel of working together and children should benefit from having a range of adults to help them. It may lead to a total commitment to team teaching. Here two or more classes plan all their work together often designating areas for particular activities in part of the space so that children go to a mathematics area for their mathematical work and to a different area for some of their art and craft work. It makes it possible to have such areas well set out with material displayed and arranged in ways which makes its use easier.

There are many ways of organising the work in a team teaching situation. Teachers may plan the use of space together and each teacher may teach his or her own class which uses the whole of the space available. Different teachers may be responsible for different parts of the curriculum so that the children go to one teacher for mathematical work and another for language work. The day can be split up into different activities so that children circulate or there can be a range of activities going on all the time with children making decisions about the order of part of their work with groups withdrawn for teaching during the day.

The advantages of team teaching are that it offers a greater range of teacher expertise to children and a greater range of space and re-sources. All the children get the benefit of the staffing ratio of the school. Teachers learn from each other and increase their own expertise and many find working with other adults a rewarding experience. Teacher absences and changes of staff make less impact because the work of the team is established and children will carry on more easily. It also makes it possible for a teacher to work with a group without interruption because there is another teacher to go to. Team teaching also makes it possible to consider the appropriateness of group size for a particular activity. There are some activities where a very large group can profitably work together. For example, watching a film or video-tape can be done in a very large group. A small group of about ten to twelve pupils which is a very good size for teaching and discussion becomes a real possibility. In a class group children can opt out of discussion but it is difficult to do this in a small group.

The disadvantages are that it takes teacher time and planning; not all teachers like working with other people and teams need to be put together carefully. Some children may find the size of the group rather daunting and it is more possible to lose track of a child who is not keen to work.

Classroom organisation

Classroom organisation will, of course, vary from one teacher to another but children will benefit if the patterns of organisation in different classes are not too different from one another. There is also a good deal of research which should now inform how teachers organise their classes.

Alexander suggests that a framework for primary practice involves the following:

Context – first the physical and organisational features of furniture, resources and participants and second the relationship observable among and between these participants.

Pedagogic process – teachers adopt particular strategies, particular combinations of class, group and individual work, particular patterns of interaction; and pupils are organised so as to facilitate these.

Content – these processes are focused on specific tasks and the acquisition of specific knowledge, skill and understanding or attribute, the content of teaching and learning.

Management – what we see and what the participants experience is subject to the teacher's management: it is planned, implemented and evaluated.

(Alexander 1992: 182)

Generally speaking too much emphasis on individual teaching tends to be limited in effectiveness simply because the teacher cannot get round all the children sufficiently often. The most effective teaching seems to be a mixture of class, group and individual teaching with teachers selecting appropriate strategies for the work in question. The ORACLE (Galton *et al.* 1980) study found that teachers who used class discussion a good deal asked more questions which required higher levels of thinking and their children performed better than those who worked more individually. They also used praise more often, used demonstration a lot and gave more feedback than other teachers.

Galton (1992) surveyed research into group work in classroom. He gives a useful summary of research findings on small group work which includes the following points:

- Children sitting in groups in a classroom are likely to achieve more if they are encouraged to cooperate either by working towards a common shared outcome or by making an individual contribution towards a common goal.
- Groups function best when they are of mixed ability and include pupils of the highest ability. It is important that the teacher encourages the group to be responsible for the activity and tries to reduce dependency on the teacher for group decisions.
- Children in groups perform differently according to the nature of the task. Levels of conversation on action tasks are higher but the quality of slower exchanges on more abstract tasks tends to be high.
- Problem-solving tasks with a clear testable outcome tend to generate a greater degree of collaboration than more open-ended tasks. With open-ended tasks children tend to stop after finding one solution.
- Children need to be taught how to work collaboratively

Dunne and Bennett (1990) point out the importance for the adult world of being able to work with other people as well as its value as a learning technique. They also note that the teachers with whom they worked found that children helped each other with minor queries leaving the teacher free to deal in greater depth with individual children. They made the following point. 'Cooperative group work led to real cooperation, the sharing of ideas and knowledge, the solving of problems together and real concern for the progress of the group as a whole' (Dunne and Bennett 1990: 12).

They suggest (*ibid.* 1990: 3–15) that there are three patterns of group work:

1 Children work individually at similar tasks but are encouraged to discuss them and help each other
2 Each child works at part of a combined task
3 The whole group work together at a task

They suggest that, according to research, groups of four are the best size for group work.

DEVELOP AN EFFECTIVE MANAGEMENT STRUCTURE

The need for a management structure depends upon the size of the school. A very small school does not need one, but as soon as the school becomes larger there is a need for the headteacher's responsibilities to be shared by others so that the school is managed effectively. In any case all staff should have job descriptions which define their roles and are known to all. This does not detract from the need for a culture where the staff work as a team and everyone is involved in some of the decision making.

Handy (1981: 199) suggests that there are four sets of activities in any organisation:

1 Steady state
  This implies all those activities which can be programmed in some way, are routine as opposed to non-routine
2 Innovative developmental
  All activities directed to changing what the organisation does or the way it does them
3 Breakdown/crisis
  This is largely self-explanatory but includes the unexpected as well as the disasters
4 Policy/direction
  The setting of priorities, the establishment of standards, the direction and allocation of resources, the initiation of action

All the staff of the school have a good deal of work in the 'steady state' category. 'Innovative/developmental' work can be anyone's task. In a small school innovation and development will be a matter for the whole staff but in a larger school it may be a matter of forming groups to consider a particular problem and how best to makes changes. Many headteachers find that their young and inexperienced staff have a good deal to offer and problem-solving groups are a very good staff development opportunity for everyone concerned.

'Breakdown/crisis' tends to be the responsibility of the headteacher or the deputy if he or she is not a full-time class teacher because they are the only people free of a class and available at the time the crisis occurs. Many crises also need the authority and experience of the headteacher.

'Policy/direction' is in the first place the responsibility of the headteacher and senior members of staff but much of the thinking here needs to be shared with other teachers.

The deputy headteacher

Mortimore *et al.* found that the deputy head in a primary school was important:

Where the deputy was frequently absent, or absent for a prolonged period (due to illness, attendance on long courses or other commitments) this was detrimental to pupils' progress and development. Moreover, a change of deputy tended to have detrimental effects. The responsibilities undertaken by deputy heads also seemed to be significant. Where the head involved the deputy in policy decisions, it was beneficial to the pupils.

(Mortimore *et al.* 1988: 251)

An important decision which depends a good deal on the size of the school, is whether the deputy headteacher should have a class. Deputies in the Mortimore study who had classes felt that it was an advantage in many ways. It enabled them to continue having direct contact with pupils and to provide an example for colleagues. However, they also felt that the dual role put pressure on them because they had too little time to get to know all the children and parents and to support colleagues.

If deputy headteachers are to make a real contribution it is important that they have some well defined responsibilities. These will differ from school to school. They may include administrative responsibilities for matters such as day-to-day administration, care of the environment, financial arrangements, public relations and much else. They may also include professional tasks such as responsibility for staff development, appraisal arrangements, support for newly qualified teachers or record keeping. In most schools the deputy needs to take responsibility for an aspect of curriculum. These responsibilities need to be clear to everyone and the deputy held accountable for work in the chosen areas. It will also be important to see that the deputy has time to deal with his or her responsibilities, particularly those of supporting other staff.

Head of first school or infant department

In a large school, particularly if it contains infants or first school children as well as older children, there may also be a senior post of responsibility for the infant or first school department. Here again it will be important to define the responsibilities of the post clearly.

Curriculum coordinators

The demands of the National Curriculum make it valuable to have co-ordinators for each curriculum area. The actual responsibilities of the coordinators will vary from one school to another and from one subject to another but are likely to include the following:

- Supporting colleagues in that area of curriculum by offering advice
- Overseeing the total programme children experience in that area
- Working with colleagues to select appropriate materials
- Inducting new colleagues into the work of the school in this area
- Ensuring that adequate records are kept of children's work
- Advising the head on the specialist needs of the area of work and on the standards being achieved

- Keeping up-to-date with developments in the area and keeping colleagues informed about them
- Undertaking some specialist teaching if this is required or, if the staffing of the school allows it, working alongside colleagues who want help.

The problems about this arrangement are the practical ones. Primary schools are not staffed for specialist work and although as new appointments are made the school can look for particular skills, in some cases the coordinator will be whoever is willing to take on the area and learn about it. There is also the practical difficulty that most primary schools are not staffed to allow for any free time for teachers and it may be difficult to plan for coordinators to have time to see what is happening in their subject in other classes in the school. In addition some primary schools are too small to have specialist coordinators in every area of curriculum.

Some of these problems could be overcome by using some part-time staff, but this will make classes larger. Another possibility is for a cluster of small primary schools to try to have all the specialisms among them and provide for a measure of specialist teaching by exchanging teachers on some days of the week. Each school has to look for the best solution to this problem.

It will be important for coordinators, as for the deputy head, to have their responsibilities clearly delineated, not only for the coordinators themselves, but also for the rest of the staff. Sometimes in the past postholders have found it difficult to advise colleagues and visit their classrooms because they felt that other teachers did not really accept their role. The role is more accepted nowadays but it is still important to make the responsibility of the coordinator clear to the rest of the staff and also demonstrate that coordinators have the authority of the headteacher behind them.

In a large school, with two or three classes in each age group, it will also be necessary to see that work across the year is comparable. This is mainly a matter for the way in which the staff work together on the curriculum, with teachers of the same year group planning together in the ways described in the last chapter and curriculum coordinators as well as headteacher and deputy looking at the continuity from year to year.

DEPLOY STAFF EFFECTIVELY

The headteacher's first task in deploying teachers is to arrange which teachers should teach different groups of children, as far as possible matching the skills and interests of teachers with the needs of the various groups. We saw earlier that where teachers are consulted about these decisions the school is likely to be more effective, but in the end the headteacher has to make the decision if only because more than one teacher may wish to teach a particular group.

There are development possibilities for teachers in teaching different age groups but teachers need more than one year with any particular group in order to get to know the National Curriculum requirements for that year. As the National Curriculum in a given year becomes more familiar to the teachers concerned they may be ready to consider moving to a different year group in order to gain experience. Experience at different levels makes teachers more knowledgeable about the school as a whole and more likely to become ready for promotion. It can also make the job more interesting to know where your work fits into the total pattern. Where teachers have taught at a variety of levels in the school, their contribution to staffroom discussion is likely to be greater. Changes should not be too drastic, however. A move to a class a year younger or a year older minimises the necessary adjustment though it will still be considerable.

A second consideration which comes into deciding which teacher should teach each class is the teacher who had that class the preceding year. A class which has had a year with a fairly traditional teacher may benefit from a year with a highly creative teacher.

ENSURE THE EFFECTIVE USE OF TIME AND SPACE

Time

Denham and Lieberman (1980) and others have found a connection between children's achievement and the time given to learning, especially the time 'on task'. It is therefore worth examining the way time is being used in the school to see if any more learning time can be achieved.

Any study of the use of time needs to start by analysing what is happening already. This means sampling what is happening in different areas of the school. The school day needs examining, looking at its length, at assembly time, breaks and lunch time and any time spent in moving about the school.

DES *Circular No 7/90* deals with the the management of the school day. It notes that the differences between schools are very considerable, varying from fewer than twenty hours lesson time a week to more than twenty six hours. This amounts to more than a day a week difference. It points out that the governing body is responsible for the starting and finishing times of each school and quotes Regulation 10 of the *Education (Schools and Further Education) Regulations 1981* which state that:

> Classes mainly for pupils under the age of eight, other than nursery classes, must provide three hours of 'secular instruction' (i.e. teaching)

a day; classes for pupils of eight or above must provide at least four hours.

(DES Circular 7/90: 6)

The first consideration in thinking about time is therefore whether the school day is long enough and whether it might be lengthened. This is not easy to do because so many other things depend on it. Parents plan their working lives around getting the children to school and may have children to get to other schools in the area; some children may come by bus; some staff may find a change of time difficult and so on. The circular suggests that it is necessary to take account of any centralised arrangements of the LEA over transport, for example; to discover the views of parents and the interests of other schools who may be involved in some way; to discuss the problem with staff; to consider any community use of the school and any local characteristics such as transport.

A second possibility is to shorten the length of the lunch hour, but this again may not be possible. In the end most schools will come down to considering whether they are using time as effectively as possible.

In general there is probably only a very limited amount of time to be saved by looking at the school day. The real differences are in the classroom and teachers need to be conscious of the importance of using classroom time to the full.

There is interesting information in the study by Tizard *et al.* (1988) about the way time is used in top infant classes. They found that somewhat less than half the day was devoted to work activity and 43 per cent of the time was used for routine activities such as registration, toilet visits, lining up, tidying up and so on. On the other hand the level of 'on task' activity was 66 per cent of all observations. This suggests that there might be a more effective use of time at this stage. It could be that the use of teaching assistants here would relieve the teacher of some of the chores which take up this amount of time.

Findings from the ORACLE study (Galton *et al.* 1980) suggest that some 48 per cent of children they observed were what the study calls 'intermittent workers' who worked when the teacher was watching them and did not otherwise. The time spent not working, on average, added up to a day a week and with some pupils to as much as half the week. There were more intermittent workers in the classes of teachers who worked on an individual basis. Here again there may be a better use of time in the classroom.

Alexander's study of the Leeds Primary Project (1992) found that while language and mathematics had the largest share of time, this was often not well used. In English, for example, the time 'on task' was on average 55 per cent. Girls spent more time on task than boys and older children than younger children. Children rated above average by their teachers worked less hard than those rated average or below average and were more likely to be distracted. In mathematics more time was spent 'on task'. Girls worked for more of the time than boys who spent a lot of time waiting for the teacher's attention. Above average pupils worked harder than in English and were less distracted than those who were rated below average or average.

In environmental studies and art the level of demand was low and teachers used art in particular as a way of finding time for dealing with work in other subjects.

Alexander also found that teachers tended to leave to their own devices the more able children, the best-behaved and girls as being undemanding. There was a considerable amount of using writing as a low level time-filling activity.

Teachers discussing the use of time should be prepared to find a way of analysing how they are using time in the classroom. If it can be arranged, it is very helpful if they can observe each other, looking at the use of time and recording what is happening. As headteacher, you need to be on the lookout for practices which waste time such as children queuing for the teacher's attention. To what extent are children practising work they already know? How far do able children spin out their work rather than try to work as efficiently as possible?

It is also part of the task of management to provide any timetable needed. This will be needed for shared facilities, like the hall and games field or playground and it may also be necessary to timetable specialist subjects like music and some television programmes. A basic decision is whether to plan time so that teachers have some free periods and the purpose of these. They could be regarded as preparation or planning periods or periods for work in their role of coordinator.

Another possible way of making time for teachers to plan together is for you to take assembly on your own from time to time allowing the staff to meet during this time. Another possibility is to supervise an uninterrupted period of silent reading in the hall while teachers discuss work or deal with children with learning problems. Alternatively two classes can come together to do this, leaving one teacher free.

Children also need to made conscious of the importance of using time well. There should be some opportunities for training them to plan work and it may be interesting with older children to get them to record what they are doing every ten minutes or so using a chart which shows whether they were on task or doing something which was nothing to do with work. If a timer is used to mark the periods it is interesting to note whether the fact that children wish to be on task when the timer sounds increases their concentration. However, this should emerge from discussion about the use of time.

Space

The headteacher has the final say in who works in the different rooms in the school. The extent to which rooms are occupied by class groups dictates whether there is space for specialist work. In an open-plan school there may be spaces planned for work like science but in a classroom-based school it may be difficult to find space for such activities. It is worth looking to see whether there are areas which could be converted. Is there more cloakroom space than really necessary, for example? It is also worth considering whether having rather larger classes and leaving a room empty for specialist work would benefit the school. This is a matter for staff discussion. Much depends on how far the teachers want to work on a specialist basis, but there are problems in doing everything in one classroom.

A further consideration in the use of space is storage. Have teachers appropriate storage for the things they need to store and is this also the case at school level? It is helpful to think about how best to store efficiently all the items people want to use. Storage in school is often in unsuitable cupboards and further thought about what is most appropriate can be helpful.

As headteacher you also need to see that the school looks attractive. Entrance halls and corridors should look attractive and welcoming and show children's work. Grounds should offer a variety of learning opportunities in addition to space for physical education. Some schools have involved children, teachers, governors and parents in thinking about the school environment and how to make the best of it and create a learning environment.

Resources

It is the headteacher's task to see that sufficient resources are available to implement the curriculum as far as this is possible within the funds available. Teachers will, of course, recommend to you the resources they need and there is much to be said for delegating sums of money to curriculum coordinators for purchasing resources for their areas of work.

You and the coordinators need to see that resources are being used to the best advantage. It is not unknown for the resource that one teacher needs to be lying unused in another teacher's cupboard. There should be an inventory of all the resources the school possesses and teachers should know what is in the school for them to use. There is much to be said for a number of pieces of equipment being held centrally to be borrowed when needed.

Chapter 6

Managing change

Change is part of living and is always with us. In recent years schools have had more changes than many would like and it is much to the credit of headteachers and teachers that so many changes have been assimilated so well.

Whatever the changes coming from the centre, any headteacher and staff are likely to have their own programme of change which is particular to the school. When a headteacher comes new to a school the changes in the school development plan will tend to be those coming from outside and accepted as necessary by all the staff. If you are a new headteacher you will have your own programme of change and it is to this aspect that the first part of this chapter refers although it is relevant to changes of all kinds. The difference is that with changes coming from the outside, the headteacher is not in a position to time the point of change according to the readiness of staff to make the change.

Any change in school involves some change in the attitudes of those involved. This is a slow process and takes time. Makins comments that 'unless a critical mass of teachers in a school come to share values and a view of what makes for quality, any improvement is likely to be fragile and short lived' (Makins 1993: 10).

Change appears to be good if it accords with one's values. This has been one of the problems for teachers over recent changes coming from government. Not all of the changes required have accorded with accepted values in primary education and teachers have had to adapt some of the changes to fit their beliefs about the way in which children of this age learn.

Change is a process rather than an event although planning for change involves a series of events. Fullan and Stiegelbauer (1991: 127–8) suggest that teachers use four main criteria in assessing change:

1 Does the change potentially address a need? Will students be interested? Will they learn? Is there evidence that the change works? i.e. that it produces claimed results?

2 How clear is the change in terms of what the teacher will have to do?
3 How will it affect the teacher personally in terms of time, energy, new skills, sense of excitement and competence and interference with existing priorities?
4 How rewarding will the experience be in terms of interaction with peers or others?

They also suggest that 'Good change processes that foster sustained professional development over one's career and lead to student benefit may be one of the few sources of revitalisation and satisfaction left for teachers' (Fullan and Stiegelbauer 1991: 331).

Little (1982: 325) found that school improvement occurred when:

• teachers engaged in frequent, continuous and increasingly concrete talk about teaching practice [their practice in teaching]
• teachers and administrators [headteachers] frequently observed and provided feedback to each other, developing a shared language for teaching strategies and needs
• teachers and administrators [headteachers and senior staff] planned, designed and evaluated teaching materials and practices together.

As headteacher you have an important role in innovation and change. You may be the change agent or you may be taking up changes suggested by someone else. On many occasions you will decide when to start people thinking about the possibility of change. You seek out the best starting points, spend time talking with teachers about the best way of proceeding. You coordinate the plans for change. It is your responsibility to see that staff are prepared for change and that there is adequate staff development. You support teachers as they try out new ways of doing things and help them to evaluate the outcomes.

Decision making is an essential part of the process of change. If change is to be effective staff need to be involved in the process of making decisions about it. There are other groups of people who need to be concerned with change. The governors need to play a part. So do parents and children. Ancillary staff may also be concerned. There are three ways in which people can take part in change:

They can be involved

Involving people in a decision implies actually letting them make the decision. This will commit them to what is decided but it will also commit you. You may therefore wish to set parameters within which the decision can be taken, identifying those solutions which would not be acceptable before the discussion starts. The most likely people to be involved are staff and governors. In some situations the ancillary staff may also be involved.

They can be consulted

Here you are discussing a decision with people which will eventually be taken by you or by the staff group or the governors. For example, you may like to consult parents and ancillary staff and possibly discuss some of the ideas being considered with some of the children but they will not take the actual decision.

They can be informed

Whatever is decided will need to be conveyed to some people who simply need to be informed about the decision. Those who have been consulted will need to know the outcome and the reasons for it.

It is important to be clear which of these three activities you are intending to pursue with each group and to make this clear to others. If they think they are involved when in fact they are being consulted this will cause dissatisfaction.

Managing change involves the following management tasks:

Identify the changes needed
Assess the situation
Plan and implement changes
Evaluate the effectiveness of changes

IDENTIFY THE CHANGES NEEDED

When you come new to a school you have to assess the need for change. You may inherit a school which is running extremely well, where you feel that the children are getting a satisfactory experience and where you feel happy to take time over changes. It is much more difficult if you come new to a school where you are unhappy with a great deal of what has been happening. As headteacher you may for a time have to accept responsibility for practice you deplore. You may feel concern abut the paucity of the experience the children are getting and feel a great sense of urgency to make changes in order to improve things.

Whatever the situation, you must assess it carefully before you act. If you try to make changes more quickly than your staff can absorb them you will not only fail to change what is happening but will set up resistance against further change. You must gain a measure of trust from everyone before you demand too much from them.

It can be helpful at this stage to set out on paper the changes you think desirable, perhaps setting them out in two columns, the first giving the present situation and the second the situation you would like. For example:

Teaching is from books and   Teaching involves first-hand
from the words of the teacher   experience and discussion with
                                     the children

Setting it out in this way helps you to identify exactly what has to happen to change practice and also gives you criteria by which to evaluate the effect of change.

You may find it helpful to use the school analysis list given in chapter 2 to compile a list of what you would like to change.

ASSESS THE SITUATION

Part of the process of assessing the situation is identifying where change is possible. Which teachers are most likely to be prepared to work in a different way? Which groups of children are most likely to respond to a different way of working? Where are parents most likely to find change acceptable? How far are your governors likely to be in sympathy with any particular change? It is usually best to start where change is easiest and most likely to succeed, because successful change makes further change possible.

When you have arrived at some idea of where you would like to start it may be helpful to assess the preconditions. There are a number of basic preconditions common to many kinds of innovation and others which may be relevant to a particular school and to the ideas being considered. The analysis on page 93 presents these items so that you can assess how far you have suitable conditions for a particular development.

The first column should be completed by putting down a lettered grade to represent the importance of this aspect for the particular innovation you have in mind. The five columns on the other side are to assess the situation in the school, so far as any particular project is concerned. The two assessments together should give you a clear idea of how difficult what is proposed will be. It also identifies the preliminary tasks to be undertaken.

It will vary from one innovation to another how far each of these items is involved, but assessing them in some detail will help you to judge whether a particular innovation is possible. If you find that there are too many items where the grade is high but the state of things is low at a particular time you may do better to shelve your plans for the time being or break them up into component parts and take a step at a time. It may

Grade	Preconditions	++	+	av	−	− −
	Motivation of those involved					
	Experience of those involved					
	Ability/skill of those involved					
	Knowledge of those involved					
	Attitude of teachers					
	Attitudes of children					
	Attitudes of governors					
	Attitudes of parents and community					
	Relationships: teacher/teacher					
	Relationships: teacher/headteacher					
	Relationships: teachers/children					
	Relationships: school/parents					
	Resources: space					
	Resources: time					
	Resources: materials/equipment					
	Other preconditions					

Figure 6.1 Preconditions for change

be that you have to work to increase skill or knowledge before you can start on an innovation or you may need to wait until you can afford materials and equipment or can change the use of space in school.

PLAN AND IMPLEMENT CHANGES

If you are to make successful changes you need to carry everyone with you. The ideal is change by consensus. Some changes can be made by working with individuals and small groups and if you are clear about the changes you want to see you can use situations as they arise. For example, you may wish to see more done to provide for very able children; in talking with a particular teacher the problem of children who work more quickly than the rest may come up and give you the opportunity to talk about some of the ways in which such children can be extended.

The best place to start making changes is usually where people see the need for change. By talking with people you will gradually identify their views of the problems they find in what they are doing. These problems give you a starting point. By discussing some of these as a group and perhaps visiting other schools and teachers' centres, the staff will gradually come to some conclusions about what they could do about the problems they have identified. It may also be helpful at this stage to invite an adviser or a consultant to set out possible ways of dealing with the problems people feel they have. In the process of these discussions you may be able to influence the direction of the discussion and staff will certainly influence each other so that there is a gradual move towards overall development.

Once people come to see change not just as something forced upon them from outside but as a normal way of working, it becomes possible to work together to plan ahead. The changes you want can then become part of the school development plan.

Suggestions for implementing change have already been given in chapter two. You may also like to consider the following strategies for involving people in making changes:

- Ask people what they would like to change and start with these ideas. You will get a range of suggestions about which you can do nothing but some of the things people would like to change may lead into those which you would like to change.
- Create situations which bring people up against the need for change. For example, you might ask a teacher or group of teachers to study a particular problem in the school or teach a group which exemplifies the problems which need to be tackled. This may make the people concerned more ready to consider change.
- Arrange visits to another school where seeing change in action may make some people enthusiastic about it.
- Make a change seem attractive by putting resources into it.
- Establish working groups with a task to do. Make sure that the group contains some people who are sympathetic to the sort of change you want to see so that they may influence others in the group

- Invite people who have something to offer to pioneer changes. It is important that such changes are successful, because their success will affect the readiness of others to undertake similar changes.
- Create situations in which people want to be seen to do well. For example, you might invite a postholder or a small group of teachers to research something for the whole staff and report at a staff meeting.
- You may be able to organise so that you release someone for a time to work at a particular change. You might, for example, offer to take a teacher's class every morning for a week in order for that teacher to get some work done for the school.
- Use brainstorming with the staff group to generate ideas for dealing with an accepted problem.
- Break up the topic under discussion into as many sections as there are people in the group. Write one of these at the top of each of a number of overhead projector transparencies. Pass these round the group asking everyone to write an idea for dealing with the part of the problem identified. When everyone has exhausted ideas, project each transparency and examine the ideas suggested.
- Take the possible solutions and ask each member of the group to write down comments for an against and any points of interest about each solution suggested. This should help towards selecting a final solution.

You may find it helpful at the next stage to use the network analysis described in chapter two.

EVALUATE THE EFFECTIVENESS OF CHANGE

Evaluation has already been discussed in chapter two and evaluation is discussed in more detail in chapter fifteen. It should be planned at the same time as the change itself so that information about the success of the change can be gathered as it proceeds.

In planning change it is important to remember that you must carry not only the staff and governors but also the parents with you. If you have been in post a long time, you may have the trust of parents and community to the extent that they will accept a great deal that you do. This cannot be assumed. You need as part of your planning to involve parents. This may be a matter of giving them information or of involving a group of parents in some way in discussion about change.

You also need to give some thought to the schools from which your children come if you do not receive them at the beginning of schooling and the schools to which they may go. Both sets of schools have an interest in how you work and you need at least to inform them of any major change.

Change is often difficult because people find uncertainty and unfamiliarity difficult to live with and changes in teaching approaches carry a measure of de-skilling. Teachers find unfamiliar ways of working worrying because they are uncertain about the outcomes of what they are being asked to do. Children may be resistant too and parents may be concerned because they do not recognise and understand what you are doing. You may need to explain over and over again. Many changes are not successful at first but go on to work well. Teachers and parents may need a good deal of reassurance at the early stages.

It is especially difficult to get people to look at change when a school is in difficulties. A school which has become unpopular with parents, where work is not good by any standards, will be one where everyone will resist change and wish to retreat into what is known in the hope that this will turn the tide. This is the most difficult task for a headteacher who has to gain people's confidence and constantly reassure everyone while change is taking place.

Another difficult situation is where a school is working in a limited way but satisfying parents because they recognise what is happening as similar to their own experience of school. In this situation change needs to be made very slowly and teachers and parents need to be led to see that different approaches will produce better results.

In both these situations teachers may spend a good deal of discussion time in talking about those aspects of change which are the responsibility of others and about which they can do nothing and avoid discussing aspects of change which they can undertake themselves. Sometimes they put all their energy into defending what is currently happening. There may be a long period of ritual blaming of other people for everything which has gone wrong before anyone is ready to get down to thinking what can be done.

In these situations you need to be patient and keep working with individuals and groups until they are ready to discuss change more positively and openly.

Another problem is that of the status of teachers. A teacher senior in service may find it difficult to change, not only because change becomes more difficult as we get older but also because it may seem an admission that previous work was unsatisfactory. Somehow you have to talk such a teacher round, perhaps using the fact that he or she is very senior to suggest that it would be possible to set an example of someone who is willing to change in spite of long service.

It is important to recognise that change will very often involve some conflict because it challenges teachers' existing values. Some teachers will take readily to the change and will challenge colleagues who disagree. You need to be ready for this and provide opportunities for talking through the areas of conflict.

Galton makes the following point

To be able to cope with the potential conflict and develop the necessary commitment requires . . . [a] collaborative structure. For this to happen teachers must be confident that the headteacher and the local authority adviser fully understand how it *feels* as a participant in the classroom, to be part of such change.

(Galton 1992: 192)

Chapter 7

Marketing the school

Schools are now in competition for children and they therefore need to take marketing the school seriously. A school in a small village where there is no other school within easy travelling distance may not be subject to the same pressure as a school in a town where parents have a choice of school. However, there is still a need to satisfy the community that the school is a good one. All schools are now in the business of public relations.

Oxley defines public relations as 'the management of all the relationships that exist between a complexity called an organisation and all the individuals or other groups with which it interacts' (Oxley 1987: 15). Planning for good public relations involves identifying the groups with which the school interacts and finding out their characteristics.

Barnes describes marketing as follows:

> It is a philosophy or approach to providing education services which is essentially consumer oriented; it involves identifying needs and wants of specified clients, designing (with due regard to prevailing educational and professional standards and ethos) appropriate education services to satisfy those needs and wants, communicating the existence of the education service to clients and delivering the desired product to them.
>
> (Barnes 1993: 1, 2)

He goes on to make the point that marketing for schools is non profit making and states that 'the legitimacy of educational institutions derives from the social value society places on them and their services, not a capacity to generate profit' (*ibid.*: 2). He also points out that consumers' needs may be consciously subordinated to educational ends.

He suggests that schools should think in terms of 'segmentation' by which he means 'the identification of the numerous sub groups which make up the mass market' (*ibid.*: 8). This makes it possible to target specific audiences. This will be particularly necessary when a school serves an area which is socially mixed.

Public relations cannot now be left to chance. The urban school that relies on its previous good reputation to ensure that children keep coming may gradually be outdone by other schools where there is a greater awareness of the need to sell themselves to the parents and it is to these schools that this chapter is mainly addressed. However, the rural school with little competition still needs to carry its parents with it and many of the suggestions below will still apply. For the urban school money spent on the right kind of public relations will be well spent if it brings more children into the school together with their budget allowances.

The following management tasks are involved.

Make regular surveys of parental views
Analyse strengths, weaknesses, opportunities and threats
Set public relations objectives
Plan and implement a public relations programme
Evaluate the success of the public relations programme

MAKE REGULAR SURVEYS OF PARENTAL VIEWS

One of the major problems about marketing schools is that people have different values. Teachers have their own values and, in a good school, individual values come together to create a philosophy and values which may not be those of the community the school serves. In any case the community will consist of different groups, each of which has its own values. The school therefore has to be aware of the values of those it serves, while at the same time remaining true to its own values and making these clear to those who are considering sending their children there. A school which submerges its own values to meet those of the groups it serves may end up pleasing no one. One of the things it is marketing is its values.

Good public relations involve identifying the characteristics of the various groups the school serves and this will be necessary in order to be able to set realistic and detailed objectives. In the first place this will be a matter of studying the local environment and the range of children for whom the school is the nearest primary school. It may then be a matter of going further afield and identifying further groups whom it would be valuable to attract. Target audiences will be parents of children now in the school, prospective parents, headteachers and staff of any feeder schools or schools to which children transfer, neighbours of the school, estate agents, local shops, local media, local churches and so on. It may also be a matter of finding out what the opposition is offering.

Governors should be an important factor in the school's public relations work. The governing body represents the local community and should be able to reflect for the headteacher and staff some of the views held locally and also represent the school to other people in the community. It is therefore important that governors share the overall philosophy of the headteacher and staff and this demands a partnership between them.

Studying the local environment in terms of the kinds of parent the school is serving may best be done by sampling the views of parents. It would be unrealistic in most schools to ask for views from all parents because of the time involved in analysing this kind of survey. It is therefore a good idea from many points of view to make it clear to parents that different groups will be asked for views from time to time so that, over the period their children are in the school, most parents are likely to be asked for their views. Where the clientele is largely middle class, it will be comparatively easy to get views on different aspects of the school from parents by sending them a questionnaire. Where it is not, and particularly where there are numbers of parents who do not speak English, it may be a good idea idea to involve children in helping to compile and get replies from their parents to questionnaires which sample parental views about schools and what they consider to be important in education. It may also be valuable to get older children' views on similar questions, since they too are clients of the school. It may be helpful to involve someone who speaks the languages of some groups of parents, to visit those who are hesitant about visiting the school and talk with them about their views of it and what they want for their children from the school. A parent or retired teacher may well be ready to do this, especially if an honorarium is paid.

A study of secondary schools by Elliott *et al.* (1981) suggests that many parents value the human qualities of schools and the happiness of their children at school above examination results although they see these as important. They found that parents 'associated happiness with the child's personal and social development at school, their increasing capacity to communicate with others and thereby create satisfying personal and social relationships.' (Elliott *et al.* 1981: 43) This view tended to be more widely shared by middle class than working class parents. They wanted schools to balance academic provision against social and personal development. If this is so then children's views about the school will be important. Although this study refers to secondary schools it is likely that parents hold similar views about primary schools.

Adler *et al.* (1989) found that Scottish parents, who have had choice of schools for much longer than parents in England and Wales, chose schools mainly on the basis of proximity, pupils' safety and the kind of children who attended rather than on the curriculum, teaching methods or examination results. They found that there was little evidence of the market functioning as a self-correcting mechanism. 'Schools with diminishing rolls lose resources and parental support and frequently experience a fall in morale, all of which make it more difficult for them to attract additional pupils.' (Adler *et al.* 1989: 52)

Macbeath and Weir (1991) who also studied parental choice in Scotland found that parents chose schools on the basis of accessibility, safety, friendship groups and the local reputation for discipline and high standards of teaching. It is likely that English and Welsh parents make decisions on similar grounds.

ANALYSE STRENGTHS, WEAKNESSES, OPPORTUNITIES, THREATS

Cave and Demick (1990) suggest that the whole group of people whose views need to be consulted be regarded as stakeholders, a group which should be taken into account in marketing the school. They suggest that the school might ask itself the following questions:

- how clearly have we identified our stakeholders?
- in what ways can the various stakeholders influence or make demands on us?
- how thoroughly are the needs of our stakeholders identified?
- how can the needs/wants of the various stakeholders be identified?
- how can the needs/wants of the various stakeholders be reconciled?
- what priorities do we establish in relation to these?
- how effectively do we manage key stakeholders?

In the case of a primary school the major stakeholders are the governors and parents, but others include contributory schools and transfer schools and people in the immediate neighbourhood of the school who could be affected if children misbehave on their way to and from school. Church schools also have the church authorities as stakeholders.

Cave and Demick (1990) go on to suggest the 'SWOT' analysis in relation to stakeholders – an analysis of the schools' Strengths, Weaknesses, Opportunities and Threats. This is not the same kind of analysis as a school may make for its own benefit, but one which analyses in relation to parents in particular. Thus the geographical situation of the school may be a strength if it is situated in the middle of its possible catchment area, but a weakness if it is a long walk from some of the local housing.

SET PUBLIC RELATIONS OBJECTIVES

Fletcher (1991), describing the results of a competition on marketing schools, stresses the need for detailed objectives and quotes a school where one objective was to attract articulate and middle class parents who would traditionally have chosen schools further afield in the public sector. Another school targetted parents who do not speak English, many of whom were illiterate. In general the competition found schools poor at stating marketing objectives.

The first task is therefore to set clear and detailed objectives. Oxley (1987) suggests that the first objective is for the organisation to be known and understood. This is undoubtedly an important objective for schools who need to be proactive in making the school known to the public. A school might look for ways of making itself widely known and have as one objective attracting positive comment in the press. Another objective might be to ensure that all parents know the work that will take place in their child's class in the coming year. Yet another might be making the school building attractive to visitors. Many primary schools, particularly those in old buildings, do not have a very obvious entrance and visitors are often confused about how to enter the school and what to do once inside. Barnes suggests that signposting areas of the school is part of making visitors welcome. It might also be regarded in infant schools as part of learning to read. The way the telephone is answered is also important in the impression it makes on parents and others.

ORGANISE THE MARKETING OF THE SCHOOL

The picture a school creates in the mind of the public depends upon a number of factors. Some of these are the result of a direct attempt to influence the views of the school held by the various stakeholders. They include all the ways in which schools have attempted to sell themselves in the past – school events, newsletters, press articles, contribution to local radio, the governors' annual report to parents and the annual parents' meeting and so on. In future there will also be four-yearly inspection reports. Although the way in which these are presented will be dictated, there is nothing to stop a school providing a commentary, showing in particular, the progress which has been made year by year.

Fletcher (1991) noted that it was important to get the whole school committed – teachers, ancillary staff, children, parents, governors, everybody involved in the school. If people who are part of the school show that they have mixed feelings and mixed ideas about what it stands for this is not good publicity.

Barnes stresses the importance of building a public image of the school and the value of having a school logo which is on all the material that the school issues.

Behind the direct methods are all the indirect methods which are often very important in forming opinion.The following might be noted.

- A welcoming attitude both on the telephone and in meeting people may make a great deal of difference to the way people subsequently view other aspects of the school. They can easily be put off at the beginning. The time someone is kept waiting and the readiness to make and keep appointments is also important.

- The impression a school makes does not stop at reception. New parents who have a choice of schools may visit to see what the school is like and will be comparing schools. Time needs to be allocated to this task. Meetings for prospective parents also need to be well organised and opportunities provided for children about to start school, to visit in small groups with their parents and spend time with the reception class teacher if this can be arranged. It can be tempting to lecture too much to prospective parents on the grounds that there is so much to tell them. It may be better to leave more time for them to ask questions and find out what they really want to know.

- The appearance of the school is an important selling point. The entrance is particularly important. If there is an entrance hall it needs to be attractive, with comfortable seating for anyone who is waiting and perhaps examples of children's work as well as plants and flowers. The outside of the school is also part of the impression the school makes and needs well-kept grounds and as little litter as possible. Children need to be constantly made aware of the way in which the appearance of their school matters.

- The appearance of children coming to and from school is seen by the neighbourhood which will draw its own conclusions. The appearance of children and their behaviour requires constant vigilance by staff.

- Written communications of all kinds carry more than the obvious messages. The school needs a logo and its own style in the layout of communications. It is now also easy to provide high-quality written communication with desk-top publishing and no school has the excuse for poorly laid-out or badly duplicated material. The school prospectus is a particularly important item. It is also worth noting what makes people attend to written messages or ignore them. People will attend to messages that are:

  - written to them personally
  - clearly of use to them
  - in language that they can easily understand. It is worthwhile being aware of what is jargon in the eyes of those not involved in education as well as trying to put messages into fairly short sentences, with important points highlighted in some way. At the same time the message should not be patronising. It may also be necessary to arrange for written material to be translated into local languages.
  - well laid out so that what is important is easily seen. Plenty of space in laying out type helps to make the message more obvious.

- short enough to be read by busy parents. If possible important messages should be kept to one side of a page.
- in tune with their own views and values.

- The extent to which parents are consulted about their views and the way in which this is done and is seen to be done may make all the difference to their feelings that they are genuine partners in the education of their children.

A large school needs someone for whom public relations is a major responsibility. This could be a job for the deputy head. In a small school it must be a responsibility for the headteacher. It may be that a governor or parent might be willing to work alongside the headteacher undertaking some aspects of the work. Whoever is responsible should be particularly good at making relationships. The tasks of that person include the following:

- surveying the views of the stakeholders at intervals so that public relations work is properly informed
- working with colleagues to identify the school's strengths, weaknesses, opportunities and threats so far as public relations are concerned
- working with colleagues to develop and implement an action plan for public relations
- making all members of the school, teachers, children, ancillary staff aware of their responsibilities for the picture of the school which is developed by parents and by people locally
- making contact with people who provide possible avenues for showing what the school is doing, for example, local press, radio and television
- evaluating the school's public relations programme.

The action plan needs to include a description of all the activities which are part of the plan, the phasing and scheduling of these activities, their cost and the way in which they will be evaluated.

Chapter 8

School administration

As headteacher, you are the administrative leader as well as the educational leader. Your background will have prepared you for educational leadership but although you may, as deputy, have had some experience of the administrative role, your experience in this area is likely to be a lot less than that in the educational role.

In the literature of many countries, the word administration is synonymous with management. In Britain we tend to see administration as the backup to management; the tasks that need to be done for the management of people to function effectively. It is in this sense that the word is used here.

The management tasks are as follows:

Oversee the administrative work of the school
Manage the school finances
Take responsibility for the school building and environment
Ensure conformity with health and safty regulations

OVERSEE THE ADMINISTRATIVE WORK OF THE SCHOOL

Every school has a number of tasks to be done which are not part of the teaching process, some of which require the knowledge and expertise of a teacher. It would be easy for you as headteacher to feel that all the administrative tasks must be your responsibility but many of them could be delegated to the deputy head or to other members of the staff. You also need to consider whether tasks actually do need teaching experience or whether they might be done by the secretary or even a volunteer parent.

On pages 107–8 is a list of some of the many tasks which need to be undertaken. Of each task it might be asked:

- is this a task which must be done by the headteacher or a senior member of the staff?
- is it a task which must be undertaken by someone with teaching skill and knowledge or could it be done by the school secretary or a teaching assistant?
- could it be shared with a more junior member of staff as a development opportunity for him or her?
- could it be done by a volunteer parent?
- is it being done as efficiently and effectively as possible? Would a greater use of micro-technology make it easier to do?

It is likely that you will put your own name opposite many of these tasks. It may be a good idea to go down the list to see whether more of the items could be delegated to other members of staff who might learn from the experience. You may be fortunate enough to have the services of a bursar. You also need to see that your deputy experiences all the administrative tasks you undertake over a period and many tasks could be shared. There are also some tasks which other members of staff could undertake, either in their role as postholders or as a specific opportunity to learn about the administration of the school; and there are some, like circular letters to parents, where a parent might help with the duplicating and addressing.

The school office

As headteacher you find yourself in charge of the school office. Very few headteachers have experience of office work and, although in a large school where there is a good secretary things may run smoothly, there is a need for you to know as much as possible of what takes place so that you know what is needed in an emergency. The smaller the school, the more important your role as far as the office is concerned. The more you know of the work of the office, the more effectively you can use the support it offers.

Every school requires non-teaching support for the administrative and clerical tasks required of it. These have increased considerably with Local Management of Schools (LMS). Some of the tasks are part of the accountability structure of the LEA or DFE. There are also tasks concerned with the governors, parents and the community.

Within the school there are clerical tasks related to the day-to-day life of the school, to the curriculum, to individual teachers and children and to personnel issues. There is also now a considerable area of work for the governing body in relation to school finance.

Clerical work in school may be broadly classified under the following headings:

MAJOR ADMINISTRATIVE TASKS	Persons responsible
Preparation of school prospectus, any school handbook, newsletter or other material for parents	
The provision of statements on school policies	
The organisation of the curriculum	
The organisation of teaching groups	
The production of any timetable needed	
The administration of Standard Assessment Tasks (SATs) and any other assessments	
The overall maintenance of records of pupils	
Reports on pupils and subsequent meetings with parents	
Arrangements for children with special needs including the exceptionally able	
Recruitment of teachers and other staff	
Deployment of teachers and other staff	
Arrangements for staff appraisal	
Organisation of staff development programme	
Preparation and updating of staff handbook or similar material	
Arrangements for induction of new staff	
Arrangements for support of newly qualified teachers	
Arrangements for cover for staff absence	
The maintenance of staff records	
Care of the staffroom	

Figure 8.1 Major administrative tasks

MAJOR ADMINISTRATIVE TASKS	Persons responsible
Care, supervision, deployment and development of caretaking staff	
Care, supervision, deployment and development of office staff	
Care, supervision, deployment and development of paid and unpaid teaching assistants	
Care, supervision, deployment and development of lunch time staff	
Lunch provision	
Arrangements for staff and children at break and lunch time, including those for wet weather	
School finances	
Maintenance and care of building and grounds	
Maintenance and care of equipment	
Stocktaking and requisitions	
Health and safety	
Transfer of pupils between schools	
Parental involvement	
Public relations	
Statistical returns to LEA/DFE	
Other responsibilities	

Figure 8.1 continued

- the collection, organisation, maintenance, storage, retrieval, provision and communication of information
- staff records, salaries, time and other personnel matters
- accounting and management of the school finances
- the processing of orders
- the provision of curriculum materials
- correspondence and telephone
- enquiries and reception
- inventories
- sales
- school meals
- filing

It is your task to see that this work is done as efficiently as possible. This means that you need firstly to make yourself familiar with the work of the office so that you have some idea how time is being used. It then means looking at what you yourself do as well as looking at what your secretary does with his or her time. Is the way you deal with the various returns as efficient as possible? Do you spend time writing letters out in longhand or dictating them to your secretary when investment in dictation equipment would allow you both to use time more efficiently? Are there times when the pressure is exceptionally high and is there any way that the work can be spread so that this is avoided? How much interruption does your secretary get and could some of this be avoided or kept to particular times, leaving time for uninterrupted work? Are you making the maximum use of information technology?

Filing is another area where headteachers are untrained but responsible. In principle it seems fairly simple and it is not unusual for a headteacher to leave it entirely to the secretary. This has snags. If your secretary leaves or is absent, you are left with a filing system which you may not understand and in which you are unable to find anything. It is better to agree a system with your secretary and mark things up for filing so that you are aware of where you are putting them. This has the advantage that anyone can do the filing of non-confidential material and it also makes filing a much quicker job for your secretary and thus a job more likely to get done. It also makes it easy to return papers to the right places.

One of the problems of paper shuffling is that you always seem to have a large collection of paper which is of action pending. You have copy letters to which you are awaiting a reply, problems you cannot act on immediately and so on. One way of dealing with this is to have a set of files, one for each month of the year, into which you put all this material plus notes of items of which you want to remind yourself. Thus, if you have asked someone to undertake a piece of work by the end of term you put the information regarding it in the last month file for the term. If you then go through your month file regularly you can take out material you need to deal with and file or throw away paper no longer relevant. Your notes about action to be taken by other people will come to your notice and you can enquire about what has happened.

The use of information technology in administration

Information technology is increasingly used to deal with the administrative tasks of the school. Its great advantage is that information can be reformed to serve a variety of needs. Desk top publishing is enabling schools to produce materials for many purposes which look attractive and present a good image.

The use of information technology offers you the following advantages.

- It reduces the time required to provide letters, reports and documents by using word processing and enables you to personalise circular letters.
- It offers the provision of a single database of pupil information capable of producing information in a range of different formats to meet specific requests.
- It enables you to produce standard statistical reports requested by the local authority or the DFE.
- Spreadsheets provide the means of analysing, controlling and auditing all your financial transactions.
- It provides a single database of staff details from which you can extract essential information when you need it

Other management information which might be held on computer includes:

- timetable information
- a list of names and addresses of supply teachers
- attendance rates
- children's names and addresses
- information about parents (for example, with whom the school should communicate and telephone numbers to use in case of a child's illness)
- children analysed by age
- groupings of children
- National Curriculum assessments
- schools from which children have come
- secondary schools to which children have gone
- equipment and materials purchased and held
- consumable supplies used including energy
- services provided (for example, those of maintenance operations)
- selected performance indicators

A further necessary consideration is that of security. School hardware needs to be marked so that it can be traced and recovered if stolen. There is also the matter of security of data. Staff and parents need to be convinced that information about them held on computer is available only to certain people. They should be made aware that they are entitled to access to any information about themselves or their children held on the school computer. This suggests that access to the computer that holds the majority of the school information should be via passwords. It will also be important to make and keep backup disks for all the standard information; and, in view of the possibility of fire in the school, they should be kept in a fire-proof safe. Databases take a long time to build up and their loss creates a considerable problem.

MANAGE THE SCHOOL FINANCES

One of the biggest changes that has happened in education over recent years is local management of schools. This has given schools much more freedom in managing their affairs and opened the door to better ways of managing the money available. At the same time it has posed considerable problems for headteachers and governors for many of whom much of the work of managing finance on this scale is new.

It is interesting to note that the movement to give schools this kind of freedom is happening in other parts of the world as well as in Britain. New Zealand, Holland and parts of Canada, Australia and America have all developed schemes giving schools greater independence. It remains to be seen whether this move will result in higher standards of achievement. It should result in better spending, since those nearest the action should be in a better position to make decisions about spending than those further away.

Delegation within the school

If the principle that spending is most effective when it is near the action is true, this implies that there should be considerable delegation within the school with individuals responsible for the budget for their area of responsibility. This means that all the teachers and some other staff must become knowledgeable about accounting. It also means that there must be clear systems for dealing with the budget which cover the way the money is allocated, the way that accounts are kept and the way spending is monitored. These systems will be needed not only by the headteacher and the school bursar if there is one but by all members of staff.

Caldwell and Spinks (1988) suggest that budgeting should be set in the context of collaborative management in which policies are worked out for every area of school life. Each area then develops a programme for work which must be seen to conform to the various policies, not only for that area of work but to policies more generally. The programmes are then costed and put in priority order and are presented in an agreed structure on no more than two sheets of A4 paper. Suggested forms for this kind of planning were given in chapter four.

Caldwell and Spinks (1988) also suggest that the plans and costing for each area of work in the school should show how they relate to the school policies and that the broad planning and costing should be outlined according to an agreed structure so that all can be gathered together in a booklet which everyone can see. They suggest that this structure should include statements about the nature of the programme, its aims or purpose, a statement of broad guidelines, a plan for its implementation, a list of the resources required, a plan for evaluation and a list of the team which has been involved in drawing it up, together with a note of the school policies which it meets. Their suggestions include the idea that the programme should be written out on a form so that all the programmes have a similar format and that proposals should be given priority labels 1, 2 or 3. Programmes should include not only the academic work of the school, but issues such as pastoral care and care and maintenance of the building and grounds.

They go on to suggest that there should be a 'reconciliation' group whose task it is to reconcile all the programmes with the overall budget. This would be a group of senior staff who would use the priority ratings from each teacher to decide how best to reduce the programmes to a level possible within the overall budget where this is necessary. The programmes would then be revised in the light of this and would eventually go to the policy group which would check that they met all the policies.

This seems rather an elaborate way of working for a small primary school but for a larger school it has much to commend it. In particular it ensures that everyone is involved in thinking about the resources needed and that what is planned fits in with the school's aims and objectives.

Budget responsibility allows the school to ask questions about the cost of educating children. It is possible to know how much is being spent on each child and on each subject and this leads to questions about whether money is being spent in the most effective ways for achieving the aims of the school.

Strain (1990) suggests that there are two ways of looking at budgeting. Incremental budgeting means taking last year's budget and modifying it appropriately to meet this year's targets. This gives stability and limits the debate but may neglect problems. Alternatively a school can use zero budgeting which involves reconsidering spending each year. This means budget holders justifying their budget requests in terms of existing and new activities and giving a valuation of the benefits accruing from each.

Most schools will probably use a modified version which incorporates some aspects of both incremental and zero budgeting, asking people to decide their priorities and give the costs of each individual activity. Priorities above an agreed cut-off line are continued and those below rejected. It is also possible to consider the implications of discontinuing existing activities. It is important that budgets reflect realistically the work that is planned. This may require a good deal of discussion and negotiation. If they do not reflect planned work, the budget holders will not feel committed to achieving their targets.

In drawing up budgets it will be helpful if items are allocated to particular heads of budget agreed by the school as a whole. Rolph (1990: 16) lists the following categories of expenditure:

- salaries
- energy costs
- rates (local taxation)
- equipment (education) purchases
- resources materials – library etc. (education)
- equipment (maintenance and administration)
- materials (maintenance and administration)
- services (educational, maintenance, insurance)
- rental cost of equipment
- staff training and travel

He also categorises planned expenditure into four levels:

- mandatory
- essential
- useful
- it would be nice if we had one of those

Mandatory costs are those which are a legal responsibility. Essential costs are those which are inescapable but not a legal obligation.

Salaries

The major element in the budget is salaries. This is about 67 per cent of the total budget. The local management in schools initiative (CIPFA 1988: 4–7) notes that schools may be concerned with the following categories of staff:

- full-time teachers
- part-time teachers
- supply teachers
- welfare assistants
- administrative and clerical staff
- nursery nurses

- technicians and resource assistants
- caretakers and cleaners
- mid-day supervisors
- school meals and grounds maintenance staff

Each of these categories of staff has its own salary pattern including the time at which salary increments become operational and its own conditions of service. You need to be familiar with all of these.

The same paper notes that schools need to compile a list of appropriate salaries and associated costs for each of the categories of employee. The following points may be noted:

- schools will need to calculate allowances for employers' National Insurance and superannuation. National Insurance varies according to whether or not individuals have contracted out of the state pension scheme.
- pay awards must be allowed for in annual budgeting and this includes National Insurance and superannuation. Superannuation will be proportionate to the pay award.
- schools are now free to decide on the number and levels of allowances within the rules laid down by the Pay and Conditions document. There should be a policy on this which is reviewed regularly.
- vacancies and staff turnover may lead to savings or to higher expenditure. It is not wise to anticipate savings from vacancies.
- overtime is difficult to estimate. It is easiest to build on last year's figures, but it should be monitored carefully.
- schools need to make an assessment of their possible need for supply cover for both planned and unplanned absence. It is important to consider how absence for INSET can be dealt with. It may be possible to timetable so that supply cover is not always needed. Some members of staff may also need cover for public duty as magistrates, councillors or trade union activities or jury service. Some of these costs are recoverable. A number of LEAs are arranging insurance for cover for long term absence. The school can also arrange its own insurance and would be wise to do so if it is grant maintained.
- it will be necessary in many places to budget for advice and consultancy where these are needed. This may be a matter of budgeting for specific advice on certain aspects of work, perhaps for an advisory teacher to work with the staff on a particular aspect of curriculum; or there may be the need and the opportunity to budget for more general advice on an agreed regular basis. This may come from LEA sources or from higher education or professional consultants or from industry. It may also be necessary to budget for peripatetic teachers for special needs or for instrumental music. In some cases it may be necessary to include the cost of superannuation and National Insurance in the fees

charged but in other cases these will be paid by the person's main employer or by the person concerned if he or she is self-employed.

- some schools may wish to share staff with other schools so that the teachers concerned can be fully employed and minority interests catered for. In this case superannuation and National Insurance will be *pro rata*.

Income

The main source of money for LEA schools will be through the formula funding but there are other sources of money which might be considered. Rolph (1990: 10) lists the following among others:

- income from lettings
- school fund and parent-derived income
- home-school association/ Parent Teacher Association (PTA) funds
- covenanting schemes
- industrial sponsorship or subsidy

In addition charges may be made to children for individual music tuition, education and transport outside school hours and the cost of board and lodging on residential trips, subject to remission in the case of hardship. The school may fix these charges.

A school is free to decide its policy over lettings. A charge must be established which covers caretaking, cleaning, heating and lighting. It will also be necessary to state what facilities will be available for the fee; kitchens, for example.

It is important to have proper accounts for all these funds. Parents have a right to know how money they have collected is being spent and it is a safeguard to get such accounts audited annually.

Monitoring control and expenditure

There should be clear pattern for the control of spending. The LMS Initiative (CIPFA 1988: 4–26) suggests the following means of control:

- All expenditure must be authorised by staff with appropriately delegated authority. Staff with responsibility for placing orders should not be able to initiate payment. This will require a separation of duties between teaching staff and administrative support staff.
- Payment of invoices (with the exception of petty cash) should be through the school's bank account, where it has one, or through the local authority creditor payment system if the local authority acts as banker.

The use of the computer as part of the record-keeping pattern allows regular monitoring of expenditure. Cave and Wilkinson (1990: 43–4) suggest that the following information should be made available to budget holders on a monthly basis:

- expenditure for the month
- budget for the month
- variance over/under
- total cumulative expenditure to date
- budget to date
- variance over/under

BE RESPONSIBLE FOR BUILDINGS AND ENVIRONMENT

This involves:

- Ensuring that the building and the environment are functional for the purposes of the school
  This means overseeing the work of the caretaking and cleaning staff, which may be a matter of working with the caretaker to deal with the firm supplying cleaning services. It also means ensuring that furniture is in the right place at the right time and seeing that the cleaning and organising the use of the building and grounds support the work of the school.
    This is more likely to be successful if the caretaker and cleaning staff are kept well informed about the work of the school and if the caretaker is involved in decision making where it affects his work. Teaching staff and children also need to be encouraged to see things from the point of view of the caretaker and his staff and support their work by being careful.
    You are also responsible for lunch-time arrangements and this too involves an important set of relationships. However you and your staff view the lunch arrangements, it is difficult to escape the idea that in a primary school they have educational possibilities. The kitchen and dining room staff need to know something about the way the teaching staff view social behaviour at lunch time if they are to work with you in training the children.
- Seeing that the building and grounds are well maintained
  The state of the school premises is an important selling point with parents. A school that looks in a bad state of repair is unattractive and not conducive to good work. Staff also look at facilities when accepting appointments and are likely to be drawn to schools where the facilities both for teaching and for the staff are good. It is also false economy to allow the building to fall into disrepair because the costs will eventually have to be met, as many LEAs have discovered. It is therefore worth spending money on the building even in difficult circumstances.
    The LEA school's responsibilities for premises will depend to some

extent on the delegation formula but all schools are likely to be responsible for furnishing, minor repairs and alterations, although they may have to accept a contract negotiated by the LEA for maintenance of the grounds and for cleaning. Building maintenance may or may not be delegated. Schools are also responsible for energy costs, water, rents and the council tax. They need to see that the necessary insurance is allowed for and that it covers everything the governors wish it to cover. This may be undertaken by the LEA but the cover which this allows should be checked. The LEA may also charge for the service. The governors are also responsible for health and safety, and arrangements must be made to check on this regularly.

Planning for work on the premises needs to be long term with plans made for several years ahead, which is difficult in a situation when the amount of money coming in is not assured and may be cut. It should nevertheless be given a high priority when money is available. It is a good idea to have a small amount of money reserved for minor repairs but it will be necessary to get competitive estimates for more major work.

- Creating an attractive environment
  If children are to care about their environment it needs to be interesting and attractive and both children and teachers need to be involved. An environment committee of staff and children may provide ideas about what is wanted to make the school a pleasant place. There should be changing exhibitions of children's work on show in different parts of the building. Children and teachers may also have ideas about making the outside environment interesting and pleasant perhaps by designing areas for different activities.

- Ensuring that there are adequate systems for selecting, storing, maintaining and using materials and equipment
  The budget should allow each year for the purchase of some major items of equipment. In some cases it will be possible, and perhaps preferable, to rent equipment. In this case, the agreement should be carefully considered since some schools have found themselves in difficulties when they no longer needed a piece of equipment. The basic questions to ask about equipment being purchased are those about product and price. It is also important to consider whether there would be a hiatus in the use of the equipment if a particular member of staff left. Rolph (1990: 26) suggests that the following questions may also be useful:

  - will the equipment use other materials?
  - does it have to be serviced at regular intervals?
  - are there any legal implications?
  - will staff have to be trained?

- can the equipment be stored?
- are there any security implications?
- are there enough power sockets?
- are any other supplies required, for example, water, mains drainage?
- in the case of large and bulky equipment, can we get it into the proposed room and will the floor loadings stand it?

A further point to consider is whether there are any safety implications and how these will be met. It may be helpful to get expert advice before purchasing and perhaps visit another school where the equipment is used. Rolph (1990: 37–8) also suggests some useful points in relation to security practice:

- the identification of visitors coming on site
- how the equipment is stored when not in use
- security measures when the equipment is in use
- how equipment issues and loans are managed
- whether the premises are protected by alarms when unoccupied
- who holds the keys to equipment and material storage areas
- whether duplicate keys can be readily obtained
- joint use of premises outside school hours
- whether the equipment has been marked to show ownership
- arrangements at holiday time
- responsibility and liability for equipment taken off site

Space is sometimes taken up in schools because things are badly stored. Different kinds of material and equipment require different kinds of storage. The right storage takes up the minimum of space and makes the materials or equipment easily and immediately available. It also takes into account the need for security both against theft and against injury. A good technology workshop often provides excellent examples of this with tools, equipment and materials stored conveniently. These principles for storage apply equally elsewhere in the school.

A second important point about storage is that a combination of storage and records must enable any teacher to see what is available. Teachers need open access to lists of what is available. It is a mistake to buy cupboards without considering exactly what is to be stored in them. Very often storage which is home made or improvised or made locally is more effective than bought storage.

The school not only needs to build in maintenance of certain items of equipment on a regular basis but also needs systems for reporting and dealing with minor breakages and deficiencies.

The combination of storage and records should enable any teacher to see very quickly what is available. There is much to be said for curriculum coordinators providing lists of what is available in their specialism with copies for each teacher. These lists should include material in classroom cupboards so that teachers know where material can be borrowed if it is not available centrally. There also needs to be a system for borrowing from central stocks of materials which avoids their disappearing into someone's cupboard or being mislaid or lost.

ENSURE CONFORMITY WITH HEALTH AND SAFETY LEGISLATION

Governors have a duty to be concerned with health and safety in school. Doe reminds us that 'where the local authority continues to be the employer (in county and controlled schools) it remains responsible under the *Health and Safety at Work Act* (1974) for safeguarding employees and persons, such as children, who may be affected but who are not employees' (Doe 1922: 20). Governors in aided, independent and grant-maintained schools also bear these responsibilities and all governors have a responsibility for seeing that the school is managed safely. Teachers and other employees must also keep to advice on health and safety in managing their work. The school needs a health and safety policy and a health and safety representative on the staff.

Governors need to check on the following:

- are there any hazards in the school building arising from maintenance?
- what are the arrangements in case of fire?
- are there dangers arising from vehicle movement which could be avoided?
- are there any hazards arising from cleaning arrangements?
- are there any hazards in the playground areas or the grounds generally?
- what arrangements are being made for safety on school transport or on buses transporting children to and from school?
- if there are contractors on the premises, what arrangements are being made for the safety of teachers and children?
- are accidents being properly reported?
- is there adequate provision for first aid?
- are there staff trained in first aid?
- is there staff involvement in health and safety through staff representatives?
- are children being given safety training where this is appropriate?

In addition curriculum coordinators, particularly in practical subjects, need to be conscious of health and safety hazards and all staff need to be aware of the school health and safety policy.

Chapter 9

Managing children's behaviour and social education

School plays an important part in socialising children. During the primary school years children are developing and learning socially and emotionally. At five children find it difficult to see from another person's point of view. This may make it difficult to share things with others or to understand what their behaviour means from other children's view-points. Gradually as they grow through the school they become more able to see other points of view. They become able to share of their own accord and become genuinely able to work with others and the school needs to set out to foster these skills.

Children come into the primary school not knowing the demands school will make. Gradually they learn acceptable school behaviour so that by the time they leave for secondary school they know what is expected from them in all kinds of situations. This behaviour may differ somewhat from what the secondary school expects but most children will also have become adept at working out what teachers will let them do and adapting to it.

The tasks of management are as follows:

Establish a philosophy of care
Establish and maintain acceptable behaviour patterns
Ensure provision for personal and social education
Establish and maintain a record-keeping system

ESTABLISH A PHILOSOPHY OF CARE

Primary schools have a heavy responsibility in caring for children who are not yet able to care adequately for themselves. It is the task of the headteacher and staff firstly to establish patterns of caring which ensure the safety of children while they are in school and then to work to make them increasingly independent.

This means having clear agreement with teachers about such matters as supervision before, during and after school, ensuring that journeys out of school are properly prepared and supervised and meet the requirements of the LEA where this is appropriate. It is necessary to make sure that precautions are adequate in any work which has inherent dangers, such as physical education or science and also to see that the school building does not present unnecessary hazards for children or teachers. This is a very important set of responsibilities made more difficult by the fact that it is not easy to foresee the things that children will do.

Caring also involves caring for children as people. There is a great deal of evidence now about the number of children who are experiencing various kinds of difficulty at home, from family break-up to incest, and for some, school may seem the only stable part of their lives. There is also evidence that some children are ill-treated by their parents and school may be the only place where this can be identified. These matters pose considerable problems for teachers and headteachers.

The normal pattern of primary school organisation in which each child is part of a class group and spends a good deal of time with the same teacher makes problems rather easier to identify than they might be in the secondary school. However, not all teachers are equally observant or equally good at caring for children and it is part of the responsibility of the headteacher to be aware of the problems children may be experiencing and to discuss these with the class teacher. As headteacher you can make class teachers more sensitive to children by the way you discuss children with them, by the way you draw attention to children who look tired or out of sorts and by the way you share knowledge which comes your way about home circumstances. You also learn about children by looking at their written work or art work. Fortunately most parents care a great deal about their children and the school shares with them the process of helping their children become social beings. The Plowden Report (1967) suggested that teachers and parents should be partners in the education of their children and this means that teachers need to know parents well and discuss children with them as individuals, listening to what parents have to say as well as telling them how children are doing in school. The patterns of talking with parents which the headteacher sets up in the school may help to ensure this.

Roberts (1983) makes the point that the headteacher needs to explain ways of handling children to all newly appointed adults, not only to teachers; explaining the work of the school and how they can help in incidental ways. She suggests that there should be occasional meetings for all the staff of the school, creating a sense of involvement.

ESTABLISH AND MAINTAIN ACCEPTABLE BEHAVIOUR PATTERNS

The Elton Report makes the following statement:

> We recommend that headteachers and their senior management teams should take the lead in developing school plans for promoting good behaviour. Such plans should ensure that the school's code of conduct and the values represented in its formal and informal curricula reinforce one another; promote the highest possible degree of consensus about standards of behaviour among staff, pupils and parents; provide clear guidance to all three groups about these standards and their practical application; and encourage staff to recognise and praise good behaviour as well as dealing with bad behaviour.
>
> (Elton 1989: 13)

The way children behave in school is a product of what the school demands of them. The important thing is that everyone is in agreement about the demands to be made. Teachers need to involve children in identifying appropriate school and classroom rules so that they can help in keeping them.

You also need to discuss as a staff what you expect from children by way of conventional good manners, such as opening doors for other people, letting adults go first, greeting visitors and everyone needs to insist that these rules are kept and praise children when they behave accordingly. These are only conventions, however, and conventions vary with the community and differ at different points in time and you must bear this in mind in what you decide to establish. On the other hand, the fact that the behaviour you wish to establish is not current in your community should not deter you, since it is part of the job of the school to make children socially mobile so that they can fit into quite different communities. You may therefore wish to set standards of behaviour that allow this.

The basis of good manners is thought for other people and this involves much more than following conventions. It involves the ability to see from the other person's point of view. This has implications in a number of aspects of school life. Very often children's misdemeanours happen because children do not see the implications of their actions for others and the task of the teacher is to help them to reason through and see after the event what they should have seen before it. The pressures of school life make it difficult to do this on every occasion but, if you make a habit of dealing with misbehaviour in this way as often as you can, children will gradually start to think before they act.

Galton suggests that teachers might more often deal with misbehaviour in class by putting their own point of view. He describes a situation where a teacher worried by the fact that too many children wanted her attention made the following comment to them:

> When you all come out like this, I don't know what to do and feel very frustrated. I know you want my help and I'm really interested in what you're doing. I want to talk about your work with you but all the time I keep on thinking of the others who are waiting and this makes me try to get through with you as quickly as possible so that I can start on the next one. Can you help me solve my problem?
>
> (Galton 1989: 158)

The result of this was that the children decided to keep a record of the reasons why they came out and whether there were alternative solutions to their need for the teacher.

You can also do a great deal to help children to see from other people's points of view through stories in literature, through drama and religious education and through general discussion of events. The necessary thing is to be agreed as a staff that this is part of your policy for helping children to live together in harmony.

Children's behaviour is to a considerable extent an outcome of the school climate and the way children are treated. Children in most primary schools are well behaved. There are, nevertheless, problems which occur with some children.

A school also needs a policy about discipline and rules which are agreed by everyone. School rules need a lot of discussion with parents and children as well as teachers and there needs to be agreement about how matters of discipline are to be dealt with. Different teachers will have different ways of managing their classes but there needs to be some overall agreement about ways of controlling children.

There are a number of possible approaches to this. Wheldall and Merrett (1984) suggest a behavioural approach. This involves identifying clearly the behaviour that is wanted and consistently reinforcing it by rewarding by praise or in some other way each time the behaviour is achieved. There is some evidence that teachers reward work by praise but less often praise children for the behaviour they are trying to establish. This approach can be particularly helpful with children who pose problems in class. The restless child, for example, might be set the task of working for ten minutes without getting up or disturbing anyone else and then being given the opportunity to mark it up on a personal chart if he or she succeeds. The time limit can then be extended or made less according to how well the child succeeds.

An American study reported by Makins (1991) suggests that teacher and children should agree no more than five simple rules for classroom behaviour. These must be rules which can easily be seen to be broken and there must be a succession of penalties for breaking the rules, ranging from putting the child's name on the board to seeing the headteacher and having their parents informed. Penalties are non-negotiable and because the rules are agreed by the class everyone is concerned that they are kept. Along with this is a policy of praising children for good behaviour and possibly using badges and stickers and visits to the headteacher as a reward.

Galton (1989) suggests that the behaviour of a class should be a matter shared by teachers and children, with children involved in setting ways of coping with any difficulties arising from their behaviour.

Lawrence *et al.* (1984) stress that children's misbehaviour may be the result of the situation in which they find themselves rather than sheer wilfulness. They also point out that if a child is labelled as disruptive, teachers may start to expect that child to produce certain kinds of behaviour and this in turn may provoke the behaviour. They stress the importance of making the child feel valued and capable of good behaviour.

Roberts also stresses the importance of teacher expectation:

> There is every reason to suppose that teachers who minimise the disadvantages or handicaps that their children may experience, who keep a watchful eye on their own prejudices and who concern themselves with future possibilities, rather than past failures, may help children to achieve higher standards of work and behaviour than would normally be thought possible.
>
> (Roberts 1983: 11)

She also notes the need to be both consistent and persistent:

> The child needs to know that you will make it clear what is expected of him and what the limits are; that your standards will not vary from one area of school life to another or from one day to the next; that you will be invariably fair in your dealings with him; in other words, that you can be relied on to declare the rules of the game and not then to change them. He also needs to realise that you will not give up, however much easier that might be.
>
> (Roberts 1983: 80)

Mortimore *et al.* (1988) found that there was a link between poor reading attainment and behaviour. This may well be a matter of children with reading problems having poor self-esteem.

Managing children's behaviour is a matter of rewarding what is good as well as providing sanctions for poor behaviour. Mortimore *et al.* (1988) also discovered that schools which used stars and badges and other ways of demonstrating approval found these effective. Harrop and McCann (1983) found that positive letters to parents were a valuable reinforcer.

Suspension

However well the school is run and however good the teachers skill in managing children, there is likely to be from time to time a child who poses serious problems and who continues to pose problems in spite of everything that the school can do. As headteacher you may eventually find it necessary, after you have tried everything else, to suspend a child. There are three types of exclusion – fixed term, indefinite and permanent. Any exclusion for more than three days must be reported to governors and to the local authority if it is an LEA school. Parents can make representations to the governors, and governors or the LEA can direct that the child be reinstated. In the case of an indefinite exclusion, the LEA must set a date for its ending. In the case of a permanent exclusion the parents can make a formal appeal to the governors who must hold a formal meeting to hear the appeal. If the governors support the headteacher, the LEA must decide whether or not to confirm their decision. If the exclusion is confirmed, the parents can appeal to an independent tribunal. If the LEA overrules the governors and reinstates a pupil, the governors can appeal to the independent committee.

ENSURE PROVISION FOR PERSONAL AND SOCIAL EDUCATION

The personal and social education of children is an important part of the work of the school. It involves a positive approach to the development of all children and a clear idea of the social and personal skills being developed

Children at the primary stage are developing as personalities and trying out behaviour and discovering the kinds of people they are. Home and school react to their behaviour and demonstrate that some is acceptable and some unacceptable. Some therefore becomes part of their vocabulary of behaviour and other behaviour is dropped. Children who experience different behavioural demands at home have the problem of matching behaviour to situation and may find it more difficult at the early stages to adjust to school demands. The teacher plays an important part in rewarding certain kinds of behaviour by praise or by drawing attention to what is good as well as commenting on what is undesirable. It is worth noting in this context that there is a lot of evidence to suggest that praising and encouraging is much more effective than commenting adversely on undesirable behaviour. A teacher wishing to change children's behaviour needs to praise as many positive activities as possible.

School will also play an important part in children's moral development, both by the behaviour which is rewarded and by the moral questions which are discussed. Stories and drama may well play a part in this and teachers need to discuss the moral ideas which they wish children to acquire and seek ways of reinforcing these. The OFSTED inspection schedule places moral and spiritual education among important aspects of the school to be inspected.

School is also the major learning place for children's social skills. Children must move from the egocentricity of early childhood to being able to live and work with other people. Part of learning to live in the adult world involves learning conventional behaviour so that one is able to move with ease in different social environments. A person who is confident will probably cope in many situations, but confidence is greater when you know what to do. It is helpful if children have learned how to greet people, how to make introductions, how to use the telephone, how to entertain someone during a meal and so on. Very often this kind of learning can be put into practice by asking children to greet visitors and show them round the school. Again the school needs some policy about this.

Most schools are concerned with developing children's ability to take responsibility. This needs to be a deliberate policy if you want to make all children responsible and not merely those who show that they are able to be responsible. Very often those who are able to take responsibility get all the practice and those who need the practice do not get it. You need to think through as a staff what you mean by being responsible and think how you train these skills and the practice children will need if they are to develop them.

At an early stage children need to learn to share with others and take turns. Later they need to acquire the skills of working in a group which involves the ability to discuss the work in hand, agree on the part each person shall play, bring the work of the group together and present it as the work of the group and so on.

We have already seen that a number of studies (Galton *et al.* 1980, 1990, 1992, Mortimore *et al.* 1988, Dunne and Bennett 1990) note that although primary school teachers generally arrange their classrooms so that children sit in groups, there is actually a limited amount of collaborative work. Although there were ten years between the reports of the studies by Galton *et al.* they found that only a small amount of change in the amount of collaborative work that went on. The tendency was for children to sit in groups but work individually.

If the ability to work with others is really part of what we wish children to learn, then we have to consider it carefully and see that it is given a proper place. This means identifying the skills required as well as the work done.

Galton *et al.* make the following point about group work:

Effective group work in the classroom concerns not only the capacity of the groups to complete tasks successfully but also the capacity for each pupil to be able to take on different roles within the group according to the nature of the task and the composition of the other members.

(Galton *et al.* 1992: 23)

Children need to be taught the skills of working together. Leadership skills are part of personal development and some children will show these from an early age. It is part of the task of the school to enable as many children as possible to experience leadership and to help them to consider what is involved in leading a group. In particular they need to learn that leading others involves supporting and helping them and drawing ideas from them rather than telling them what to do, although there may be situations when this is appropriate too. They also need to learn that there are situations when they should be prepared to follow. This again needs discussion with staff and children.

Perhaps the most important contribution the staff make to children's personal and social learning is the example they offer. Children tend to treat others as they themselves are treated and as they see others treated. A teacher who demonstrates that he or she is caring of all the children in the class and shows respect for all of them no matter what their ability, is likely to have children in the class doing likewise, especially if these matters are discussed.

The way teachers appear to children to treat each other and the way the headteacher treats teachers is also important as an example to children. In particular it is valuable for children to learn that there can be disagreement among adults without hostility; that there can be more than one valid point of view and that others may see things differently from ourselves.

ESTABLISH AND MAINTAIN A RECORD-KEEPING SYSTEM

Every school and every teacher needs to keep records of each child's progress. It should be possible to see a child's whole school career through the school records. The National Curriculum and the demands of its assessment has made this even more important. It is the responsibility of the headteacher to see that adequate records are kept, that appropriate records are passed on to the next stage of education and that parents are informed of their children's progress.

Bennett (1992) makes the point that teachers do not use assessment for diagnosis to a sufficient extent. Children come to school with ideas about many of the things they learn about and unless the teacher has some idea of what and how they are thinking much teaching may fall on deaf ears. Bennett comments:

What in fact is found in contemporary classrooms is a great deal of assessment, some informal and unrecorded, and much assessment characterised by ticks, crosses and brief comments. There is a lack of diagnosis and this is often accompanied by teachers concentrating on what children produce (for example, a page of completed sums) rather than on how it has been achieved. Yet both are necessary for diagnosis. An analysis of common errors in written work, or in number work, gives teachers a first glimpse through the 'window'; further questioning of the child concerning strategies used when coming to these typical errors opens the 'curtains' even wider.

(Bennett 1992: 20)

The record-keeping system of a school needs to include the following at school level:

- Background records for each child giving information about family, any previous schools, serious illnesses or handicaps and any other information likely to be relevant to the child's progress in school.
- A record of the work a child has done in school. This will be mainly in terms of the National Curriculum but the approaches also need to be recorded in some way. This may be dealt with by providing a duplicated sheet for the class and identifying the specific aspects of the work of the class which the particular child has experienced. This can then be complemented by information about what the child has actually learned, by comments from the teacher about any problems the child has experienced and by the record of National Curriculum assessment. This will give a diagnostic record which provides a background for further learning.
- A record of personal development. This might include social development, and a note about the child's development in such skills as the ability to work with others, take responsibility and social and learning skills.
- A quick reference record giving each child's home address, names of parents or guardians and telephone numbers of where they can be reached in an emergency. This is best kept on a computer so that it can easily be accessed. In addition other information frequently required, such as children's dates of birth, might be part of this record. If this is put on a database, information can easily be extracted when needed.

Alongside the school records each teacher needs to keep day-to-day records of children's progress. The assessment required for the National Curriculum now dictates much of what needs to be kept, but the kind of diagnostic record described above might be kept in a file, in which there is a sheet for each child on which the teacher makes notes of information about the child as it is revealed.

Schools are now required to send written reports to parents and these will give information about where the child stands in relation to the National Curriculum.

There is a strong case for involving the children themselves in keeping records of their own work and progress. At the early stages these may be simply ticks on a list to show work covered, but the teacher should discuss progress with individual children, encouraging them to think about how well they have worked, so that they are able at the later stages of primary education to keep records of their own progress and comment on how well they feel they have done. All children need to become able to evaluate their own work.

Some schools arrange for children to have a personal file into which they put work they are proud of. This forms a good record of their work and involves discussion about which pieces of work are good enough to go into the file. Children who do this show a great deal of pride in their files and the discussions serve to increase their ability to evaluate their work.

Schools must now report to parents on children's progress and the school record of achievement forms the basis for this. Parents will want to know how their children are doing in each aspect of the National Curriculum. There is much to be said for arranging for children and their parents to add to the child's record and this provides material for discussion with the parent when teacher and parent meet to discuss the child's progress. A school may also like to agree some goals with children and record progress towards them.

Teachers need to take care over what they record about individual children. It is no longer possible to have records which are confidential to the school. Teachers need to maintain their records in the knowledge that they may have to make them available to parents and that a court could demand to see their records in the case of a dispute.

Chapter 10

Managing people

Management in schools is primarily about managing people. All teachers have to manage children but managing a school means managing adults so that the work gets done. The following management tasks are involved:

> Lead and motivate staff
> Delegate effectively
> Agree staff salary policy with governors and implement
> Deal with staff problems
> Have knowledge of relevant legislation

LEAD AND MOTIVATE STAFF

Margerison (1978) writing about advisory work in industry, lists a number of different kinds of influence:

- *Force influence* People in senior positions can influence because of their power to make things difficult if other people do not do as they wish. This influence is there whether or not the person influencing wishes to work this way and it is important to take it into account because people may not show their true reactions to those in power. The problem in exercising force influence is that those being influenced in this way may not be convinced of what they are being asked to do and may therefore do it very superficially.
- *Knowledge influence* Influence also arises from the skill, knowledge and expertise of the person influencing.
- *Reward influence* As headteacher you are in a position to reward people for moving in certain directions. The reward could be in support for promotion or in provision of materials and equipment for further development of good work or it could simply be in terms of praise and

recognition for work well done. If the school pay policy includes performance-related pay it could include additional pay.

- *Positional influence* As headteacher you have influence because of the position you hold. Your deputy and other senior members of the staff will also have positional influence. This is akin to force influence and has the same advantages and disadvantages.
- *Personal friendship influence* People are influenced by those whom they like and respect. From this point of view it is important to win over staff when change is contemplated.

Other types of influence include:

- *Persuasion* This relies on reasoning and is usually the preferred method of influencing others.
- *Exchange* This is really a subtle form of bargaining in which A offers B something in exchange for acting in a certain way. It happens, for example, if you offer teachers extra resources in order to encourage them to change in a certain direction.
- *Environment* It is possible to influence people through their environment. Thus a teacher might be influenced by being next door to another teacher working in a certain way. Teachers may also be influenced to work differently if their working conditions are updated making it easier to do certain things.
- *Magnetism* This is an aspect of charisma. People are influenced by those who have some kind of drawing power for others.

The human need for satisfaction in relating to other people and for achievement are very important. Many people rate these above salary in their list of requirements in their jobs, although salary will take priority if it is not seen to be a fair reward for work done. Over three decades ago Herzberg *et al* . (1959) wrote of a study in which two hundred engineers and accountants were interviewed about events at work which had either resulted in a marked improvement in job satisfaction or had led to a marked reduction. The major findings of this study showed that strong determinants of job satisfaction were achievement, recognition, work itself, responsibility and advancement, the last three being of greater importance for a lasting change of attitudes. The major dissatisfiers were company policy and administration, supervision, salary, interpersonal relations and working conditions. The dissatisfiers he named the 'hygiene factors'. The findings of this study still have relevance for managers in all kinds of organisations.

Teachers and other members of staff may vary in what motivates them and any one planning staff development must take this into account. Motivation will probably operate differently at different periods of a person's career and men and women tend to differ in some aspects of what motivates them. Knowledge of the motivating forces is valuable in helping individuals and in thinking out how to provide a programme which will be effective for as many people as possible.

Teachers may be motivated by:

- children developing and learning
- enthusiasm for subject matter
- recognition, praise, interest and encouragement
- a chance to contribute and to shine
- a chance to take responsibility
- a challenge to professional skill
- the inspiration of others
- career prospects.

Other staff may be motivated in somewhat similar ways. The stimulus of the content of their work and the children, can be an active ingredient in the motivation of ancillary staff as well as teachers.

Leadership behaviour

The various ways outlined above in which people can be motivated come down in the end to the way the leader of a group behaves towards others who are part of it. Leadership behaviour is in the first instance part of personality and most good leaders act instinctively without thinking about how they are operating. But just as teaching behaviour is partly a matter of personality and partly learned, so is leadership behaviour. A leader has various tasks to undertake. The way they are carried out affects the extent to which others are prepared to follow and be influenced.

Many of the characteristics of the effective headteacher listed in chapter one are relevant to the management of people and the following additional points should be noted. The effective leader:

- makes others feel secure
  Some people in leadership roles create an atmosphere of security from an early stage because of their personality. However, every leader must eventually earn the trust of colleagues through performance. Security is created through predictable behaviour. People like to know where they stand and how you are likely to react. They need to know the issues in which you wish to be involved and those which can be left to other people. This does not mean that you should always behave in expected ways but that you must first satisfy some of the expectations of those being led.
- is consistent in behaviour
  Consistency in behaviour is important in creating security and pre-dictability. There must be seen to be rational principles behind your

decisions. Every decision made in the early days is creating a precedent for the future. No decision can be taken in isolation.

- is seen to be fair in dealing with people
This is another aspect of consistency. You must be seen to treat people impartially – and normally make the same decision in a similar situation for one person as for another.

- shows support, interest, recognition, praise and encouragement to individuals
A leader in any organisation has to do more by way of praising and encouraging than seems obvious and it must be done consistently and impartially. Over a period, you need to demonstrate interest in all staff whether teaching or ancillary and offer them encouragement. In many schools where there is dissatisfaction staff will say that no one takes an interest in them. It should be remembered that the cleaner and care-taker, the school secretary and the kitchen and dining room staff need praise and encouragement just as much as the teachers.

- is honest
One of the most important factors in managing people is the creation of trust. This is not easy because to get trust a person has to give trust and there is risk in this. Trust is most likely when people know that you will be honest with them in a supportive way. This means saying what you mean but following it up with an offer of support and some genuine steps that the person can take. It is also important not to promise anything which cannot be carried out. It is better to err on the cautious side and then please people by being better than your word than to promise and have to go back on your promise. Trust is also important in obtaining openness. If you want staff to explore ideas you have to create a situation in which people feel that they can say what they think without being afraid that it will be held against them or that readiness to explore an idea will be taken to mean agreement with it and a readiness to see it implemented.

- is flexible and adaptable
Flexibility in a leader and readiness to have a change of mind if you are convinced that you are wrong is a sign of strength not weakness. What is needed is an ability to stand back from a decision and assess it according to principles.

DELEGATE EFFECTIVELY

Many people taking on a leadership role for the first time have difficulty in accepting that their task is no longer to do the work themselves but to get it done by others. It is tempting to take on tasks because you know that you can do them well, when the tasks are really the province of somebody else. This means that you are using time which should be spent in other ways and taking opportunities which others may need to acquire and practise skills.

It is very important to be able to delegate. Even in a small school there should be some delegation. Delegation provides ways of sharing work equitably. It provides training for staff to develop in their existing posts and an opportunity to prepare for more demanding management roles. In a school where there is much delegation, there are often good candidates for promotion when vacancies occur. It should be part of the professional development programme. If you delegate you are able to spend more time on evaluation and planning, two aspects of management which can be neglected when pressures build up. You can also spend time on those areas of work where attention is most needed. If you delegate and have trained colleagues to take responsibility you know that work will continue to be done well in your absence. Headteachers who are frequently pursued by telephone calls when they attend meetings out of school should question whether they are delegating satisfactorily.

When tasks and responsibilities are delegated, sufficient authority must also be delegated. If you delegate authority you must make it clear to everyone concerned that a specified person has been asked to shoulder certain responsibilities and that he or she will be supported publicly.

It can be helpful to any leader, even one who delegates well, to analyse the way he or she is spending time and to consider whether enough is being delegated. Details of ways of analysing the use of time are given in chapter sixteen. It may also be helpful to work through the following programme:

- Make a diary analysis for the previous month (or as far back as you can remember or have recorded sufficiently well) listing all the tasks you have undertaken personally. Add any other regular personal tasks and then mark each item with one of the following categories:

    A. A task which must be done by the headteacher. This should be done stringently and only tasks which cannot be delegated should be graded A.
    B. A task which you have done because you have particular skill and knowledge which at present no one else can offer.
    C. A task which requires your skill and knowledge but which could be done by somebody else, with help if necessary.
    D. A task which ought to be done by somebody else.

- Review all the tasks listed under D and plan to delegate any likely to recur. Then review the tasks under B and C and consider which could be delegated.
- Discuss with likely members of the staff the possibility of delegating B tasks and make plans for delegating them when staff have acquired the requisite skills.

- Consider whether any of the C tasks can be delegated.

One sometimes hears people say that they cannot delegate a task because they do not feel that it will be done properly. People who say this are often unaware that they are admitting their own failure as managers. It is the manager's job to train others to do a job adequately, not to do it for them. This involves working towards full delegation, helping and supporting the person concerned until he or she can work independently. It will involve the following stages:

- Define the task
  If you are delegating something for the first time you would be wise to set down exactly what is wanted in terms of the outcomes and the limits of the tasks.
- Talk it through
  Discuss with the person concerned to discover how he or she intends to work. It is good practice for the person to go away and think out how to do the job and then to come back and discuss it. This enables you to check that everything has been thought of or to feed in suggestions. Remember that there is usually more than one way of doing a job well and your colleague may be effective working in a different way from the one you would have suggested.
  There is also a need to determine the proposed programme of action. Many tasks require a timetable. Ask for dates by which different stages of the task will be accomplished and note these for future reference.
- Monitor progress unobtrusively and supportively
- Review what is happening at regular intervals

Part of your task is that of evaluating how things went. If, for example, you have delegated the arrangements for a school event, you will want regular reports on how things are going and you may also want to sample any practice arrangements or preparations. If things seem to be going badly, it is best not to take over the job or give it to someone else unless this is unavoidable, since this may damage the confidence of the person concerned and lose the learning which may take place if he or she tries again. It is useful to ask the person concerned for views about how his or her performance could be improved and then to recommend appropriate changes as a starting point, perhaps supporting in a different way, possibly by involving a member of staff whom you know would be supportive.

If you are asking someone to report back at regular intervals you need to develop a reliable reminder system about this since it is important that people know that there will be a check.

Evaluating the process should involve sampling what is happening. It is also important when mistakes are made to analyse what went wrong, remembering that errors and failures are a legitimate part of learning.

This analysis should be as objective as possible, looking for pointers to the solution of the problem. Vague criticisms are no use for learning and your task is to see that your colleague learns and improves in skill. If he or she can be led to see criticism as objective and supportive, concerned with actions rather than personality and leading to development and growth, this is a valuable tool for staff development.

Things may go wrong for many reasons. If you have not defined the tasks and the responsibilities adequately, they may be misinterpreted, both by the person with the responsibility and by others. This may give rise to various kinds of difficulty.

An adequate briefing may be misinterpreted because the person to whom the task was being delegated was preoccupied with something else at the time. Or your colleague's planning of the task may have been inadequate. It is often useful to go through it step by step looking for mistakes and omissions and trying to draw out a strategy which could be applied in future situations. You then need to seek an opportunity to let the person concerned undertake a similar task doing the planning with him or her.

It is not impossible for someone enjoying authority for the first time to use it unwisely. Sometimes a person will act autocratically if he or she has not understood what is involved in leadership. In such a case it is important to get the person to see from other people's point of view and to anticipate the outcomes of certain actions. This may require quite specific discussion about actions which have upset others, perhaps painting a picture of how they see the situation.

A quite different problem is when nothing gets done. There are all kinds of reasons for this and an assessment of the reasons will influence the way the problem can be tackled. A clear brief and a firm date by which action is required will persuade most people to start work. The person may have been asked to do more than he or she is able, however. If there seems to be difficulty in taking steps towards the necessary action, try making them smaller still.

Discussion of what has happened should lead to discussion of points for improvement and points which might be relevant elsewhere; for sometimes someone coming new to a task discovers ideas or ways of working which might be of interest to others. In such a case the information needs to be appropriately disseminated.

Finally you need to come back to a personal analysis and look at whether your skills in coaching are adequate. Delegation is not easy and the final responsibility is yours. Every time you delegate there is a risk, but if there is periodic review you will get better at delegating. It is a learning situation for you as well as for the person to whom a task is delegated.

The situation is different if you work in a very small school. Here you have a limited number of people to whom you can delegate and what is needed is a sharing of some aspects of the work. It is also worth considering whether you do anything personally that could equally well be done by children or volunteers.

AGREE STAFF SALARY POLICY WITH GOVERNORS AND IMPLEMENT

Governing bodies now have greater freedom to determine pay policy for teachers than ever before. This means that the governing body needs to draw up a pay policy which is made known to everyone on the staff and is seen to be fair. If the school is a large one it may be that they decide to have a salaries committee. It will certainly be important that some governors at least, as well as the headteacher, are familiar with the pay and conditions legislation. Arden (1991: 3) suggests that pay policies must ensure the following for teachers:

- any discretionary payments are awarded in a fair and consistent manner
- the criteria for awarding discretionary supplements are lawful and drawn up and annually reviewed in consultation with staff
- awards are only made in accordance with the written criteria
- appropriate pay differentials are maintained between jobs in the school

The pay policy also needs to meet the aims of the school and encourage recruitment and retention of staff as well as the legal requirements. There should also be agreed practice on how vacancies, allowances and acting posts are made known to staff. Careful records of salaries need to be kept.

There is pressure from government to move towards performance-related pay and some schools may wish to use this. If this is the case there must be a clear statement about how performance will be assessed and by whom and the conditions under which additional pay for performance will be awarded. Hitherto appraisal has been seen as staff development. Where there is performance-related pay it will be difficult to avoid using appraisal to make decisions about pay. This would seem likely to make it less valuable for development in that people will be less prepared to discuss their problems openly.

In recommending any changes in salaries, governors must remember that there will be costs for National Insurance and superannuation.

DEAL EFFECTIVELY WITH STAFF PROBLEMS

Working with people involves you in dealing with many different kinds of problems. Some of these are personal and need human sympathy and care. Some are professional and involve the competence of teachers. Some are to do with conditions of service of teachers and with various forms of industrial action. Yet others are legal problems arising out of conditions of employment. More recently there have been difficult decisions to make about redundancies. The headteacher of a school is likely to encounter problems of all kinds.

Personal problems

A person with a problem at home cannot avoid bringing it to school. You cannot take the view that such problems are nothing to do with you for they may affect the professional work of staff who are sometimes unable to concentrate because they are preoccupied with other matters. In some cases the problem will gradually resolve itself. The marriage will break up and the partners start to make new lives; the illness will move into a period of recovery; the mourning will become dulled by time. In other cases there will be no solution but a need to cope from day to day, as in the case of parents with a handicapped child. Sometimes the problem is part of the individual's personality and all that anyone can do is listen and support as far as possible. A good deal of what is said in the next chapter is relevant here.

When you deal with problems of this kind it is important to keep your own balance. You need to be sympathetic and caring but your first duty is to the rest of the school and hard decisions may have to be taken. You may find that your LEA, if you are an LEA school, has various kinds of help available for some problems, particularly the medical and psychological ones and it is worth checking on this.

Professional problems

In all schools there will, from time to time, be teachers who fail in some way, perhaps not pulling their weight in a more senior post or simply failing to function adequately as teachers.

The first task is to identify the nature of the problem. If anything is to be done about it, it needs to be analysed in some detail. This means going beyond the statement that Jim Smith finds it difficult to handle a group of more than twenty children or that Margaret Jones upsets other people because she tries to fulfil her role as deputy head in an excessively bureaucratic manner. This means observing them at work and trying to collect as much evidence as possible which will enable you to help them.

Part of any problem is the way that people see it. You therefore need to know not only what the problem seems to be but also how it is viewed generally by those concerned with it. The views people hold may not be an accurate picture but that in itself may be part of the problem. You are likely to hear a good deal of how people view the kinds of problem described above.

The next step is to get the person concerned to see the problem in a way that allows progress. People often find it difficult to acknowledge that there is a problem and getting acceptance of this may be a necessary first step. For others the problem may seem so enormous that you have to work to get the person concerned to see it in perspective so that he or she has enough confidence to work at overcoming it. People who have problems in relationships often have difficulty in accepting that the problems are of their own making and it can be useful in these cases to concentrate on suggesting that they try a different approach without necessarily insisting that they acknowledge the problem. Such people often press for details of the evidence which it may not be possible to give. Others refuse to agree that what has happened is in any way their fault even when evidence is given.

It is not unusual to find that a school is desperately concerned about the problems a teacher is posing but that no one has actually talked to the teacher directly about them. This is less likely to happen now that we have regular appraisal, but even here problems can be side-stepped. This is mistaken kindness. If someone is failing, it is your responsibility to see that everything is done to improve that person's performance. At some stage this means discussing the problems frankly and setting them out in terms which are unequivocal and which lead to positive outcomes.

A useful first step is to identify the kind of improvement required in terms that the person concerned can understand and to agree goals which can be seen to be achieved. Thus in dealing with a teacher who is having problems in class because of poor organisation you might ask for written preparation listing what is needed for each lesson with plans for changes of activity. This could then be discussed at a regular weekly meeting with you or your deputy. In dealing with a teacher in a senior management post who is failing because of personal relations one possible solution might be to arrange for him or her to attend a course on assertiveness in order to learn how to work more positively with other people. You might also discuss with the person a particular situation in which it is necessary to ask for cooperation and consider with him or her how this can be done so that people do not get upset. It may be that past practice has been a matter of ordering people around instead of requesting action and a change in the actual words may help. It may be the way that things are said and perhaps the person concerned needs to smile more. In such cases it is best to ask for a step at a time but steps must be detailed and it must be clear that they have been taken.

You may also have the problem of the teacher who will not accept that anything is wrong. If this view persists after you have done everything you can you will need to spell out, preferably in writing, the ways in which improvement is needed. This may lead to union action and you therefore need to be sure of your ground and have involved other colleagues before arriving at your opinion.

If these approaches are not successful it may be necessary to consider what further help is needed or what disciplinary action is required. This may still be action from within the school or you may call in outside help. It may be necessary to involve governors if it seems that disciplinary procedures may be needed, but initially this will be a matter of informing rather than asking for action, since the governors may be required to act in a disciplinary role later.

Where failure continues and, in spite of support and help, is at a level which could be regarded as serious enough to consider dismissal on grounds of incompetence, you will have to embark on the formal processes leading up to this. This area is covered very thoroughly by employment legislation and it is important to follow procedures correctly. For local authority schools there will almost certainly be procedures laid down and agreed within the authority and it is essential to involve the education office as soon as the situation seems to be serious enough to warrant it, to find out the local practice.

Before moving on to a formal warning it is normal to give a person at least one informal warning that his or her work is unsatisfactory in some respect and to offer help and support for improvement, including both help in school and opportunities for appropriate training. A formal warning may follow if there is no real improvement. This must be in writing, setting out how the person must improve and giving a period during which there must be improvement. If the improvement is not sufficient within the time allowed there may be further warnings leading to a final formal warning. The governors may decide to recommend dismissal in the case of a local authority school or to dismiss the teacher themselves in the case of other schools.

At any disciplinary hearing the teacher concerned has a right to be represented with a friend at the governors' meeting. In the case of dismissal there is also a right to appeal subsequently to the education committee in the case of a local authority school and and/or to an industrial tribunal. The teacher has the right to receive copies of any reports that you or others may be making to the governors, fourteen days in advance of the meeting. Governors may also be involved in an appeal and those involved in the appeal may not be the same people as those who were involved in the case in the first instance.

Where a teacher or other member of staff is failing, the keeping of notes becomes very important. A failing teacher needs to be seen in the classroom regularly and these lessons must be recorded in some detail and a note given to the teacher setting out what he or she must do to improve. It should be remembered in doing this that written statements could become evidence at an industrial tribunal. You would be wise to arrange for the teacher to be seen by another senior member of the staff who also records what was seen. Discussion should take place while the event is fresh in the observer's mind.

You should, if possible, arrange for someone outside the school, such as an adviser or inspector, to see the teacher in question. Your presence or that of a senior member of staff in the classroom changes the situation and children are likely to behave better simply because you are there. It is also difficult for you to allow a serious level of bad behaviour to continue unchecked. This problem is less likely when the visitor is unknown. Headteachers in grant-maintained schools may like to invite a colleague from a neighbouring school to act in this capacity.

It is also important to remember that a tribunal will wish to be assured that procedures have been correctly followed and that everything possible has been done to help and support the teacher. They will look for evidence of work observed and discussed, advice and help given, in-service and other opportunities of various kinds provided. It is therefore important not only to make such help available but to record that it has been done.

A rather different set of problems occurs when a teacher does something which is professionally unacceptable and which warrants disciplinary procedures. This includes sexual offences, assault, theft or mishandling of money or other criminal offences and similar matters. In this circumstance a headteacher may wish to suspend the teacher from duty pending enquiry and inform the governors. Again, for local authority schools, it is important to consult the local office as well as the governors so that the action is correct at each stage. Where a headteacher is in doubt about what to do, the teacher can be sent home while investigations are made. It will eventually be the responsibility of the governors to decide what should be done and, in the case of a maintained school, to make recommendations to the authority.

A school should have its disciplinary rules for all staff in writing as well as those for pupils. These should ensure that all staff know what is expected of them and should cover such matters as absence, time-keeping, health and safety, race and sex discrimination, performance and behaviour. They should state the kind of offence which will be regarded as misconduct and the penalties which can be employed. In the past disciplinary codes have been laid down by the local authority but as schools become more independent they need to develop their own codes of practice. Local authority statements, which have usually been agreed with unions and with legal advisers may be a useful model but may need to be brought up to date with more recent legislation.

Relationship problems

A number of problems in school are to do with relationships between people and you may find yourself trying to resolve a problem which is basically one of people not getting on together.

There may be conflicts about territory and who does what. There may be conflicts over ideology where one person does not agree with another person's handling of a situation because it does not conform to his or her frame of reference. There may also be conflict between people who just dislike each other to the point where they find it difficult to work together.

Caldwell and Spinks (1988) suggest that agreement in conflict situations might be achieved by getting people to collaborate in the goal-setting process, having considered needs and formulated policies. This may be a good way to deal with conflict over ideology and over the distribution of resources. Many conflicts about territory may be resolved by defining more carefully the limits of each person's responsibilities. If there is conflict over territory this probably means that the boundaries are insufficiently clear.

Conflict can be dealt with in a number of ways:

- A discussion chaired by you can be arranged to talk out the problem and arrive at agreed solutions. This is an essential first step in trying to resolve problems.
- Time can be spent agreeing needs and possible ways of meeting them, going on to agree goals.
- Rules and procedures can be devised and used or job descriptions revised. This can be a useful way of resolving conflict over territory where the task is to sort out which people are responsible for which activities.
- The people concerned can be separated if this is possible.

Much of what is said about negotiation in chapter eleven is relevant here.

Stress

Stress affects most people in education today. There are many reasons for this. A fundamental reason is that the aims of the government for education and the values these represent are at odds with the aims and values held by most teachers. Teachers generally do not see education as a form of competition and as a commodity to be purchased by the community but as a service and a liberating influence aimed at developing each child as an individual. The general tendency to denigrate the work of teachers and to attribute the success they achieve to other causes, such as examinations becoming easier, also contributes to stress. Stress can also be caused by poor management and working conditions, by role conflict and role ambiguity and by children's behaviour.

Headteachers are experiencing greater stress as a result of their greater responsibilities as well as their position at the boundary of the school where they must interact with the public and work with governors. Deputy headteachers are in a particularly stressful position in that they stand between the headteacher and the staff and are expected to mediate in situations where there is a difference.

What is stress? Kyriacou (1989: 27) states: 'Teacher stress refers to the experience by teachers of unpleasant emotion such as anger, tension, frustration, depression and nervousness, resulting from their work as teachers'.

As headteacher you have not only to consider your own problems of stress but also those of your colleagues. It is important to be aware of teachers who are becoming stressed so that you can support them. It is also important to create a situation in which people feel free to discuss the problems they are experiencing without feeling that this is an admission of failure. People also feel less stressed when they are able to manage their time well and it may be worth spending a professional development day on time management.

Teacher stress can lead to teacher burnout, described by Kyriacou as follows:

> Teacher burnout refers to a state of mental, emotional and attitudinal exhaustion which results from a long period of stress. Such teachers are still able to function as teachers, but they have largely lost their commitment and enthusiasm for their work and this inevitably shows in aspects of their job performance.
>
> (Kyriacou 1989: 27)

Mancini *et al.* (1984) found that burned out teachers gave less information and less praise and showed less acceptance of their pupils' ideas and interacted less frequently with them. Burnout may lead to more serious forms of illness, such as depression and other psychological disorders and to prolonged absence from teaching or to people leaving the profession altogether.

Woods (1989) suggests that the following people are most at risk:

- probationers and inexperienced teachers who have not yet learned how to cope with the dilemmas and contradictions of the teacher's role
- teachers who find it difficult to 'orchestrate their teaching' in the classroom
- senior teachers who are in a position of greater role conflict.

You need to be on the alert for signs of stress in colleagues and in yourself. Dunham (1992) lists among many other signs over-sensitivity to criticism, feelings of inadequacy and insecurity, exhaustion, irritability, headaches and other physical symptoms, poor sleep patterns, over-reaction to changes and difficulties and the appearance of being rushed.

Stress is affected by various aspects of the working environment. Where the demands on people are greater than they can reasonably expect to achieve, they are likely to experience stress. However, the extent to which individuals experience stress depends also on their personal resources. People who see themselves in charge of their lives are less likely to experience stress than those who see their lives directed by others. Stress is less likely to occur where people have been involved in decision making about the work they do and where there is strong support from colleagues and a problem-solving attitude in the school. The current experience of change beyond the control of the profession has resulted in considerable stress on many people.

Handy (1981) speaks of creating 'stability zones' which he describes as places for rebuilding energy reserves. Holidays and weekends, home and family, are important stability zones. It is valuable for people to be able to turn to some quite different interest or occupation from time to time and there seems to be evidence that physical activity helps to combat stress, whether this is a strenuous game or a mild activity such as gardening. Making things also seems to offer a way of relaxing. Relaxation techniques and meditation have also been used as a way of managing stress.

It is not easy for those who are deeply involved in their professional lives to switch off and it may help to be able to talk through problems and difficulties with a friend or with one's partner. Handy also suggests that routines are a way of coping with stress, enabling a person to do some things without thinking about them because they are habits. Routines are particularly useful when a person is tired and flagging.

You need to be preparing for the stressful situations when you are not under pressure. This is the time to organise the routines and the systems and arrange the delegation, the time to develop stability zones and hobbies and outside interests and activities. People who can organise their professional lives so that they run smoothly for most of the day have time left for the problems and strategies to cope with the stressful situations.

HAVE KNOWLEDGE OF RELEVANT LEGISLATION

There has been a great deal of employment legislation in recent years as well as other legislation affecting schools. Headteachers need to be aware of some of the provisions of the following Acts as well as the various Education Acts:

- The Equal Pay Act 1970 (as amended)
- Trade Union and Labour Relations Act 1974
- Health and Safety at Work Act 1974
- Employment Protection Act 1975
- Sex Discrimination Acts 1975 and 1986
- Race Relations Act 1976

- Employment Protection Acts (consolidation) 1978
- Employment Act 1980
- Employment Act 1982
- Trade Union Act 1984
- Wages Act 1986
- Teachers' Pay and Conditions Acts 1987
- Employment Act 1988

The major provisions of most of these pieces of legislation are comparatively straightforward but you would be wise to seek advice in any case where you are uncertain.

The issue of redundancy is very much with us and each school needs to have a clear and agreed practice for deciding who should go when staff are to be declared redundant. The process must be seen to be fair, although it must also be influenced by who can be spared. Probably the most usual principle is 'last in first out' but there certainly need to be criteria by which the decision is made which are known to everyone.

You may also have to deal with union problems. Your staff may bring grievance procedures or collective disputes and you need to know how to deal with them. If you are head of a maintained school you can turn to the education office staff though you may be charged for legal advice. Your professional association should also be able to offer you advice. There will be some situations where you need to to act quickly and you need to be clear about your rights.

Where there is major union action, it is usual for a local authority to issue guidance to its headteachers making it clear what is expected from them. This may contain problems for you but you will be sharing those problems with other headteachers and with officers of the LEA.

You would be wise in any case to work closely with any union representatives in your school. These provide a kind of consultative machinery and reflect a different and useful point of view. It is also wise to look at any major change as it might be seen by the various unions. Even if the staff are not strongly unionised it is a valuable exercise in seeing things from a different view.

Chapter 11

Skills with people

Your success as a headteacher depends a great deal on your ability to make good relationships with people. Good relationships come about partly because of the person you are and the sensitivity you show in dealing with others. They also involve certain skills. People learn skills in making relationships as they grow up and most teachers develop these skills further as they progress towards headship. However the tasks you may be called upon to undertake as headteacher and the kinds of relationships formed are rather different from those practised at earlier career stages because the role is a different one. Other people also have strong expectations of what someone in the role of headteacher should do and, while it may be a good idea to surprise them occasionally by doing something different, it is necessary to fulfil their expectations if one is to have their trust.

The term 'skills with people' covers the following:

Presenting material to a group
Interviewing individual people
Negotiation
Leading a group

COMMON FEATURES OF INTERPERSONAL SITUATIONS

There are common features to most interpersonal situations. They include the following:

The effect of the venue

Environment affects what happens. The way a room is arranged affects interaction. For example, in some situations you may choose to talk with someone sitting on a level with you in an easy chair and this creates a particular kind of relationship. On another occasions it may be politic to stay sitting behind a desk in order to make a different impression and create a different relationship.

People are also affected by the degree of privacy, and inferences are drawn from the place where an interview is conducted. The headteacher's room has overtones which affect reactions in different ways. The head-teacher is always more at home there than other people. People will also draw conclusions if a serious interview is constantly interrupted by the telephone or a secretary. It suggests that they are not important enough to be given your full attention.

Discomfort interferes with listening and attending to what is going on. If it is difficult to see or hear a speaker, if the seats are uncomfortable or the temperature too hot or too cold, an audience may make little effort to listen. This is also true to some extent in a face-to-face interview, though the content may be of such vital importance that the people concerned attend to the business in hand in spite of discomfort.

The way the interchange starts

The beginning of any interpersonal activity sets the scene for what follows. In a talk the speaker's first words may gain or lose everyone's attention. In an interview or negotiation the scene may be set by the way you make the other person feel at ease or threatened.

Where an interview deals with a difficult topic it is probably best to start with more general conversation and then move into an explanation of the purpose of the interview. If you wish to make notes, it may be wise to explain this and give the reason for it so that the other person does not feel threatened by it. It is also helpful at an early stage to define what the interview is about. All of this applies to appraisal interviews and to any face-to-face discussion.

The way people react to each other

It is very important to be able to read the body language messages which people send which tell how they are reacting to what is being said.

The following signs are common and are relevant when speaking or working with a group as well as in dealing with individuals:

- Eye contact
  We signal the beginnings and ends of exchanges and many other ideas with our eyes. Keeping eye contact in talking to someone is very important if the person concerned is to feel that the conversation is sincere.
- Interest, involvement, concern

Attention and interest are signalled by eye contact, smiles, nods, sounds of agreement. These are also signalled when someone sits forward.

- Tension
People show tension by adopting an uncomfortable sitting position; by clenching and unclenching their hands; moving their feet about; by facial expression in which the muscles of face and jaw are tight; by frowning; by exhibiting signs of dryness of mouth.
- Lack of interest, impatience, boredom
These are signalled by losing eye contact, looking at the time, playing with something, sitting back and looking far away.
- Embarrassment, anxiety feelings or hurt
These may occur in the course of a meeting with an individual or group and it is important to recognise them quickly in order to be aware of what is happening. All the tension signals may also convey emotional involvement. Eye contact may be dropped when the situation is emotionally charged.
- Views of relative status
People convey messages about status to a greater extent than is usually realised. It is usually possible to recognise very quickly who is the senior person in an interview or discussion. He or she will exercise a degree of control over what is happening, summing up the discussion occasionally and moving to a new topic, perhaps 'talking down' the other person on occasion or using status to dismiss or encourage the other's ideas. The more senior person will speak with a greater degree of confidence and authority than other people and may hold eye contact until the other person drops it.

Conversely those who see themselves in more junior positions will reverse these actions, backing down easily when someone else talks them down or retains eye contact. They may put ideas forward more tentatively than their senior colleague and it may be his or her role to draw out ideas from them so that they are able to make a contribution.

PRESENTING MATERIAL TO A GROUP

People in management roles find themselves required from time to time to put something over to a group of adults. The task of communicating with a group varies from one occasion to another in a number of important respects, including group size and composition, subject matter, context and the state of the audience. A speaker can choose from a range of possible approaches to achieve the optimum communication within the particular set of circumstances, choosing subject matter and language for the particular audience and using voice and gesture to stimulate them.

Preparing a talk involves considering the subject matter to be covered, the approximate size and composition of the audience, the time available, the context of the particular talk and the environment in which it will be given. A good beginning captures the audience and makes them feel that the speaker is with them and a good ending sends people away with something to think about. If you have prepared the end of a talk you can jump to the end if time is running out although a good speaker should be able to time a talk accurately.

If you are frequently giving talks or regularly giving similar talks, it can be useful to prepare notes on cards or on overhead projector (OHP) transparencies, in very small units. These can then form the nucleus of materials from which you can select for a particular talk. If OHPs are made with water based markers, they can be changed in detail to match a particular talk. Once the outline has been prepared, the use of visual aids or handouts can be considered. These must add to or reinforce what is said as well as providing variety.

Experienced speakers take time over starting and they look at the audience, who at this point are making judgements about whether this speaker will be worth listening to. It is helpful to scan the audience, making eye contact with individuals and noting the behavioural clues listed earlier.

A talk should end with something memorable, perhaps a summing up, a quotation or story which emphasises some of the main points.

TALKING TO AN INDIVIDUAL

There are many situations in a which you have to deal with individual people in a one-to-one situation. You may see someone in order to gain information, deal with a problem, counsel, receive or give criticism, make a request, appraise a situation or the work of an individual or for many other reasons. These may all be regarded as interviews.

All interviews call for a high degree of skill. Moreover many of them have to be dealt with as and when they arise, although some may be programmed.

There are a number of different kinds of interview:

Interviewing for information

Interviewing to obtain information is one of the commonest types of interview. It is also a necessary beginning to interviewing for problem solving, appraisal, counselling and selection and is frequently necessary in its own right.

Interviewing for information involves getting as much accurate information as possible in the shortest time compatible with maintaining good relationships. Your task as interviewer is to create a situation in which information is freely given and to check what you are told by asking questions and by offering summaries for comment. It is often valuable to go beyond the facts and try to find out how the other person feels about what he or she is saying. This may give some indication of its accuracy, since people are more likely to misinterpret matters they feel strongly about. It may also offer clues to acceptable action.

Problem-solving interviews

A problem-solving interview involves getting information about the problem, including finding out how people view it, exploring and considering solutions, considering how people are likely to feel about them and possible action.

Try to make sure that you have got down to the real problem before starting to explore solutions. A person's feelings about a problem may lead to an illogical description. Minor problems may be used as a route to discussion of major problems and getting to the nub of the real problem may take time.

It is easy to assume that what worked for you in a similar situation will work for someone else and suggest this solution at an early stage. Different people work differently and it is wise to be wary of offering solutions too quickly and to try instead to lead people to formulate their own solutions when possible. These are often the most successful.

It is important to preserve a measure of professional detachment. Problems may be emotionally charged and it is essential that you are seen as sympathetic yet calm and able to see the problem in perspective.

Many problems come down to issues of behaviour and relationships. Some of these can be eased if the person concerned can identify and agree something to work at as suggested in the previous chapter.

Most schools have some problems which are very difficult to solve. In a few cases there are no good solutions. In the majority of cases, however, the situations should be viewed positively, especially where they concern human behaviour. One can reflect that teachers in schools for children with severe learning difficulties achieve results by breaking down tasks into very small steps until they reach a point where the pupil is able to succeed. Each minor success is rewarded with praise and comment and minor successes gradually add up to greater achievement. These techniques can be applied to almost any situation.

Receiving a complaint

One common interview situation which all headteachers encounter is that of receiving complaints. A complaint may be against you personally or against a colleague or the school or some part of it. Some people making complaints are aggressive. Others are apologetic and negative, sometimes starting by apologising but then getting increasingly aggressive as they become more emotionally involved. It is easy to respond to this situation by being aggressive or defensive in return. Neither approach is satisfactory.

A few people make complaints all the time but for the most part a situation has to become bad before people voice their concern. Consequently you may face someone who is in an emotional state and who has rehearsed the scene many times before coming to complain. It is often helpful to encourage the person to talk without interruption until the tale is finished. When the end comes, the story can be filled out and checked by asking questions and running through the information as it has been given.

What happens next depends upon whether the complaint is about something which involves other people and whether the evidence is available. If the evidence is only the story according to the complainant, then, after listening sympathetically, you may offer to investigate and give some idea of what may be involved, arranging to let the other person know in some way the result of investigations.

If the whole story is there, you have to decide on a course of action. If you personally are in the wrong to any extent, the best course may be to apologise. A person never loses by apologising when wrong and it is more likely to lead to good future relationships than a defensive reaction.

Whatever the rights and wrongs of the situation, the person complaining wants to go away feeling that something will happen as a result of complaining. You have to decide what this can be.

A difficult situation is when the complaint is against one of the teachers and you agree wholeheartedly with the complainant. There is no point in refusing to accept that the teacher is wrong. However, most people accept that a headteacher has to be loyal to the staff and is therefore unlikely to join those complaining about teachers. A parent will normally be mollified by a promise to talk to the teacher concerned about the problem without too much comment about how you views the incident.

It is always wise to end an interview of this kind with a summary of what has been said and a plan for action on the part of the interviewer and possibly on the other person's part, sometimes following this with a note of what has been agreed.

No one likes receiving complaints, but this is part of the headteacher's role. However, they can be seen as an opportunity to learn how matters seem as seen from a different viewpoint. The situation then becomes more positive.

Criticising someone's work

All managers need from time to time to be critical of someone else's performance. The way you do this will determine whether or not the person concerned leaves the discussion feeling that it is important to do everything possible to improve and that you will do everything possible to help, or goes away feeling thoroughly bloody-minded and determined to retaliate at the first possible opportunity. Between these extremes will be the person who feels miserable or defensive about what was said in the discussion but uncertain what ought to be done about it. In this situation a person will probably try to forget an unpleasant incident without doing very much about it. It is therefore important to criticise in a way which brings a commitment to improvement.

It helps if you can choose the time and place for the discussion. It is easier to discuss a problem when the person concerned does not feel that a reprimand is being fitted in before you dash off to deal with something else. The matter is vital to the person being criticised and it is reasonable to expect it to be the same for the person criticising.

It is unwise to criticise someone in front of another person except where a witness is needed or a fellow interviewer can help.

The way you conduct such an interview affects the seriousness with which the other person regards it. It is possible to create a relaxed or a formal situation. When a problem first comes to light it is usually best dealt with in a relaxed way, perhaps with both parties seated in easy chairs or at least on the same level. At a later stage it may be necessary to make the situation more formal, but usually the informal methods of dealing with people are more productive.

It is important to think out beforehand how best to run such a discussion. It is particularly important for you to be sufficiently in control to avoid expressing feelings unintentionally. The expression of anger, for example, is a tool to be used rarely and deliberately and with considerable forethought about the outcome. 'Tearing someone off a strip' may relieve your feelings, but is more likely to produce an aggressive response than a desire to improve. Conversely it is necessary to avoid being so gentle and kind that the person is left feeling that the matter is not important. The ideal is to be sympathetic but firm and to state the criticism clearly.

It is important to listen carefully to what the person has to say, questioning to ensure that his or her point of view is understood. It is often a good idea to start by asking for an account from the other person's viewpoint of whatever is being discussed so that both sides can be seen. This not only gives you a chance to sum up the situation but tends to take the steam out of it, because it can be seen that you are trying to be fair. People often see their own actions more clearly if asked to describe them and sometimes the other person will say all that is necessary by way of personal criticism. Your part is then to help that person to reflect on performance and identify possible action which can be taken. Such an interview should end with an agreed commitment to action and a date for reviewing the situation.

Refusing requests

Saying no is not always easy, but a headteacher who has not learned to recognise the occasions when it is the best answer will rapidly run into difficulties. It is also easy to go to the other extreme and say yes too rarely.

The first task is therefore to define the criteria for saying no, thus providing a yardstick by which to measure requests. The following are possible criteria, although they may need to be modified and extended for a particular situation:

Does what is requested:

- further the broad aims of the school?
- further your own aims for the school?
- further the aims of the individual making the request?

Is what is requested likely to:

- take an unreasonable amount of time from other activities?
- use an unreasonable amount of resources of other kinds?
- create problems for other people?
- Is what is requested contrary to any agreed policy or practice or in conflict with any other activity?

Saying no is not just a matter of deciding what to do against criteria, but of actually saying it. This can be difficult when someone comes along enthusiastic about a scheme which must be refused because of the problems it poses.

It may be possible to help the person to change the request so that it becomes acceptable. If this is not possible, then it is important to share the criteria so that the person concerned can not only see why the answer is no but can also make this judgement for him or herself on a future occasion.

A further problem about saying no is to discern the occasion when you should have a change of mind after getting further information. It is not a sign of weakness to give way if matters begin to be seen in a different light. On the other hand, if this happens too frequently, other people will not accept an initial no and will spend a lot of time and effort trying to get a different answer. Here again, the criteria are important. If you can say that you are having a change of mind because the request now seems to fit the criteria in a way that it did not before, it makes for rationality all round.

Interviews which go wrong

Interviews sometimes go wrong because there is some form of misunderstanding. Words, gestures and movements are misinterpreted and every interviewer should try to check the understanding of the other person by summarising and questioning further.

Sometimes matters go wrong after the interview, when the person concerned has had time to think it over. This is particularly likely if the interview was an emotional one. It is wise to make a note of the content of any interview in which decisions are made or where the content has been emotional or possibly threatening. Notes are best made while the information is fresh in mind and if appropriate a copy sent to the other person so that there is no misunderstanding.

In a situation where an interview is likely to prove threatening in a serious way, for example, in a situation where you are giving a member of staff an informal or formal warning, it may be wise to involve a witness. This also provides the possibility of another mind on the problem.

NEGOTIATION

Everyone in a management role spends a good deal of time in negotiation. Negotiation, in this context, is not only negotiation with trade unions or professional associations, but with the day-to-day task of bringing people closer in their views so that profitable action can ensue, of interpreting one person to another and persuading people to work together, of finding a way forward acceptable to everyone.

Negotiating involves attempting to understand the frame of reference from which the other person is working and looking at where it matches your own. This gives a basis for arguments towards any particular end.

There is a sense in which all leadership has to be negotiated. A teacher in charge of a class is its designated leader but maintains this role by negotiating with the children. One sometimes hears a teacher indulge in a kind of trading with children: 'When you have finished your writing you may choose an activity.' Occasionally children ask a question such as: 'Do we *have* to do this?' A teacher also has to establish the level of work expected from children and the children try to find out what the teacher will accept. Similarly teachers and other staff negotiate what is acceptable with the headteacher and senior staff.

There is also negotiation with parents and children about such matters as uniform, homework, rules and discipline. Teachers negotiate over who teaches particular groups or parts of the curriculum. As headteacher you have many negotiating tasks inside and outside the school. Inside the school you will be continually discussing and agreeing patterns of work, negotiating with teachers, secretary, caretaker, cleaning staff, the cook and dinner helpers. You also have to negotiate with parents, governors, local authority officers, advisers and inspectors, the local community and others on many different issues.

Every school has to draw together the philosophy of its headteacher and staff and the views of parents, governors, students and community. Aims and objectives will not usually be shared unless a deliberate attempt is made to explain the school's viewpoint, listen to the views of others and take them into account. This involves negotiation.

Teachers negotiate with headteachers and others for the resources of time, materials and accommodation. Headteachers may negotiate with their governors over the use of the resources they have and with parents and sponsors for additional resources.

Children negotiate behaviour with teachers and teachers negotiate behaviour with the headteacher and senior staff. The school negotiates behaviour with parents and the community. If the community dislikes the behaviour of the children, parents will not send their children to the school.

All teachers with a management function in school have to negotiate their role. Generally speaking the headteacher's role is understood and you may therefore have less negotiating of role to do than some other people. A new headteacher will still need to negotiate a particular way of working, however.

Many deputy headteachers find that they need to negotiate their role, partly because the deputy headteacher's role may be ill-defined, even when there is a clear job description, because it depends upon the management style of the headteacher and what the individual in post has to offer. In the course of a deputy headteacher's first year or two in the school, he or she will be modifying personal views in the light of the views of the headteacher and colleagues and they will be modifying their views in the light of the deputy's performance, so that the deputy's role eventually becomes acceptable to everyone.

This is the most common use of the word and it includes day-to-day resolving of differences between individuals as well as management/ worker or trade union negotiation.

Fisher and Ury (1987) describe negotiation as getting what you want from others. They suggest that what is required is what they call principled negotiation. This involves looking for mutual gains and then making decisions about areas of conflict by agreeing standards. For example, a governing body is concerned and doubtful about the the way in which children with special needs are being supported in the classroom. They feel that such children should be in a separate group for some of the time. The staff who have experienced the current way of working are convinced that the arrangement they have is right for these children and that they make better progress both academically and socially when they work with more able groups. It may be possible in this situation to get governors and staff to agree that if it can be shown in an agreed way that these children are making progress suitable to their ability then the staff are probably right in their view.

This would mean deciding on and agreeing the criteria by which this would be judged. If, on the other hand, the criteria agreed show that there is substantially less progress than staff thought there would be then perhaps the staff should think again.

Fisher and Ury (1987) argue that taking positions should be avoided and that discussion should be concentrated first on the areas of agreement and then on the criteria by which decisions about the areas of conflict should be decided. They suggest that the more one knows about the views and feelings of the other party, the more chance there is of resolving the conflict in a way which is satisfactory to everyone.

Negotiation involves much of the thinking about aggressive and assertive behaviour. Back and Back (1982) contend that there is a midway between being aggressive on the one hand and making only a very limited attempt to express and maintain a point of view (non-assertiveness) on the other. This midway is what is described as assertive behaviour. Assertive behaviour is where an individual states his or her views firmly, clearly and politely in such a way that it evokes a positive response. The right kind of assertive behaviour may also deflect attention from what seems to be an attack on a person, to a supportive analysis of the nature of differences and problems.

Negotiation takes place either between people who are equal in status or where one is senior to the other. It may also be between individuals or among a group. These aspects makes differences of approach necessary in different situations.

Negotiation between equals means that people start with equal rights to be heard and to make the final decision. It may therefore be more difficult to achieve a decision, but those involved need to make an effort to see the others' viewpoints because they need to understand in order to argue their own views. Sometimes the conclusions reached in these circumstances are good ones where all parties have modified their original views to arrive at consensus. On other occasions, the discussion may take a good deal of time and the outcome may be one that nobody likes or even a stalemate which effectively prevents action. This is what tends to happen in strikes.

This kind of situation is most frequently resolved by a third party who may be a neutral arbitrator (such as the Advisory, Conciliation and Arbitration Service in the industrial setting) or by the involvement of someone more senior.

Negotiation between groups or individuals who are not of equal status also has its problems. Negotiation between the headteacher and a member of staff is conducted in the knowledge that you, as headteacher, have the right to have the last word. The effect of this knowledge on the staff member may be that he or she tests out your views and when they appear to differ from his or her own, backs down quickly without pressing a point of view or explaining the ideas sufficiently for you to assess them adequately. This is something that you need to recognise and try to avoid.

Alternatively the member of staff faced with the likelihood that you will disagree may start to act aggressively and try to press you into agreement. Somewhere between these two forms of behaviour comes the assertive approach which achieves a proper consideration of the issues and an outcome which is acceptable to both parties. This is not to suggest that you should keep silent about your views. In this situation you need to give a good indication of the parameters within which you are prepared to work in such a way as to appear open to new ideas and ways of doing things. This is not easy.

Negotiation does not always go smoothly or have a satisfactory ending. Sometimes one person will manoeuvre another into an impasse, where neither can move without losing face. When discussion takes place in a group, it is the task of the chairperson to resolve this kind of conflict and it is sometimes useful to suggest that the problem is set aside for a while and returned to later, when it is not unusual to find that resolution is easier.

LEADING A GROUP

Group leadership is an important part of management. There are many situations when a headteacher is expected to take the chair, sometimes formally and sometimes informally.

Although the skills required for leading different kinds of groups vary from one group to another, the majority are common to most groups.

Preparation for the meeting

You need to do some preparation for every meeting. This may simply be a matter of going through the agenda of a regular meeting and considering how to deal with each item. If the meeting is one for discussion of a particular topic or topics it may require the following kind of preparation:

study the material for discussion and clarify:

- the objectives of the discussion
- what needs to be put in writing before and during the discussion. This may include an agenda, discussion outline, members' list, background papers
- possible starting points or ways of presenting items
- what should be achieved by the end of the meeting.

prepare:

- a plan for getting started. If a meeting has an agenda this will not be needed, but where a meeting is concerned with exploratory discussion the starting point is important

- a series of points and questions which need to be covered in the course of the discussion
- a plan for drawing the meeting to a close, particularly if it is an exploratory discussion. A group leader needs to have some idea of how far the group might get and of possible ways of finishing the discussion
- a time plan for discussion.

If there is a formal agenda it may be useful to put a rough time by each item. It is also wise to set a finishing time and make people aware of it before the meeting.

consider the venue and seating plan

> Discussion can founder if people are not comfortably seated so that everyone can see everyone else. A circle is usually the best arrangement or a horseshoe if you plan to use a flip chart or OHP. Try to avoid a straight line of chairs if possible because people in a line do not see each other.

decide whether to take notes

> Some people find it easy to chair a meeting and take notes but it is usually better to ask someone else to act as scribe and it is wise to arrange this before the meeting. If notes are not taken it can become difficult to sum up and draw conclusions and much of the discussion may be lost.

The working session

The way a group starts work is important. When a group is newly formed, people may have all kinds of views, fears and prejudices, especially if the group and its leader are unfamiliar to each other or participants are overawed by the status of the group leader or some group members.

It is helpful to provide an opportunity for each person to speak as soon as possible and reward each contribution with some kind of acknowledgement – a smile or nod or comment. See that the task of the group is clearly stated and understood and watch for those who are ready to speak. During the discussion your main task is that of controlling the discussion and drawing together the thinking of the group. This means that you need to:

- set and maintain the rules of discussion. In a formal meeting the rules are laid down and as chairperson you have to see that they are followed, establishing the extent to which you are prepared to allow divergence from the task in hand, recounting of anecdotes, discussion between sections of the group and so on. In an exploratory group it is possible to be more flexible than with a more formal group with an agenda.

- maintain a relationship with each member of the group by the way you react to contributions. Your skill in questioning and extending contributions, rewarding them in various ways and your interest in what members say, does much to determine the readiness with which people speak and the degree of frankness they offer. Try not to talk too much.
- scan the group from time to time, looking round to see those who may wish to speak. Someone may be trying to catch your eye and is perhaps sitting forward or in the process of drawing breath to speak. Look for anyone who appears to be bored or detached or becoming interested in something outside the discussion and draw that person back in.
- maintain the direction of the discussion by extending contributions and relating them to the task in hand, looking for trends and directions in what people say or patterns in the contributions. You need to be analysing and classifying what is being said so that you gradually help the group to create a coherent body of thought.
- sum up and move the discussion on when it seems the right moment to do so. You need to make the group aware at intervals of the direction of the discussion, perhaps summing up points of agreement and difference at the apparent conclusion of a section of discussion. There is a right moment to do this. A group which is not ready to move will usually refuse to start thinking of anything else until they are ready to change direction. Where there is a formal agenda you may need to sum up the findings of each item.
- deal with any problems arising. For example you need to be on the look out for silent or over-talkative members and draw the former into the discussion and find ways of ensuring that the latter give others a chance to speak. There may be cases of conflict or emotional tension where you have the choice of talking this through or alternatively changing the direction of the group. Your decision depends upon whether it seems to be worth the trouble of working through the conflict and whether you feel able to handle it.

A group sometimes decides that it does not wish to work at the task in hand, and its members will introduce red herrings, act negatively or helplessly and refuse to think constructively. This kind of behaviour has to be worked through but there will eventually be a moment when they are ready to move if you keep trying to get them going in a constructive way.

Where you know this is likely to happen it may be a good idea to get everyone to start by writing down something positive about the topic and using this as a starting point.

It is your task to watch the time during discussion and at a suitable point sufficiently long before the end, stop the discussion and start summing up. This should normally include a summary of the main points and suggestions for action.

Leadership roles in different groups

The information above applies generally to most groups. There are some differences in the leadership behaviour required in some groups, however, and different styles may be appropriate in different situations. If you know your own style you are more likely to know how to make the most of personal strengths and limitations.

In exploratory or learning groups it is particularly important to be able to make and maintain good relationships. In this context you need to be encouraging; to extend people's thinking; to draw contributions together and build on from them, being patient while people work through their own thinking.

A group with a task requires firm leadership and a determination to achieve. This means keeping people to the point and making them work at the task.

A problem-solving group may need firm leadership to get everyone working at the task and then a middle course between encouraging wide-ranging thinking and keeping people to the point. Your skill in drawing together points of agreement and finding a way forward will be crucial.

A review group is one which meets regularly to deal with day-to-day business, staff meetings, for example. Leadership of review groups may vary. You may wish to let coordinators chair staff meetings concerned with their specialism, for example. The leader of a review group must know the rules for running a formal meeting, what it may and may not do or decide and what its responsibilities are.

A briefing group is one which meets for the dissemination of information. In some schools the whole staff may meet for a short time daily for this purpose. Anyone running a briefing group needs skill in giving lucid and brief explanations in a way which is acceptable to the group.

CONCLUSION

The skills described in the various situations above are part of the same family of skills. You gradually learn to observe and interpret the behaviour of others, develop skill in identifying the important points in any situation and where to go next, the skill to put something to another person in an acceptable way and a set of skills for meeting most situations. A person can acquire these skills by observing others, by being self-critical and by analysing and evaluating situations, as well as by formal training. You need not only to acquire these skills yourself, but also to see that your deputy and perhaps other senior members of staff have the opportunity to acquire and practise them in preparation for possible future promotion.

Chapter 12

Communication

The work of an organisation is only as good as its communication. Every school needs to give thought and care to communication both within the school and with the world outside. It is easy to think that, because a primary school is small, communication is easy and there will be no problem. In practice even quite small schools need to give a good deal of thought to the way any communication takes place. Too much reliance on the odd word over coffee can be a mistake.

No school can ever afford to be complacent about the adequacy of its communication. Every organisation of any size has problems of communication from time to time and needs to work constantly to maintain communication if problems are not to multiply.

Communication is fundamental to the whole process of education. Education is about helping children to communicate effectively. Children's learning depends upon the ability of teachers to communicate. Each child must communicate with the teacher if the teacher is to be aware of the child's progress and match work to the child's stage of development and learning needs. Classroom behaviour is about communication and much that applies in the classroom also applies to communication between headteacher and staff, teacher and teacher, pupils and pupil, school and parents and school and community. Even in schools where the communication is good, there will be people, who, for one reason or another, do not get the messages sent.

If two people are to understand each other, the words each one uses must mean approximately the same to them both. Yet each person's understanding of language is dependent upon his or her experience. For example, a parent whose own experience of education was entirely formal will have a different view of the process of teaching from that of a teacher who believes in a great deal of practical work and first-hand experience of many kinds. The parent's interpretation of the language they both use will be different from that of the teacher because of the differences in their frames of reference. We are currently seeing this kind of misunderstanding at national level between professional educators and politicians. Words used in common do not carry the same meaning for both parties. Teachers need to recognise this and allow for it if they are to communicate effectively.

In a similar way a child who has never seen the sea will have difficulty in understanding what people are talking about when they describe it. All teachers need to remember that the experience of primary school children is very limited and it is easy to overestimate it and in doing this to underestimate children's intelligence.

Teachers also interpret each others' words differently because of their differences in view and experience and it is important that there is suffi-cient discussion to enable teachers to understand each others' views if children are not to be confused when they change teachers.

There is, in particular, a difference in the educational views of teachers and the classroom behaviour expected between the primary and secondary stages of education. Primary and secondary teachers often use different language in talking about their work and when they are using the same language they may accord it different meaning. They also differ in the way they use language to talk about the same processes. This must be remembered when primary and secondary teachers meet to discuss the children who will be transferring to the secondary school.

Oral and written language are important modes of communication but in any piece of communication the message is conveyed not only by the content but also by the way it is presented, by the language chosen, the tone of voice, facial expression and body language in the case of speech and by appearance, choice of words, sentence construction and layout in the case of written communication. These may modify or change the meaning of a message and the choice of language carries messages both about the speaker and about his or her view of those receiving the mes-sage. Where the words of a message conflict with the way it is conveyed there can be uncertainty and misunderstanding. Inexperienced teachers sometimes have difficulty because they have not learned to convey messages with body language as well as words.

It is wise to use oral communication as a starting point, when anything disturbing, threatening or critical needs to be communicated. In emo-tional situations people tend to hear what they want to hear. If information is given orally, it is possible for them to ask questions and for the message to be repeated in different ways. This can then be followed up in writing. If information of this kind is initially given in writing, there is even more opportunity for misunderstanding and rumours can proliferate. It is also important to see how the listener is receiving a message which is critical or threatening and to react accordingly.

The written communication which arrives on your desk each day may well be more than you can read. Even if you are fortunate enough to have a good secretary sorting out the mail for you, there is still a great deal of mail which you must read yourself. You therefore need to develop skill in skimming written material to decide which parts need to be read carefully, which need no more than a glance, which should be kept for reference and which can go straight into the waste paper basket. There is much to be said for trying to reserve about half an hour each day for reading, perhaps first thing in the morning if you arrive well before staff and children. Your time will often be disturbed but you will have some mornings when you get through much of the material.

It is also important to write as economically as possible, arranging the text so that the eye catches what is important and so that there are few dense patches of text, which tend to put people off starting to read what is there.

The written word has certain advantages and disadvantages compared with the spoken word. It is, in a sense, permanent and this is both an advantage and a disadvantage. People can retain written communication and go over it at their own speed if they wish. The writer can go back over material and revise it until it seems to convey the message adequately. Word processing makes this easier and desktop publishing allows a similar revision of layout and presentation. But writing is a more limited form of communication than speech, since it lacks the messages conveyed by movement, facial expression and tone of voice. Although written language conveys messages by format and choice of language, there are fewer clues from which to make inferences than there are in spoken language and since there is no opportunity to check that inferences are correct, the possibility of misunderstanding is greater.

All communication must be appropriate if it is to fulfil its purpose. This means it must match purpose, situation and audience or readership. It is particularly difficult to match language to the parent group because it is likely to contain people of widely differing backgrounds. It is important to avoid jargon, remembering that what seems to be perfectly normal language in school is read as jargon by those outside. It is also wise to avoid complex language.

It is useful when considering any problem to think of what information is required in order to solve it. It can be helpful in sorting out an issue to make a flowchart and to add to each link in this the information which will be needed.

Written communication may pose problems of confidentiality. The school must decide what should be recorded in writing and who should have access to it. Similarly the information on computer comes under the Data Protection Act and the school will need to register and adhere to its conditions.

Notes need to be made on various occasions. For example, it is wise to note important points made in discussions with parents and colleagues. It is also wise to make careful notes as soon as possible after the event of incidents which might escalate into cases for the courts and tribunals. As assault of any kind or a serious accident certainly requires this kind of treatment and any interview with a teacher or other member of staff which could lead to disciplinary action should be fully recorded. Interviews with a child which might lead to suspension also need careful recording and this includes interviews with the child's parents.

Reports on teachers' work have now become more open than formerly, but confidential reports are still used in some contexts. Whatever the system of reporting, a headteacher should normally make a teacher acquainted with any criticism of that teacher's work, so that if something critical is included in a report, it cannot be said that the criticism was unknown to the teacher.

It should also be remembered that one can no longer be certain that what is recorded in confidence will remain confidential. Those conducting enquiries and tribunals may legally demand to see information in confidential files and it is therefore even more important to be careful in recording and retaining material.

Communication involves the following management tasks:

Ensure appropriate communication with everyone
Create and maintain a communication system
Ensure that information travels in all directions
Seek information and feedback from all levels
Evaluate the effectiveness of communication

ENSURE APPROPRIATE COMMUNICATION WITH EVERYONE

The adults in the school

Adults in the school community include the headteacher, teaching staff, non-teaching staff and others, such as supply teachers, voluntary helpers and student teachers who may be in the school for a period.

The lists which follow on pages 166–72 are intended to provide both a summary of the information required by each group and a way of analysing the particular situation in a school. The 'source' column is intended to be completed giving the way in which the particular information is conveyed, except where the source is obvious.

Teachers

Information for teachers is often provided through school handbooks of various kinds. If the school handbook is built up as a loose-leaf document

INFORMATION REQUIRED	SOURCE
Salary; conditions of service	Letter of appointment
*Person to whom responsible	Job description
People for whom responsible	Job description
*Tasks/duties for which responsible	Job description
Premises, equipment, materials for which responsible	Job description
Standards of work expected	Job description

Figure 12.1 Information needed by adults in the school

* Information needed by all adults, paid or unpaid

INFORMATION REQUIRED	SOURCES
The school philosophy and policies	
The school development plan	
Information about school finances	
*Curriculum	
*School organisation	
School patterns of responsibility	
Communication channels	
*Routines e.g. lunch arrangements	
*Patterns of assessment of children	
Staff appraisal	
Staff development programme	
Normal contacts with parents	
*Information about individual children relevant for teaching/pastoral care	
Information about the governing body	
Normal contacts with other institutions and bodies. e.g. feeder and transfer schools	
Relevant LEA policies	
Services available from the LEA	

Figure 12.2 Information needed by teachers

* Items needed also by teaching students and supply staff

INFORMATION REQUIRED	SOURCE
Other staff or volunteers for whom they have responsibility	
Tasks for which they are responsible	
Equipment/materials/space/finance for which they are responsible	
Relevant school policies	
Arrangements for making contact with feeder or secondary schools	

Figure 12.3 Information needed by teachers with additional responsibilities

INFORMATION REQUIRED	SOURCE
Attendance of staff and children	
Behaviour of staff and children	
Effectiveness of organisation	
Effectiveness of teaching/learning	
State of school finances	
State of building and environment	
State of equipment and materials	
Specific problems of organisation	
Specific problems of individual children	
Specific problems of individual staff	
Views/attitudes of staff and children	
Views/attitudes of governors	
Views/attitudes of parents/community	
Sources of help/advice/consultancy	

Figure 12.4 Information needed by the headteacher

it makes it possible to add or change material as necessary. It needs to be reviewed and updated regularly and the process of producing papers for it and reviewing it may be a valuable piece of staff development for a group.

Non-teaching staff

Information is also needed by non-teaching staff. If they are made aware of the educational intentions of the school, they can often help to implement them.

INFORMATION REQUIRED	SOURCE
Overall aims of the school	
Ways in which they can help in the development and learning of the children	
Events in the school calendar of relevance to them	
State of school finances as it affects them	
Contribution to the overall life of the school expected from them	

Figure 12.5 Information needed by ancillary staff

The children

Children need to be given information about patterns and routines and rules of behaviour. Demands upon children need to be consistent as far as possible and each child needs to know where he or she fits into the pattern. Security comes from knowing what is and what is not allowed.

They also need to be involved in some aspects of the planning and evaluation of the day-to-day life of the school. Real involvement in decision making is the best preparation for adult life in a democracy and as children grow older they need to become more involved.

A school handbook for all parents and children can be valuable in providing all the routine information such as details of any uniform, arrangements for meals, absence, together with annually updated information like a list of staff. This is likely to meet the needs of children more successfully if existing pupils are involved in some way in compiling it.

Children, especially older children, need to be given reasons for why the school/class is organised as it is and the purposes behind aspects of the curriculum and the way it is assessed. Parents tend to get a great deal of their information from their children and, if the school takes children into its confidence, this also helps to get the message to parents.

INFORMATION	SOURCE
Routines for entering and leaving the school and rooms within it	
Routines for morning assembly, breaks, lunch times	
Overall organisation of the school/classroom	
The thinking and reasoning behind the school/classroom organisation (older children)	
The major responsibilities of the various teachers with whom the children come in contact	
The names of responsibilities of non-teaching staff and volunteers with whom children come in contact	
The timetable and pattern of the day and week as it affects the individual child	
The thinking and reasoning behind approaches to learning (older children)	
The behaviour expected from children	
The school's goals in training children's behaviour	
The school rules – what is not allowed and why	
Appropriate ways of dealing with routine matters, for example absence notes, lost property, arriving late	

Figure 12.6 Information needed by children

INFORMATION	SOURCE
The intended source of each piece of learning	
The criteria for the assessment of work	
The goals of each particular piece of work, including what children should know and be able to do at the end of a given period	
The thinking behind any change of curriculum and the reasons for it	

Figure 12.7 Curriculum information needed by children

INFORMATION	SOURCE
Special teacher knowledge and skill on which they can draw	
Access to special facilities such as computers	
Out-of-school activities available	

Figure 12.8 General information needed by children

INFORMATION REQUIRED	SOURCES
The school philosophy and policies	
The school development plan	
Information about school finances	
Curriculum	
School organisation	
Patterns of staff responsibility	
Communication channels	
Patterns of assessment of children	
Attendance of staff and children	
Effectiveness of the organisation	
Effectiveness of the teaching	
Staff appraisal arrangements	
Staff development programme	
State of buildings and environment	
State of equipment and materials	
Out-of-school activities offered	
Normal contacts with parents	
Relevant LEA policies	
Services available from the LEA and elsewhere	

Figure 12.9 Information needed by governors

Children are likely to learn better if they see where what they are learning fits into the larger pattern. There is therefore a need to give them a good deal of information about the curriculum.

Children may find it helpful to know about staff skills and special facilities and arrangements for access to both. They will also need information about out-of-school activities.

Governors

Governors need to be kept informed about most aspects of the life and work of the school. Their main source of information will be the headteacher's report and the information given by the headteacher at their meetings. They should also become informed through their own visits to the school.

Parents

Parents also need a good deal of information. Some of this will be in the school prospectus and some will be given at the annual parents' meeting but there is a need for information through a newsletter and a parents' handbook. The newsletter should give current information; the handbook information about the school which is fairly standard, such as arrangements for meals, any information about uniform and so on.

CREATE AND MAINTAIN A COMMUNICATION SYSTEM

The communication task you face as headteacher is both to see that the right information reaches the right people at the right time and to see that appropriate information reaches you. This needs to happen as efficiently as possible with the least possible effort on everyone's part.

In any organisation there are three parallel systems of communication:

- The formal system
  Every organisation needs systems to communicate plans and policies and everyday information. This requires definite official lines of communication which are as short and direct as possible and which define clearly the responsibility of different members of staff for communicating information to others.
- The informal system
  The informal system is frequently more rapid than the formal system but less accurate and is often concerned with communication which is threatening or alarming. This needs to be taken into account when planning formal communication. For example, important information which could be misinterpreted should be given to everyone authorita-

INFORMATION REQUIRED	SOURCES
The school aims and philosophy	
School approaches to learning and the reasoning behind them	
Information about the National Curriculum and assessment	
School patterns of staff responsibility	
School rules	
Any uniform requirements	
Any homework requirements	
Lunch arrangements	
Timing of school day and holidays	
Admission arrangements	
Normal contacts with parents	
Information about their child's progress	
Arrangements for meeting staff to discuss children's progress	
Other meetings for parents	
What is expected of parents	
Opportunities for parents to contribute to the school	
Information about the governing body	

Figure 12.10 Information needed by parents

tively, quickly, clearly and fully, so that it is difficult for the informal system to misinterpret it. The informal system is also useful in complementing the formal system.

- The inferential system
  Every activity of people within an organisation is a form of communication. Inferences are made from a person's tone of voice, appearance, movement, choice of language, matters selected for comment, the arrangement of the environment and much else besides. There is sometimes a gap between what a school or a person thinks is being communicated and the message actually being received. For example, a school may be

keen to foster very good relationships with parents and other visitors to the school, but be unaware that people entering the school are made to feel unwelcome by the lack of indication of where to go and the attitude of the secretary.

Effective communication

No communication system ensures that people actually absorb what is offered to them. It is therefore important to consider what makes people receptive. They are most likely to take in communication when:

- it is personal, that is, it is addressed to them.
- it fulfils a need or rouses an interest.
- it is significant to the person receiving it. For example, very few people miss information about salaries or condition of service. A strong interest can sometimes be used as a lead in to other information.
- it is seen to give power or status. People tend to absorb information which comes to them because of the office they hold or if it enables them to know something which others would like to know.
- the communication requires action. Most people hate to let others down. If a communication demands action which is public in that it can be seen to be done, it is usually absorbed.
- they identify with the organisation. People will take in communication when they care about the organisation from which it comes and their jobs within it.
- the presentation is right.
- the source is respected. The person who gives a message affects whether it is taken in or not. Most headteachers will recall times when someone has said: 'You tell them because they'll listen to you'. The status and personal standing of the person communicating is important.
- the context predisposes the listener to be receptive. Communication is best when all the conditions are good. It is easy to be distracted from a communication by discomfort – for example, uncomfortable seats at a meeting or illegible writing. A frequent distraction is that of receiving too many pieces of communication at once!

Things which go wrong

There are many things which go wrong with communication.

- They may go wrong because of faults in the system.
  In a large school a communication system for passing information through the school depends upon each person in the chain taking part. A system which depends upon coordinators or year leaders both passing on and collecting information falls down if they have no

chance to talk to colleagues about the issues concerned. In a small school an arrangement which depends upon the headteacher giving out notices at break requires a good back up system for ensuring that the teacher on duty receives the information given to the others.

- A communication system which demands a radical change from the past may be difficult to work initially.

  This is not only because people may not play their parts adequately but also because the informal system which complements the formal system also needs to find a new way of working. It is often better to look at the way in which communication is currently working and look for developments which improve this than to go for a completely new system.

- Things will go wrong if no one checks occasionally that the system works.

  This does not mean insisting that there is only one way of operating, but if, for example, the system depends upon certain people passing on certain kinds of messages, they may tend to do this less carefully as time passes and as pressures increase and may need occasional reminders of their responsibilities.

- The secretary may not be able to keep up with the demands for typing. Schools are rarely generously staffed with clerical assistance and any communication which relies too heavily upon typed papers may founder.

- Things go wrong because of the presentation of communication.

  Unless they are very strongly motivated, busy people are prepared to make only a small amount of effort to understand something which is not clear. There is an art in giving people exactly the amount of information they can manage. Too much type on a page and a person does not start to read it but sets it aside to read later – but later never comes. Too much talk and people switch off. On the other hand a person given only half a message may invent the other half incorrectly. Somewhere there is an optimum for all messages. It is worth looking at how the advertising world gets messages across effectively.

- Things go wrong with communication because people are as they are. Messages may be interpreted in the light of previous experience of which the sender is unaware. They may be misunderstood intentionally or unintentionally. Mr Smith may so dislike Miss Jones that he cannot hear what she is saying. A message may be distorted by the status of its sender, receiving additional attention if the sender is very senior and being ignored if the sender is very junior.

ENSURE THAT INFORMATION TRAVELS IN ALL DIRECTIONS

Communication has to be more than a top-down arrangement. It must involve information travelling upwards and sideways as well and this is more difficult to achieve. Sometimes you may feel that you are doing everything possible to get views and ideas from people but somehow you are not getting very much coming back.

This is something to look into, because there are several possible reasons for this. Perhaps you have so many ideas yourself that people are discouraged from putting their ideas and views forward. One of the difficulties about headship is knowing when to hold back your own ideas in order to get ideas from other people.

Another reason why people do not put ideas forward is that they have experience of situations when they have produced ideas but have felt that these were not welcomed. They may even feel that ideas advanced very tentatively were not recognised. It is easy to sound unenthusiastic or to talk when you should listen and draw out and so miss ideas altogether. If you are new in post you may also be suffering from the characteristics of your predecessor and you have gradually to establish that things have changed and ideas and views are welcomed.

You can help to ensure that information and ideas travel upwards by creating situations in which staff views can be put forward. Asking a group of teachers to get together without you and put forward views about some aspect of the life and work of the school may start people contributing. A staff conference with lots of opportunity for discussion will also bring out individual ideas.

It is also important to encourage teachers to communicate with each other and to share ideas. Even in a small school teachers can work in very separate ways and there is research evidence which suggests that where teachers work together the results are better (Little, 1982). This will come partly from staff meetings, conferences and working parties, but it is also a matter of creating a climate in the school in which teachers naturally share their thinking.

SEEK FEEDBACK FROM ALL LEVELS

Part of your job as a headteacher is to find out how different people in the school view matters. This involves talking at fairly regular intervals not only with all the teachers and children but also with the secretary, the caretaker, cleaners and dinner staff and with visitors to the school about their views. Even in a small school it is easy to miss talking to some people and you need to be systematic, checking on whether you have had any conversation with particular individuals lately. All headteachers need to get around the school frequently talking with people they meet en route. You also need to make a point of talking with parents and governors who will have a different view of the school.

A headteacher gets a filtered view of what people think. They tell you what they want you to know which may or may not be the same as what you want to know. You have to work to get behind this.

EVALUATE THE EFFECTIVENESS OF COMMUNICATION

We have already looked at some of the ways in which you can check on the effectiveness of communication in the school. Perhaps the most important of these is regular discussion with everyone in the school. The check lists of information needed by the various people involved provide a tool for checking one aspect of the system.

You may also like to check the school system against the following list of characteristics of a good system. In a good system:

- The right messages get to the right people at the right time. Check by asking:

    How often do people fail to act on information which was believed to be sent?
    How often does the wrong message go over?

- There are clearly understood channels of communication upwards, downwards and sideways and these are all used. Check by asking:

    How much information do the headteacher and senior staff actually receive which has come upwards?
    If people are asked how they communicate or receive communication, is the answer the expected one?
    Does communication actually appear to come through the channels planned?

- Everyone feels well informed, but not overwhelmed by communication and people at every level appear to feel involved and conscious of participation. Check by asking:

    Does anyone complain of getting too much or too little communication?
    Are there any major gaps in communication?

- Communication takes the minimum time for its proper working. Check by asking:

    Does any part of the system take a lot of time?
    Is what is communicated really necessary?
    Does all the paper which crosses your desk really need to come to you?
    Are meetings well planned and led and felt to be worth the time spent on them?
    Are appropriate modes of communication being used?
    Is the optimum use being made of information technology?

- An overview of the system is maintained and practice is regularly reviewed. Check by asking:

Is there an adequate overview?
Should more be done to review the system?

• The inferential system gives the same messages as the formal system. Check by asking?

What views about the overall aims of the school are being put over officially to staff, parents and children?
What is actually being communicated?
Is anything happening which is counter to the official view?

Chapter 13

Staff selection and professional development

Staff selection and professional development are two aspects of the same process. When you make an appointment you are looking for someone with particular qualities and skills. Once someone joins the staff it is your task to enable the person concerned to develop professionally in ways which enhance his or her ability to undertake a new role, building on from previous experience and using appraisal as a means of identifying emerging needs.

Staff development is wider than this, however. A school needs to have a professional development plan to enable staff to meet the demands of the school development plan which will include the many demands coming from the National Curriculum and other national initiatives.

The management tasks involved in staff selection and development are as follows:

Organise and assist with staff appointments
Evaluate appointments procedure
Establish policy for staff development and appraisal
Create a development programme for all staff
Evaluate the staff development programme
Maintain staff records and provide any necessary reports

ORGANISE AND ASSIST WITH STAFF APPOINTMENTS

Although the responsibility for staff appointments has now been transferred from the LEA to governors, the number of people involved in the appointment of staff may make the headteacher's role a complex one. Chapter one referred to The POST Project report on the appointment of secondary school headteachers (Morgan *et al.* 1983) which described the system of appointing secondary school headteachers as placing far more emphasis on qualities of personality which are not easy to assess in

interview, rather than on the skills needed to do the job. Too little emphasis was given, the authors felt, to the ability to undertake the management
tasks of headship.

Although this study is now over ten years old and is concerned with
the appointment of headteachers of secondary schools, much that it says
is still relevant for primary schools. The authors point out that very few
of those involved in interviewing have been trained as assessors and that,
since the questioning is often given little preparation, what is discovered
in the course of an interview may not give the interviewing panel an
adequate idea of the suitability of the candidate for the post. They suggest
that other ways of assessing candidates might offer more information
than interviewing alone, which is known to be an uncertain way of
assessing people.

Schools are now in a much stronger position than they were formerly
to set up their own staff selection procedures and you are in a position to
persuade your governors to allow a more in-depth method of appointing
staff than a single interview, especially for appointment to more senior
posts.

The task of matching person to post involves collecting all the evidence
available about the candidate and at the same time offering the candidate
evidence about the nature of the school and the kind of philosophy which
you and your colleagues try to foster. The governors have to decide
whether a particular candidate matches the post under consideration and
the candidate has to decide whether this is the school for him or her. The
evidence on which these decisions are made is gradually revealed during
the process of appointment. It is one of the most important tasks which
any governing body undertakes.

The application

Before an appointment can be made, the job description should be brought
up to date. The job description should contain the following information:

- title of post and salary range
- person to whom the postholder will be responsible
- responsibilities for:
    teaching
    other activities
    children
    the work of other staff
    resources.

You also need a person description describing the kind of person wanted
for a particular vacancy. It should contain statements of what is required
by way of:

- qualifications, knowledge, skills, abilities
- experience
- special aptitudes and qualities
- particular interests.

Information about these points should be given in the further particulars of the post and the list made available to those making the appointment. A copy of the prospectus should give information about the school's philosophy and aims.

The further particulars should, in addition, contain the following information:

- The school and its situation
  the history of the school so far as it is relevant and any significant events
  the site and buildings – their age, distinctive features, any future plans
  the school catchment area
  the age range of the school
  the number of children currently on roll
  the size of form entry
  any arrangements for collaboration with other schools
  community use of premises
- Staffing
  current staffing ratio
  number of staff currently in post
  the staffing structure, including where the post fits into the structure
  ancillary staff employed
  arrangements for appraisal
  staff development programme
  facilities for staff in school
- Curriculum and organisation
  the way children are grouped for learning
  any relevant information about the organisation of the National Curriculum
  provision for children with disabilities, for slow learners, for the gifted, for ethnic minorities and so on
  statement of relevant facilities
- Parent/teacher links
  contacts with parents
  the existence of a PTA or school association
  the expectations of teacher involvement
- The governing body
  numbers and types of contribution

committee organisation
contacts with teachers
- LEA support
  provision for staff development
  advisory services available to the school
- Community links

The ideal advertisement and further particulars should attract the right candidates only.

Some schools may now be in a position to develop their own application forms. It is important to have an application form because in a letter of application candidates can more easily disguise the information they offer than when a form is used. The use of a form also makes it easier to compare candidates. The application form should include space for a letter or statement in support of the application which gives information about the way in which the candidate's particular experience and qualifications fit him or her for the post in question. This kind of information is more likely to be given if some advice is given about the statement required, preferably on the form itself, but otherwise in the further particulars. This too makes it easier to compare the applications from different candidates.

Once the applications have been received, they need to be sifted to decide which ones warrant seeking further information. The person description should be helpful here. It is important to be ruthless at this stage in taking out applications which do not measure up to the specifications. Even if there are very few applications you need to think very carefully before pursuing someone who is not qualified by experience and knowledge for the post in question.

At this stage you may wish to ask for further information about a number of the candidates. This should add to the information available and is more likely to do so if you ask some specific questions. If you are seeking someone who will be in a management role, for example, it is a good idea to ask about experience of leading adults. You may also want to ask questions about the candidate's approaches to primary education. A particularly useful question is 'Would you appoint this candidate to a similar post in your school?' and it is also useful to ask for strengths and weaknesses. It is a good idea to ask whether the candidate has been given the opportunity to see the report. It is wise to get more than one report on a candidate, particularly for a senior post and it is unwise to make any appointment without written information of this kind, although pressure of time may sometimes make this necessary. Interviewing is known to be fallible and even the most experienced interviewer makes mistakes.

The governors may or may not wish to be involved in making the short list. Even if they are prepared to delegate the task to you, it is wise to involve other people. However good your judgement, mistakes are less likely when more than one person is involved. Most appointments at other than deputy headship level should involve other members of staff who will have to work with the person appointed and they will therefore need to be consulted at all stages.

Other people are also useful in helping to separate prejudice from reality. It is easy to be prejudiced by irrelevancies in reading applications forms, to be put off by poor handwriting for example. There is no evidence which connects poor handwriting with poor teaching or poor management skills although the inability to present information well may be a disadvantage. It is also easy for teachers to be over-critical about spelling and minor grammatical errors. Of course these should not occur in teachers' applications in a perfect world. But in the real world some teachers are poor spellers but good teachers, are good at some subjects but not at English. Most people also have particular words and phrases which attract them or repel them. It is easy to over-play this.

An analysis of some kind is useful in studying application forms and it is helpful to draw up a proforma for comparing qualifications and experience.

Planning the interview

The time the candidates are in school should be carefully planned. Every part of the day is an opportunity for getting information from them and giving them information and even when interviews are taking place, it is a waste of opportunity to leave candidates doing nothing. Such time might be used for parallel sets of interviews or for discussion with other staff or spending time in classrooms. In addition to the formal interviews it should be possible to provide the following opportunities:

- a tour of the buildings, particularly the room(s) in which the successful candidate will work and the staff facilities. They need to get an honest picture, with difficulties and problems made plain, so that they know what they might be coming to.
- time to talk at some length with those who will work most closely with the selected candidate. This can be in a social context over lunch or coffee, but there is a good deal to be said for some preliminary planning of topics to be discussed so that necessary ground can be covered without overlap.
- some social time with members of staff. Although it has to be accepted that all the time the candidates are in school has some relevance for selection, the social parts of the day can be more relaxed and in practice offer a rather different kind of information to the selector.
- time with you to ask questions so that they are clear about the nature of the post they might be accepting.

The actual selection process should be designed to elicit as much relevant information as possible from each candidate so that they can be compared.

The education service tends to limit selection procedures to interviewing, but there is no reason why other ways of selecting should not be employed. For example, each candidate might be asked to teach a small group for a short period of time. Or where the school is seeking someone in a management post, each candidate might be asked to chair a short discussion on some topic involving all the candidates. This will both elicit information from everyone and also give information about the skill of the group chairperson. Some useful information is given in *A handbook on selecting senior staff for schools* (Morgan *et al.* 1984).

Whatever selection procedures are used, it is essential that an interview is included. This is the only way of getting some of the necessary information and it also gives governors the opportunity to play their part. If possible there should be more than one set of concurrent interviews with small groups of interviewers looking for particular attributes. This means that each candidate is interviewed for longer and there is therefore more information available on which to make a decision. If the governors are not happy to do this, it may be possible to have preliminary interviews followed by a more formal interview with governors. Governors should, if possible, be persuaded against interviewing in a large body. This does not allow for questions to be pursued and tends to put candidates off.

The governors need to know in advance all the details of the person required and the way in which the evidence is being built up. In particular the headteacher needs to explain plans for questioning and ask governors if they would be willing to explore specific areas of questioning, remembering that the governing body may well include some people who are practised interviewers able to contribute a lot and will need little guidance. Others who are less experienced may be glad to be asked to do something specific and may have a useful contribution to make because they come fresh to the procedure.

In questioning it is helpful to remember that a useful guide to candidates' ability is in what they can tell the panel about what they have actually done providing that it is followed up with probing questions to establish that the experience is genuine. Most questions should be followed up with others which probe so that there is a check on what people say.

In selection interviewing, as in short-listing, people have to guard against their own prejudices and reactions. It is, of course, important that a headteacher sees that the person chosen is someone with whom he or she can work, but it is easy to be drawn to an exciting candidate and turn aside a less exciting person who could actually bring far more to the job. Interviewers should know their own temptations and weaknesses.

At the end of the day a decision has to be made in the light of all the evidence available. The chairperson may have personal ideas about the best way to arrive at a decision, but the following pattern is useful:

- Check that everyone is aware of all the evidence, perhaps by getting someone to sum up and then ask each member of the interviewing panel to list the candidates in order of preference, using any gradings made to help with this.
- Ask everyone to state the candidates he or she would put at the bottom of the list. This usually narrows the field and avoids wasting time discussing unlikely candidates.
- Ask everyone for his or her first, second and third choice if there are that many candidates. This narrows the field and concentrates attention on a small number of names. It may even provide the final decision.
- Review the evidence about the names left in and discuss them further. This will usually produce the final decision.

Where there is a difference of opinion about the final decision, narrow the field if possible by voting. If this does not produce a clear answer, make use of one of the following procedures:

- make use of any gradings given
- recall the favourite candidates for further questioning. This needs careful planning
- decide to readvertise the post

It is also possible to use the chairperson's casting vote if everyone is happy with this way of resolving the situation.

If a conclusion has been reached and the candidates are still waiting, the successful candidate should be offered the post. Any statements made to the successful candidate about salary or responsibilities at this stage are legally binding so it is important that prior decisions have been reached about these points and that any information given is correct. The unsuccessful candidates should be thanked for coming and if they wish some feedback on performance should be given to them, perhaps sharing out this task so that each person has a chance to talk with a member of the appointing panel.

All the information from the interview should be kept for a period in case queries arise. The papers of the successful candidate become the starting point for the personal file, giving information on which further professional development can be based.

EVALUATE THE APPOINTMENTS PROCEDURE

The proof of the effectiveness of any selection process is not only in the quality of the staff built up over time, but also in the extent to which the people appointed turn out to to be better or worse than the impression they gave at interview. In the ideal situation a selector should have a good idea at the end of the day of the kind of person who has been appointed. It is useful to look over notes made at the time of appointment to see what kind of picture of the successful candidate emerges, perhaps adding to the notes if necessary in order to have something to look back at. These notes can then be reviewed after six months or so after the person has taken up the post to see how far the picture formed at the interview was an accurate one.

Immediately after the selection it is a good idea to think over the day to see if you feel that any particular part of it could have been better organised. You may like to talk to governors who took part to see how they viewed the procedure.

It may also be useful to discuss the selection procedure with the person appointed as soon as he or she joins the staff. There may be points at which it seemed particularly satisfactory or unsatisfactory from the candidates' point of view which it would be helpful to know about.

ESTABLISH POLICY FOR STAFF DEVELOPMENT AND APPRAISAL

It is your responsibility to see that teachers have opportunity and encouragement to develop in their work. This includes not only teaching staff, but there is also a case for considering the development of other staff particularly if development is regarded as important for work in the current post and not simply as preparation for the future.

Poster and Poster (1991), in discussing appraisal, suggest that it can be seen from two different points of view. These two points of view are also relevant for professional development generally. We can ask what are the aims of the school and plan for the development of staff so that these aims can be achieved. Or we can look at the needs of individuals and help them plan first to be effective in their current posts and then to learn in preparation for possible promotion.

The learning needs of teachers

Teachers enter the profession with a body of skills and knowledge from training and the beginnings of teaching skills. Schools are playing an increasing part in the training of teachers; and the school in which a teacher starts work is probably the most important single source of learning from then on and likely to affect the way he or she works for many years, perhaps throughout teaching life. This is so whether or not you and your staff make a conscious effort to help new teachers to develop. Newly qualified teachers are impressionable at the beginning of their careers and the examples they are shown and the training they receive from colleagues are important. It is in the context of actually doing the job that skills are developed and knowledge acquired and consolidated.

Teachers learn through interaction with their professional environment. They form and develop a frame of reference by which they judge their own professional activity and that of others. They acquire new knowledge and develop the skills to meet the tasks and situations they encounter.

Oldroyd and Hall (1988: 11) note that:

> institutions identified for their good staff development programmes tend to exhibit a collegial, participative style of leadership where senior staff work as a team and are ready to:
>
> - consult staff about needs and priorities
> - delegate significant responsibilities
> - encourage staff ownership of INSET policies and programmes
> - invite open review of processes and activities
> - identify and use talented staff to lead INSET activities
> - network good practice between groups within the institution
> - lead by example by themselves engaging in their own professional development
> - contribute towards a positive climate by offering professional support and personal counselling to staff.

Little reinforces this view. She studied a number of schools and in the most successful she found that:

> it was difficult to encounter teachers when they were not engaged in some discussion about classroom practice . . . . By contrast in the less successful schools teachers were likely to restrict formal meetings to administrative business and were likely to consider the faculty lounge off limits to 'serious' discussion.
>
> (Little 1982: 33)

Knowledge and skill may be developed in a variety of ways. Teachers may read, selecting books which offer what they want. They learn a good deal from each other, sometimes through staffroom discussion, but also by looking at work in each other's classrooms and discussing individual children. It is important for newly qualified teachers to see other people teach because it is at this stage that they are forming their own teaching style. They do this partly by trying out ideas of their own but also by trying approaches which seem to work for other people. The more good models they see the better their chances of forming a good style.

The school may also offer opportunities for working with other teachers to particular ends, perhaps seeking the solution to a problem or making plans for a piece of work or planning an in-service day. Appraisal will also contribute to teacher development.

Teachers also have opportunities outside the school. They may listen to the radio and watch television programmes which seem to offer something useful. They select from in-service programmes on offer. They may also take part in inter-school activities. It is your task as headteacher to see that they take advantage of appropriate programmes.

Visiting other schools is also a valuable opportunity for staff development and it can be helpful to have a plan whereby everyone in turn has a chance to visit and feedback. This overcomes the feeling in some teachers that they are being singled out. If you can possibly arrange it, it helps to have more than one person visiting or attending a course at the same time. It gives each of the people concerned someone with whom to discuss what has been experienced and makes the feedback to the rest of the staff more complete.

There are considerable problems involved in sending teachers to daytime in-service courses. Many LEAs have delegated the in-service money to schools and now charge for courses. There is also the problem of providing cover for teachers who are absent. It may be wise, if possible, to allocate a significant sum of money for supply cover for all the various purposes for which teachers may be out of school as well as for absence through illness. It is helpful if the school can obtain regular supply teachers who get to know the school and can link with teachers going out of school so that the time is not wasted. The situation in which there is least disturbance is one where there is team teaching. This ensures that at least one teacher in the team is present and knows what the children are doing and can help a supply teacher to work effectively.

Many schools now feel that some of the best in-service work comes from their own in-service programmes when these are planned to meet the needs of the school and the teachers and involve staff in their planning.

In all these learning situations teachers will be constantly taking in and sorting out new materials and ideas in their minds, fitting it into their emerging frames of reference, digesting it and making it peculiarly their own. Alongside this, new teachers will be developing in maturity and this too affects their work in school.

There is a good deal of research evidence to suggest that teacher development depends to a large extent upon the leadership they are given. Fullan and Hargreaves, for example, make the following statement 'Among the many factors which shape what kind of people and teachers, teachers become, one of the most important is how their schools and their heads treat them' (1991: 43).

The factors include not only the leadership of the school but also the leadership which comes from coordinators and others in senior roles in the school. The way in which you recognise, encourage and praise the work of teachers affects their commitment and enthusiasm and readiness to try new ways of working. Teachers who feel secure in your approval are ready to take the kinds of risk which lead to genuine innovation and improvement. One important reason why a headteacher should not teach full–time is that he or she needs time to help other teachers develop their work.

You may choose to help teachers by working alongside them. The teacher who does not believe that the children in his or her care can work in certain ways may be convinced if it is seen to happen. On the other hand your style may be so different from that of the teacher that it may not be helpful to that teacher to see how you do it. In such a case it may be better to observe the teacher and try to make suggestions which fit his or her style. Many routes are possible and a good headteacher recognises that there are many kinds of effective teaching and aims to balance the experiences children get as they move through the school. A headteacher is also in a particularly good position to team teach with colleagues and this allows a marrying of styles and can help to set standards.

It is easier for a teacher to accept help from someone else if there is an element of reciprocity. You may, for example, suggest to a teacher that he or she tries something out with your help and then feeds back the findings to the rest of the staff. This, if you present it that way, can be seen as helping you while you help the teacher.

The professional development and appraisal policy

All schools need a professional development and appraisal policy. This might include statements about the following:

- overall philosophy and attitudes
- the people whom the policy concerns (non-teaching as well as teaching staff)
- the possible professional development activities
- the organisation and responsibilities for professional development
- the way needs will be assessed
- the part played by appraisal
- provision for induction and for newly qualified teachers
- provision for management training
- the way in which provision for individuals will be built up
- the way in which teachers' progress and development will be recorded

Organisation

The responsibility for the professional development of staff is now very much with the individual school. This means that each school needs an organisation which can provide for this. Professional development needs to be the responsibility of a senior member of staff with support from the rest of the staff or, in a large school, a representative committee which meets regularly and which holds occasional meetings with other staff to discuss the development programme. It may be a good idea to include a representative of the non-teaching staff and perhaps a governor so that there is first-hand knowledge among the governors of the way in which the school is planning the development of its staff. The professional development committee should be responsible for identifying needs both for the school as a whole and for individuals, and planning and implementing the overall staff development programme.

The staff development programme needs to be linked with the school development programme so that any training needed to implement the school development plan is clearly identified in the staff development programme. The plan should take into account the need:

- for particular development and knowledge within the school at the present time
- to prepare for future needs
- to keep staff stimulated by the work
- to keep everyone up to date with what is happening professionally outside the school.

Preparation for future needs is partly a matter of looking two or three years ahead and, as far as is possible, anticipating the needs that will exist then.

A school not only needs formal plans for staff development which require assessment of the overall needs of the school and of individuals within it, and the creation and development of a programme. It also needs to use informal opportunities which arise as means to these ends. This requires clear thinking about direction and goals.

The emphasis in staff development will vary according to the particular emphasis at any given time and the particular group of staff in office. There are, nevertheless, some staff development activities which should be a permanent part of any programme although the way they are conducted may change.

- Induction
  New staff, however experienced in the work, need induction into the particular school organisation and systems. There should be a meeting, probably with the headteacher or the deputy to explain school policies and systems; the provision of information on children; briefing on relevant work already undertaken by staff; and some arrangement for checking they are settling in happily and for dealing with any problems.
- Provision for newly qualified staff
  The probationary year as such has now been abolished but the need to

support and continue the training of newly qualified teachers including licensed and articled teachers, remains. They will not only need the induction programme, but also support and further training in their work in the classroom and there should be a clear responsibility for providing this. Most newly qualified teachers need reassurance that they are making progress and opportunities to see other teachers at work, as well as being seen in the classroom fairly frequently themselves. They also need good opportunities for discussing their work with more experienced teachers. It is wise to arrange for one teacher to act as a mentor to the newly qualified teacher. The mentor should be the person the inexperienced teacher turns to with any problems. If possible they should meet regularly to discuss progress and the mentor should see the newly qualified teacher at work fairly frequently and coach him or her in skills where necessary. This could be a good way of persuading teachers to work more collaboratively.

- Opportunities for all teachers to reflect on performance, work on classroom skills and management development
  All teachers improve their work by reflecting on it. The trouble is that schools are extremely busy places where time for reflection is hard to find. You need to see that the organisation is such that you yourself make time to reflect and that you also create time and opportunity and give encouragement for others to reflect. This is most likely to happen when a group of people come together to discuss their work and one way of providing this is to use a staff development day occasionally for this kind of reflection. Another possibility which worked very well in one school was a monthly evening meal which was part of a long staff meeting. Each person contributed some food and the staff felt that this was an extremely helpful meeting because everyone was relaxed and having a meal together cemented friendships and trust.

  There is a sense in which we create reflection opportunities by giving people more, rather than less to do. The coordinator asked to work with colleagues to make a statement justifying demands for a larger part of the financial cake will somehow find time to do this because it really matters. In the process the teachers concerned will do some thinking about their work which they might not otherwise have done. One task of management is to stimulate and structure thinking by asking questions and making demands.

  Reflection on performance is further created by teachers seeing others at work. The headteacher and coordinators have a role here, but there is also value in peer-group evaluation. If two or more teachers can come together and organise themselves so that they see something of each other's attempts to achieve particular targets in the classroom, this too is valuable. It works best if it is mutual help.

Appraisal

Schools are now required to appraise all teachers. This has gradually been gaining adherents and is now being put into practice in schools. The pilot studies of appraisal suggested that it was easier to introduce it in a situation where there was regular reviewing of the work of the school.

It must be remembered that some teachers may see appraisal as threatening. Wragg (1987) notes that the fear of humiliation is very present in the minds of teachers when appraisal takes place and it can force people to confront themselves in ways they would normally wish to avoid. These problems need to be kept in mind in running an appraisal system.

The purposes of appraisal need to be clear to everyone involved. The DES *Statutory Instrument* on appraisal (1991c: 2) states that appraisal procedures shall in particular aim to:

- recognise the achievements of school teachers and help them to identify ways of improving their skills and performance;
- help school teachers, governing bodies and local education authorities (as the case may be) to determine whether a change of duties would help the professional development of school teachers and improve their career prospects;
- identify the potential of teachers for career development, with the aim of helping them where possible, through in-service training;
- help school teachers having difficulties with their performance, through appropriate guidance, counselling and training;
- inform those responsible for providing references for school teachers in relation to appointments;
- improve the management of schools.

Dean (1991) adds to this list:

- to provide help and support for teachers in a management role;
- to support teachers with management roles in their responsibility for the work of their colleagues;
- to provide an opportunity for praising what is good and dealing with unsatisfactory elements in a teacher's work;
- to provide the teacher with an opportunity to ensure that others know about his or her work and to give an opportunity for expressing views;
- to provide the appraiser with additional knowledge about what is happening and to enable him or her to have a view of school as a whole;
- to provide an opportunity for those in leadership roles to influence the thinking of others and be influenced by their views.

Sources of information for appraisal might include the following in addition to the essential planned observation of the teacher in the classroom:

- self-assessment by the teacher concerned

- planned observation of the teacher's work in the classroom
- test results
- study of children's work
- information from children
- observation of the teacher in a management role where relevant
- other observations

Appraisal involves observation of the person being appraised in his or her working environment. This requires the establishment of criteria which should be worked out and agreed by the whole staff. It requires some thought about what constitutes good teaching, what constitutes effective behaviour in a management role and what should be included about other contributions a teacher may make to the school.

The plan for observation of the teacher's work should include, if possible, some opportunity for self-evaluation and there are many published forms for doing this and for classroom observation (Suffolk LEA 1987; Dean 1991, Surrey LEA, 1993). There are also many other LEA lists. However, there is also value in schools making their own lists which can be made to match their particular aims and objectives. It is a very useful piece of staff development.

There will need to be agreement about the pattern of lessons to be observed. The appraiser also needs to establish before observing a lesson what the teacher is trying to achieve. There should be agreement among staff as to the form the observation will take, whether everyone should use similar criteria for observation, what they should be and how they should be recorded. It is also important for discussion of the lesson to take place as soon as possible after the observation while what happened is fresh in the minds of observer and teacher.

Appraisal interviewing is an important skill and, if this task is to be done adequately, at least an hour needs to be set aside for each person, if there is to be sufficient time to explore thinking in some detail.

Both interviewer and interviewee need to prepare for the appraisal interview. Classroom and other observation is only part of the necessary preparation. It is helpful if the appraisee provides some form of self-evaluation in writing before the interview. This might ask about objectives, success in achieving them and particular problems and difficulties. The appraiser needs to study any relevant background information, including the previous appraisal documents and notes of any discussions which have taken place since the last appraisal.

The appraisal interview is an opportunity for interviewer and inter-viewee to plan together. The idea is to review the immediate past, look at the current situation and agree goals for the future. It may provide an opportunity to speak frankly about areas of work where improvement is required, but this should be in the context of mutual planning for overall improvement and should be positive and supportive as far as possible. It should also be an occasion for praise and encouragement. If the interview is done well and positively it can be a powerful means of development for individuals and a valuable way for the management of the school to keep an overall picture of how people see the school, their colleagues, their work and themselves.

DES Circular 12/91 on teacher appraisal stresses that appraisal should be 'set in the context of the objectives of the school' and linked to the School Development Plan. 'Appraisal targets, when linked together, should provide an important agenda for action for the school as a whole' (DES Circular 12/91 1991d: 2).

LEAs now have to ensure that in each school there is one appraiser able to conduct appraisal interviews for each four members of staff. The need for training will continue as new people are appointed to management roles and it must be the responsibility of the school to see that training takes place before people are expected to appraise others.

Each school has to decide who should appraise whom. The DES circular made it clear that it was expected that teachers would be appraised if possible by someone who was in a management role in relation to them. The headteacher has the task of allocating appraisers. Primary schools do not always have a tidy line management organisation and while in a small school the headteacher and deputy will be able to deal with everyone between them, in a large school, selecting appraisers will probably be a matter of using the teachers who have additional allowances with the headteacher and possibly the deputy appraising these teachers.

Handy and Aitken (1986: 53) suggest that if appraisal is to work:

- the data must be recent and objective, not subjective
- the manager must be credible
- the manager must demonstrate high regard for the subordinate as a person.

CREATE A DEVELOPMENT PROGRAMME FOR ALL STAFF

The professional development programme must cover all aspects of the life and work of the school. We can start by considering what teachers need to learn. Much of this learning will start during training but the school enables it to continue developing.

Areas of teacher learning

Personal development

Teachers' personalities and their personal qualities are crucial factors in success in teaching. Most people learn better when they like and respect the teacher. A teacher who is a mature human being offers a model to young people which may, in important ways, affect their attitudes to school, to learning and to the world.

All teachers are still developing as people. The treatment they receive from those senior to them, the extent to which their views are considered and treated with respect, the attitudes shown to them, all affect their development.

Child development

Teachers need knowledge of the normal patterns of physical, intellectual, emotional and social development of children if they are to understand those they teach and recognise deviations from the norm. Knowledge in this area is continually developing and teachers need to try to keep up to date with research findings.

Teachers may also have to deal with issues which may be outside their own upbringing and personal experience such as violence, child abuse, drug-taking, alcoholism, HIV and family breakdown. There needs to be an awareness in the school of these issues and some agreement about the best way to deal with them. Teachers need the support of colleagues so that they, in turn, can support children in difficulties. Primary school headteachers also often find themselves counselling parents and it is important to have good links with social services.

Knowledge of learning and teaching

Teachers tend to be more effective when they have adequate theoretical backing for what they do and can use their theoretical knowledge to improve their practice. They also need a range of teaching methods and learning strategies so that they can select appropriately for different teaching situations.

Group behaviour

Teaching in school depends upon teachers' ability to manage children in groups. The skill with which an experienced teacher manages groups of children normally reflects an understanding of the way groups work, even if this is not consciously acquired knowledge. Knowledge of the way groups control individuals and an ability to recognise the effects of both competition and cooperation are valuable to all teachers.

Skills needed

Teachers need the following skills:

- ability to observe children recognising the needs and progress of each
- ability to communicate through exposition, questioning, leading discussion and so on
- skill in organising and planning
- ability to evaluate own work and that of children.

At a more senior level teachers need not only the skills of the classroom teacher but also management skills including the following:

- the ability to make good relationships with adults and the interpersonal skills involved in working with them
- skill in eliciting ideas from colleagues and drawing them together
- skill in identifying aims and objectives, making them explicit, planning and organising so as to achieve them
- the ability to analyse and solve problems
- skill in handling various administrative tasks.

Those in non-teaching posts may also have learning needs. These may be more difficult to define than those of teachers, but they still need to be considered. There are three main ways in which learning takes place for all staff in schools:

Learning opportunities for teachers

- They learn as part of their work
  Teachers learn by studying their own work through:
    opportunities to talk over work with more experienced colleagues
    provision of feedback on performance for a single lesson or work over a period of time, perhaps as part of the appraisal process
    use of self-assessment techniques such as check lists
    feedback from children
- They learn from other teachers through:
    formal and informal staffroom discussion
    observing children with other teachers
    observing other teachers at work
    visiting other schools
    being involved with other teachers in experimental and problem-solving activities
    being involved with other teachers in evaluation and assessment
    action research in which a group of teachers together studies methods of improving some aspect of their work
    coaching in particular skills identified through classroom observation

    experimental work in the classroom

    appraisal meetings

- They are involved in opportunities for acquiring management skills:
  These may include:

      participation in decision making activities

      being given opportunity to exercise responsibility

      being given opportunity to exercise interpersonal skills with adults

      understudying a particular post for a period as part of a staff development programme

- They learn by specific provision within the school:
  Schools now normally provide formal opportunities for staff development. These may include:

      provision of specific written material and discussion about it

      involvement in the preparation of written material such as a staff handbook or scheme of work

      staff conferences

      seminars or discussions on a regular basis.

      job enrichment opportunities – perhaps being given additional responsibility

      job exchange

      use of prepared materials with a staff group, for example, prepared in- service packages, videos

      viewing of television programmes made for discussion by teachers

      joint visits to other schools or centres by groups of teachers

      specific encouragement to undertake relevant professional reading, perhaps by requesting a teacher to read a particular book and report on it to colleagues.

- They learn through external provision:
  However good the internal programme, it is important for teachers to go out to external courses and meet teachers from other places. The cost of this to schools means that such opportunities need to be carefully chosen to service the needs of the school as well as those of the individual teacher.

  Opportunity to take part in inter-school discussions and working parties may not be labelled in-service or even be thought of as having a professional development purpose, but nevertheless may make a contribution to the development of those taking part. This kind of opportunity is particularly valuable to teachers who have been a long time in post but who feel that in-service courses are unlikely to contribute much to their development.

Needs assessment

Planning the staff development programme first requires an assessment of the needs of the school. These will have been partly identified in the course of working out the School Development Programme and the check list on pages 26–9 should be helpful in thinking about the in-service needs of the school.

Individual members of staff also have personal in-service needs, however, and the programme should include opportunities for people to develop the skills they will need for career development.

In-service needs should be reviewed systematically each year and the programme discussed by the whole staff as well as any professional development committee. In assessing needs those of the non-teaching staff should not be forgotten.

EVALUATE THE STAFF DEVELOPMENT PROGRAMME

The provision for staff development should be evaluated regularly. Each part of the programme should include some evaluation and the whole programme should be evaluated at intervals. This is a task for the whole staff or for the professional development committee. There are a number of distinct methods of evaluating which include the following:

- questionnaires
- other documentary evidence
- discussion with those who have experienced the programme
- interviewing a sample of individuals
- observation of whether suitable programmes have had an effect
- evidence from children
- value-for-money assessment.

The following questions may be useful in evaluating the programme:

- Have we a satisfactory staff development policy and programme?
- Have we an adequate method of assessing needs? Are we missing any which are important?
- What opportunities do we offer teachers to improve their teaching skills?
- To what extent do teachers work together sharing problems, experience and skills?
- What opportunities are there for teachers to acquire and develop management skills?
- What opportunities are we offering to coordinators and holders of other equivalent posts to improve their ability to do their present job?
- Are we doing enough to train the next generation of leaders for primary education?
- Are we making provision for non-teaching staff as well as teaching staff?

- What are we gaining from our appraisal programme?
- Are we getting value for money in what we spend on our own programme?
- Are we getting value for money in what we spend on sending people to courses?

MAINTAIN STAFF RECORDS AND PROVIDE ANY NECESSARY REPORTS

It is the responsibility of management to see that an adequate record is kept on each individual member of staff. These records should include information about the work which teachers have done during their time in the school and this will form the basis of any report written on members of staff who are candidates for promotion or who are failing.

One way of providing this information is to get teachers annually to write a note of the work done during the year, including both curricular and extra-curricular activities. This can then go into the file exactly as the teacher wrote it. This is slightly different from the kind of information which needs to be provided for appraisal which needs to have a self-evaluation element.

All headteachers find themselves asked to provide reports on the work of teachers who are candidates for promotion. A headteacher may receive a request which lists questions to be answered, but many such requests are more general. Information about the teacher's experience in the previous years may be helpful in this context. It is wise to give the teacher concerned some idea of what is being said. If this involves actually showing the reference to the teacher a note about this should be included.

Where the request is general the following points should be covered in the reply:

- the teacher's full name and home address
- the title of the post for which the teacher has applied
- title of present post and salary level
- summary of responsibilities in present post
- summary of previous experience in present school
- statement of your contact with the teacher, including the time you have known him or her
- assessment of the suitability of the teacher's experience/qualifications for the posts applied for. If it is a post with management responsibility a statement about experience and success in managing adults should be included
- assessment of the suitability of the candidate as a person for the post applied for

- statement of recommendation. This should be a definite statement if possible – either recommending unreservedly or stating reservations. Statements like 'I recommend X as worthy of interview' are not very helpful.

Specific questions can be answered as part of the items on this list.

Teachers should be able to see their own files upon request.

Chapter 14

School and community

As head of a school you are at the boundary between the school and the community it serves. Although members of your staff will have contact with parents and governors, you are the main point of contact for the world outside the school. You are the school's official representative and are seen to be responsible for everything that goes on. You are in a position to encourage people from outside the school to contribute to its needs and at the same time you need to protect the staff from some of the outside pressures. Schools have a life of their own which is demanding and absorbing and it is easy to become too inward looking although the parents of children in a primary school are usually too much in evidence to make it possible to forget that the school is part of a community which sees the school as serving its needs.

Schools are not only part of a wider community within the neighbourhood and nationally. They are also part of a professional community of those schools which contribute children to them and of the schools to which children transfer.

There is now a strong emphasis on meeting the needs of the school's clients, the parents and children. A primary school may be the only one in the area so that the matter of choice is largely academic. Nevertheless it is still important to carry local parents with you. This is a much more complex issue than some would have us believe, however. Parents in many areas are likely to have a wide range of frames of reference and if you make carrying parents with you the only criterion for your ways of working you are likely to be in difficulty. The school needs a philosophy and a sense of direction which is agreed with its governors and as far as possible with its parents, so that parents send their children to the school knowing its philosophy.

In relation to the community, management has five key responsibilities:

- Represent the school to the outside world
- Work effectively with governors
- Involve parents in the work of the school

- Create and maintain links with contributory and transfer schools
- Encourage the use of the community and neighbourhood for learning

REPRESENT THE SCHOOL TO THE OUTSIDE WORLD

As headteacher representing the school to the world outside, you will undoubtedly need to attend various meetings on behalf of the school in situations where delegation is not possible. This is not only interesting but may very often be of benefit both to you and to the school in providing an opportunity to see and hear how other schools function.

One problem is that of being out of school too frequently and for too long, particularly if you become involved with a number of activities taking place in school time. Some meetings will be necessary and unavoidable, but there will be others where there is a measure of choice about becoming involved. You need to develop criteria for deciding whether to attend outside activities and to be firm about this. An important criterion is whether the school will benefit in any way from your involvement in the activity in question. Another is whether you have something valuable to offer to the particular activity. There is also the question of how well the senior staff are able to manage the school, although it might be regarded as a criticism of your management if you feel that your deputy is incapable of managing the school in your absence.

There is also a difference between the beginning of your time as a headteacher when you cannot afford to be much out of school and later stages where there is a competent deputy and everything is running more or less smoothly.

WORK EFFECTIVELY WITH GOVERNORS

The Education Reform Act has changed radically the relative roles of LEA, headteachers and governors. In particular headteachers now work with their governing bodies in ways which are different from those of the past. Governors, for their part, need to establish confidence in the headteacher's ability in the first instance and you will need to bear in mind the possible differences in outlook until you and your governors are well known to each other. A new headteacher needs to go about change carefully, sounding out governors as well as staff.

A legal framework for governors in their responsibilities for staff was provided under the DES paper, *S222 Education (modification of enactments relating to employment) Order* (1988) which came into force in 1989 and included the following provisions:

- Governors were given a share in the duties and responsibilities of employers.
- The governing body will have to appear as the respondent at industrial tribunals for any cases brought as a result of its action or by the LEA at its instruction, although governors will not be personally responsible for costs arising from any decision. The order does not affect staff in voluntary aided schools.
- A local dispute between staff working at the school and the governing body is now to be regarded as a trade dispute, provided the action falls within the definition of a trade dispute contained in the legislation.
- Trade unions will be able to organise industrial action against the governing body with immunity from civil action by the governors, provided that the action itself is lawful.
- The LEA will continue to have primary responsibility under the Health and Safety at Work Act (1974) and will be able to issue directions on health and safety with which schools must comply. Governors are responsible for the safety of employees.

The responsibilities of the governing body

The responsibilities of the governing body now include the following:

- agreeing the aims and objectives of the school with the headteacher and staff
- agreeing the budget
- agreeing policies for the following and ensuring that they are implemented:
    - the National Curriculum and its relation to LEA policy
    - other aspects of curriculum including
        - health and safety
        - sex education
        - religious education
- agreeing policies for:
    - public relations
    - admissions
    - equal opportunities
    - discipline
    - charging
- receiving and acting upon inspection reports
- agreeing arrangements for staff development
- agreeing arrangements for school evaluation
- appointing staff
- dealing with staff disciplinary cases
- ensuring that all governors are trained for their responsibilities
- evaluating their own work

Roles and relationships

Joan Sallis (1990) in a paper delivered at a DES conference on governors, spoke of the relationship between headteachers and governors. She said that she believed that sound relationships could only be built on shared values, common purposes, efficient working structures and clarity about roles.

Wilkins defined the role of governors as 'the establishment of policy and monitoring and evaluation of that policy' and the role of the headteacher as 'translating broad policy in practice and establishing and maintaining appropriate structures and processes to ensure that policy objectives are achieved' (Wilkins 1990: 5).

The most difficult problems arise over territory which was until recently the professionals' preserve. Headteachers need to see their governors' work as a reflection of their management skills, and be professionally proud of it. This means having high expectations of their governors and sharing responsibility for their development. It is a considerable test of your management skills to ensure a proper involvement of the governing body in the decision making process of the school and in the development of a school philosophy.

You can foster the work of governors in the following ways by:

- encouraging them to set objectives and work towards them
- encouraging them to develop systems for reviewing the work of the school
- taking issues to them at the sketch plan stage so that they play a part in the decision making process. For example, they should be involved in the progress and updating of the School Development Plan
- helping to plan their involvement with the school so that their visits are purposeful and visiting governors have a clear programme
- making sure that governors have the opportunity to meet and get to know the work of the staff, perhaps by giving members of staff the chance to attend a governors' meeting to talk about their work
- ensuring that governors are aware of a range of techniques for appointing staff and that they employ good practice in undertaking this
- making opportunities to talk with every governor and not only those with whom you feel an affinity
- explaining your personal philosophy and that of your staff to them and demonstrating how it works out in practice as a preliminary to developing a joint philosophy
- encouraging governors to take part in governor training and using all the possible opportunities to complement this by involving them in work in school and in appropriate staff meetings
- encouraging governors to evaluate their work against objectives in a systematic and regular way

- establishing and communicating high expectations from governors
- getting every governor involved in the school by setting up structures which involve regular contact
- encouraging governors to meet parents and communicate with them.

The relationship between headteacher and chair of governors is particularly important. There must be a sharing of values and mutual trust. Where these do not exist, it is important to do everything possible to work toward them. There should be recognition by both parties of the other's role.

It is essential that you and your chair keep each other informed, probably by having a regular meeting. You have to learn to be selective here, however, and to find out from discussion what it is important for the chair to know. You need to give similar messages about the school's aims and philosophy to parents and the community.

Getting to know the school

Governors need to get to know the school well, from the inside as well as from the outside. This means that they must visit while the school is in action and become involved in some of its activities. This may be difficult for some governors and everything possible should be done to make suitable opportunities.

It can be difficult to be a visitor to a school if you do not know what is expected. It is very important that you and your staff plan governors' visits carefully and make clear your expectations. A governor might:

- spend time in particular classes observing what is happening. It will be helpful here to suggest what the governor might look out for and to explain in advance what the teacher is trying to do
- adopt classes or year groups or aspects of curriculum so long as this does not preclude getting to know other aspects of the school's work
- join the staff for field study work, helping to supervise the children
- join the staff for a staff development day on an appropriate topic
- join a staff working party with a particular task, for example, working out a programme for social and personal education
- join the staff in evaluating a particular aspect of the life of the school
- where a governor has particular skill or knowledge which might be of value to the school, talking to the staff about it or, if more appropriate, working with a group of children.

All LEAs have provided opportunities for governors' training and there are also many training packages. You can do much not only to encourage governors to become involved with training, but also to train governors in unobtrusive ways. All of the suggestions for involvement given above have a strong element of training.

Training for governors will need to be an on-going process as new governors become involved in the work. While much of the responsibility for this will remain with the LEA, it is important that both the governing body itself and the school play a part, particularly in the induction of new governors into the local situation.

The West Sussex newsletter for governors (West Sussex Education Committee 1991) suggests that each governing body appoints a 'link governor' with a responsibility for training. Among the other responsibilities suggested for this role is that of working with the headteacher to develop a pack of materials for new governors.

The more knowledgeable the governing body the more effectively it can support the school. Governors need skills and knowledge in the following areas and you should look for opportunities which help them to develop them:

- selection and appointment of staff
- personnel issues, including staff discipline
- financial aspects of LMS
- other aspects of school management from the governors' point of view
- the National Curriculum
- other aspects of the curriculum, particularly:
    sex education
    religious education
    health and safety
    personal and social education
    citizenship
    environmental education
- special educational needs
- equal opportunities
- public relations
- chairmanship and effective meetings
- assessment and evaluation in schools.

Evaluation

Governing bodies, like schools, need to evaluate their work from time to time, particularly in relation to the annual parents' meeting. Those in a position to evaluate are the governors themselves, the headteacher and teaching staff of the school and to some extent the parents, who will really be evaluating the work of the school. You can do much to encourage this kind of review. Evaluation may involve the following:

- looking at how objectives have been achieved
- discussing areas of work and expressing satisfaction or dissatisfaction;

for example, reviewing the appointments made and discussing with the headteacher how successful they have been

- circulating questionnaires to relevant groups; for example, the governors themselves, headteacher, teachers and a sample of parents, asking for comment about specific aspects of the governing body's work
- questioning headteacher, teachers and a sample of parents about aspects of the governing body's work. It is sometimes useful to follow up questionnaires with discussion with relevant parties about the issues raised by the questionnaire survey
- setting new objectives in the light of the evaluation.

Readers interested in following this further should see the paper 24 of *Building an effective governing body* (1988), published by the National Association of Governors and Managers. This gives a full list of the questions which governors might ask themselves about their work.

INVOLVE PARENTS IN THE WORK OF THE SCHOOL

There is a good deal of research evidence that parental attitudes make a difference to children's success at school (Douglas 1964, Tizard and Hughes 1984, Brighouse and Tomlinson 1991). Studies in the United Kingdom, Australia and the Unites States all show that schools in which pupils 'do well' as defined by achievement and behaviour are all characterised by 'good home-school relationships'. Bastiani notes that:

> These successful schools go well beyond the basic legal requirements to develop effective, two-way communication, are accessible in a variety of ways and at all reasonable times, work hard to find ways in which parents can encourage and support their children and provide them with practical help and above all, build a sense of shared identity and common purpose.
>
> (Bastiani 1993: 103)

Children whose parents hold high but realistic expectations of them are more likely to make good progress than those whose parents expect little. There is also evidence from a number of LEA paired reading schemes that when parents are involved in helping children with reading they make better progress.

Learning goes on throughout our waking hours. Macbeth (1993) points out that children spend only 15 per cent of their time in school but that there could be an assumption that the school's influence is greater than this because it is professionally provided. Children learn at least as much out of school as they do inside it and when home and school work together the overall learning which takes place is likely to be more soundly based. A child's problems are more likely to be solved by home and school working together than by either working alone. In addition there are reservoirs of talent and goodwill among parents which the school can tap.

Even parents who seem apathetic about coming to school events are usually concerned about their children's education and Tizard *et al.* (1988) found that interest was strong in virtually all parents of young children.

The DES paper, The Parents' Charter (1991b: 18) lays down the information which the school must provide for parents. It lists five key documents:

- A report about your child
- Regular reports from independent inspectors
- Performance tables for all schools
- A prospectus or brochure about individual schools
- An annual report from your school's governors.

The Parents' Charter also stresses the need to work in partnership with the school. 'Teachers need your support in their efforts to help your child do the best he or she can' (DES 1991b: 13).

One of today's problems about communication with parents which was rare in the past is that there may now be a number of children with three or four 'parents'. Under the Children's Act 1992, a parent of a dissolved partnership may seek from the courts joint parental rights. When these are granted he or she must be given access to school reports, invited to school functions and in all respects treated as equal with the partner who is parenting. Where a partner has not been granted these rights, the school may be in breach of the law in communicating with that partner unless the other partner specifically requests it. Divorced parents usually have equal rights. The new partner only has rights if the child is legally adopted. In such a case the new parent may well supersede the birthright parent. The school needs to be clear about the situation in the case of any child where there has been separation.

One important effect of the National Curriculum is that parents are being given a much clearer picture of how their children are doing in school. This has implications for all teachers who may now need to work more closely with parents than ever before.

Many schools have developed excellent work with parents but research suggests that there is still quite a way to go if schools are to create the kind of cooperation with parents which will truly support their children's learning. Munn (1993: 1) notes three aspects of traditional parental involvement with the school:

- it has been largely concerned with the well-being of the parent's own child
- it has been to support the largely taken-for-granted value system of the school

- collective action, such as through parents' or parent-teacher associations has been largely concerned with fund-raising, or transmitting information, and has not usually challenged the school's way of doing things.

She also notes that 'parental involvement in identifying the values which the school will embody is rare'. She suggests that this is likely to change and that 'parents operating through local federations of governing bodies or other interest groups are likely to assume greater importance in policy-making in education' (Munn 1993: 5).

Atkin *et al.* (1988) suggest that when parents understand what the school is trying to do, identify with its goals and support it efforts, understand something of their role as educators and take an interest in and provide support for their children's school work, then the effects can be both dramatic and long-lasting. They note that parents are a resource for the school and also have unique opportunities as educators. The school needs to harness this resource for children' learning.

Atkin *et al.* (1988) found that schools do not give parents enough of the right sort of information. Parents get their ideas of what the school is doing mainly from their children and from looking at their work. They may not be aware of the educational philosophy of the school, its policies and teaching strategies let alone become involved in developing them. Teachers too rarely explain what the term's work will consist of and suggest ways in which parents might help. Nor do they explain the processes by which they are helping children to learn. In general parents tend to get the message that teachers would rather they left the business of educating children to them. In practice many parents try to help and this help is a resource which is too rarely harnessed. The development of genuine partnership will involve changes of attitude on the part of both teachers and parents.

Tizard *et al.* (1988) found that teachers did not give a great deal of feedback on children's progress. They were concerned to find that only 20 per cent of parents had been told that their child was having difficulties when testing suggested that the overall figure was considerably higher. Only 12 per cent of reception class parents had been told that their child posed behaviour problems although the teachers said that 26 per cent of children posed such problems. There was also the feeling on the part of some parents that teachers tended to be defensive about problems rather than being prepared to discuss them openly. This pattern should gradually change as a result of the requirement to feed back information about progress in the National Curriculum.

Carrington and Short (1989: 86) suggest a number of ways in which the school may contribute perhaps unwittingly to the non-involvement of parents. This may happen when:

- teachers are unwilling to work with parents who are regarded as non-professional and therefore not qualified to offer anything;
- teachers foster the view that the parent's responsibilities cease at the school gate;
- the school structures visiting arrangements for parents in such a way that some parents are prevented from coming by work commitments.

There are two possible views of the relationship of parents with the school. They may be seen as partners in the process of educating the child or as customers buying (indirectly in the case of maintained schools) a service from a professional organisation.

Parents as partners

Pugh (1989: 5) defines partnership with parents as:

- a shared sense of purpose
- mutual respect, and
- a willingness to negotiate

This view of partnership has considerable implications for parents and teachers. Both parents and teachers have stereotypes of each other and the parents' view of teachers will be largely formed by their own experience of school. This has left some people very hesitant about entering a school and talking with their children's teachers. Parents may see teachers as the fount of all knowledge and wisdom, as intimidating figures, as friends or as rather underpaid employees. Teachers, for their part, often blame parents for the problems their children create in school and frequently comment that it is the parents who do not come to school whom they would most like to see.

Teachers may also hold the view that working-class parents are not particularly interested in their children's progress at school and this is particularly so where black parents are concerned. However, Tizard *et al.* (1988) noted that 70 per cent of teachers in their study made negative comments about black parents – mainly that they were 'over-concerned with their children's education', 'had too high expectations', 'lacked understanding of British education' and so on. The same study found that virtually all parents said they gave their children help with school work and more black than white parents started to teach their children to read before they started school. This study suggests that there are really very few parents who are not interested in their children's progress but some are hesitant about coming to the school to meet teachers.

If parents are really treated as partners in the education of their children then they should have some involvement in some aspects of decision making. At the very least they should be consulted about appropriate aspects of change.

Atkin and her colleagues (1988: 64) give a list of concerns and suggestions:

- The development of practical arrangements for effective communication between parents, teachers and children lies at the heart of good home/school relationships. Parents need to see, discuss and experience and develop understanding.
- Effective basic communication needs to be backed up by a range of appropriate opportunities for parents to participate in their children's schooling.
- Schools need to recognise, support and strengthen the crucial role of parents as educators.
- Parents represent a valuable but often unacknowledged resource which can be tapped to great effect in the education of children and young people.

One might add that open days which give parents a chance to see what is happening are valuable as are opportunities for parents to experience some of the learning which their children are experiencing. Schools also need to give thought to ways in which parents can support children in different aspects of curriculum and to ways of involving of parents in appropriate decisions. 'Appropriate' here means more than decisions about issues such as school uniform. Some decisions about curriculum and organisation may also be more effective if the school is aware of what parents think about them.

In a large school it would be very difficult to involve parents in decision making in any substantial way, but it is possible to consult the parents on the governing body and to consult parents in groups, sometimes by inviting sample groups of parents to take part in some aspect of discussion, sometimes by involving all those who choose to come to talk in small, teacher-led groups about their ideas on particular issues, sometimes by sending questionnaires to samples of parents and making it clear that over a child's school life all parents will have the opportunity to take part in a questionnaire survey.

Macbeth (1993) suggests that schools might usefully adopt the Scandanavian plan of the class meeting. Parents are involved in planning a meeting for the parents of the class of which their child is a member. This provides an opportunity for the teacher to tell parents about the work planned and to invite their cooperation in helping their children with it and to suggest ways in which they can help. A meeting of this size also makes it possible for parents to ask more questions than perhaps they would in a larger meeting, especially if the class meeting is held regularly so that the parents of a particular class get to know each other.

If parents are really going to be partners in their children's education they need to be taken into the confidence of the school more than is often the case. The DES papers *Planning for school development 6* (1989a) and *Development planning 7* (1991a) suggest that parents should be made aware of the School Development Plan and that governors should report on its progress at the annual parents' meeting. Many of the plans for learning need to be discussed with parents. At the level of the individual class, each teacher needs to consider how to inform parents about the work being planned. An alternative to class meetings is to have meetings of parents of one year at a time when the staff can talk about the work the children will be doing and the way in which parents can help with it. Methods need to be explained as well as outcomes so that parents can learn how to work with their children in ways which complement the work the teachers are doing. There is also a need for plenty of time for questions and discussion.

Discussion with parents needs to be two-way. Teachers have something to learn about children from their parents and there is much to be said for the kind of meeting described by one first school, where all parents of new entrants to the school were seen for an in-depth discussion about their children about a month after they started school. This aimed to do three things – to check on factual information, hear the parent's view of how the child had settled at school and listen to what the parents could tell the school about the child.

These studies all suggest that there is much to be gained from treating parents as partners in the education of their children and the school needs continually to be thinking of ways to do this. If the large majority of parents are keen to help their children to do well in school, this is a resource which teachers would do well to use. Parents who are keen to help their children will do this anyway, however much teachers discourage them.

Parents as clients buying a service

Much that has been said about parents as partners will also be true if parents are seen or see themselves as clients buying a service. In this situation the school needs to set out very clearly what it is offering. Communication will be just as important as it is if parents are seen as partners, and it needs to be two way for the same reasons.

Parents will want to get value for their money and the school will need to demonstrate what it is offering and what the child is gaining. They are likely still to be keen to do all they can to help their children and may expect the school to help them to do this. Alternatively they may take the view that they are paying the school to educate their children for them. In this case the school may need to point out that children are learning all the time and that parents make an important contribution to a child's education whether they set out to do so or not. Parents have many opportunities to foster their children's learning and the children are likely to make better progress in school if home and school work together.

Hegarty who feels that parents should be seen as clients rather than partners, makes the following comment: 'Partnership may be an agreeable concept, redolent with egalitarian overtones, but the warm glow of right thinking should not be confused with dispassionate action carefully designed to achieve significant targets' (Hegarty 1993: 129–30).

Schools need to have a clear idea of what parental involvement really means in their particular context.

Communication with parents

Parents have a unique view of their children which is much more comprehensive than a teacher's can possibly be. Teachers have therefore much to learn from parents about the children they teach. What is needed is a regular meeting where both teachers and parents inform each other. The parents inform the teacher about the child and how they view what seems to be happening in school and the teacher informs the parents about the progress that child is making, the work which the child's class will be doing and how they can help. Both teachers and parents also need opportunities to discuss frankly the problems they are encountering and how they can work together to overcome them. It involves listening on the part of the teacher as well as on the part of the parent.

The studies suggest that there are two further ways in which teachers are not always effective in communicating with parents. In talking about how parents can help, teachers tend to dwell on what not to do, rather than on what to do. They are also inclined to use what parents see as educational jargon. The problem about jargon is that one person's jargon is another person's technical language. Teachers quite properly have ways of talking about what they do which are peculiar to the education profession but are confusing to other people. It is a good idea for a group of teachers to try to think of all the words and phrases they use which will be seen by others as jargon. For example, topic work, environmental studies, not to mention all the language which has come in with the Educational Reform Act – key stages, levels, Statements of Attainment, Attainment Targets, SATs and many other words, phrases and acronyms are unfamiliar to parents because they have all come into being since they were at school themselves. Such terms need either explaining or avoiding.

Teachers may also like to consider a year group newsletter which informs parents about the work in hand and how parents can help. This might also include information about school journeys and visits and what is needed for them as well as what may be needed for different aspects of other work. It will, of course, be important not to cover the same ground as any school newsletter and it may be necessary to enlist the help of certain parents to translate the letter into other languages.

The major piece of communication with parents is now the discussion of each child's progress. Teachers must inform parents of where their children have reached in the National Curriculum and, although this can be done on paper, there should also be a meeting at which the details of what is being said can be explained.

Assessing the National Curriculum (SEAC 1990: 71–2) suggests that the intentions behind reporting are as follows:

- to widen access to information about the school's curriculum plans and objectives for individual children and classes in the case of parents and more generally for the school as a whole;
- to provide parents with the information necessary to support an informed dialogue with the school and with the children themselves about their achievements, progress and future work throughout their school career;
- to encourage partnership between schools and parents by sharing information and explaining its implications;
- to enable a school to report on the overall accomplishments of its children in ways that not only parents but also the wider community can appreciate.

Most teachers will regard it as important that children see their progress in the light of their own performance and tend to discourage too much comparison with other children. However, parents will certainly want to know, not only where their child stands currently, but how he or she stands in relation to other children of the same age. In most cases this will be a fairly complex picture with individual children being well up with the age group or beyond it for some work and doing less well in other areas.

The outcomes of National Curriculum testing will require quite a lot of explanation if parents are to understand about Levels and Attainment Targets but it helps to answer questions about how the child stands in relation to other children because it can readily be seen that the answer is a complex one. Every child will have a different profile.

Discussion of this profile needs to be followed up by discussion of what teachers and parents can do to help the child in the areas where he or she is at the lower levels. The teacher who discusses this with parents needs to have some positive suggestions about ways in which the parents can help and to give them a clear idea of what he or she is planning to do.

It is important in these discussions to keep a positive view in all that is said. Teachers need to emphasise the areas in which the child is doing well and be positive about action to be taken where he or she is doing less well. They should also try to avoid over stressing what not to do and concentrate instead on what parents can do.

Discussions with each child's parents need to go further than discussion about curriculum progress by including any problems of behaviour. Teachers, not unnaturally, feel that this is a very delicate area which could imply that either they or the parents are not doing their job. Tizard *et al.* report that in the one in four cases where teachers actually discussed behaviour with parents 35 per cent of parents responded positively; 36 per cent agreed with the teacher; 25 per cent responded negatively, and 15 per cent could not see the problem. There was also a marked difference between the views of parents and teachers. Only 30 per cent of children regarded as a problem by teachers were also thought a problem by parents and only 34 per cent of those seen as problems by parents were also seen as problems by teachers. This suggests that children often differ in their behaviour between home and school and that there is everything to be gained from parents and teachers each knowing about the problems the others find and working together to overcome them. Parents are also often grateful for the opportunity to discuss with someone else the problems they encounter.

It has been customary for most discussions about children to take place on the school premises. However, there is much to be said for visiting the children's homes to discuss them with their parents. Parents feel more confident on their own ground and usually appreciate the fact that a teacher has taken the trouble to come to see them. This kind of meeting can be more relaxed than a meeting in school where there may be others waiting to see the teacher and it gives the opportunity for the teacher to learn about the parents' view of the child. A teacher can also learn a great deal about a child by seeing his or her home setting and the discussion tends to be more valuable than it sometimes is at school. This activity takes time but is very rewarding. It is important in doing this for the teacher to acquire techniques for finishing a meeting so that he or she does not spend too long in any one home. Usually putting one's papers together and making summarising statements give an indication that the meeting is ending.

Schools now have to send parents a written report on children's progress. This needs to state where each child has reached in the National Curriculum and also report on other areas of work and on work skills, behaviour, attitudes and any problems. It must also give information about the average class performance. Decisions about the nature of such reports will be made at school level, but parents may profitably be involved in discussing the design of the report form. Again it will be important to be positive as well as honest and there is much to be said for a report which allows parents to comment and possibly which allows older children to comment also.

Ethnic minority parents

Many urban schools have a high proportion of ethnic minority parents and this poses problems of communication as well as creating a rich culture for the school. Smith and Tomlinson (1989: 135) found that 'one stereotyped belief which persists (among teachers) is that ethnic minority parents are 'just like white working class parents apart from colour and belief'.

Tomlinson and Hutchinson (1991) studied a group of Bangladeshi parents arranging individual interviews with them with a Bengali-speaking interviewer. They found that half of the mothers and a fifth of the fathers had had no education and did not read or write. They tended to have large families and often had children at several different schools. The study suggested that their contact with schools was inadequate. Twenty months after the Education Reform Act, 90 per cent of mothers and 40 per cent of fathers knew nothing about the changes in education. Schools appeared to have few strategies to overcome the language barrier and parents failed to appreciate the high level of language competence their children needed to function across the curriculum. These parents did not get the level of information they wanted about their children's progress. The researchers summarised the views of these parents as follows: 'Working class Bengali parents, often with little English, had an interest in education and a sophistication in their desires for their children which teachers did not credit them with'(Tomlinson and Hutchinson, 1991: 142).

This and other studies suggest that there needs to be a change of attitude on the part of teachers to one with less stereotyping and greater effort to keep ethnic minority parents involved on an equal basis.

Parents in the classroom

It has become common practice in primary schools to invite parents to help in the classroom or about the school. This has a lot of advantages in that parents begin to see how teaching takes place and this not only helps them to support their own children, but may well make them good advocates for the school. The teacher is also helped in many of the tasks which take time from the more professional aspects of teaching. For example, some schools have used parents to help children with learning difficulties, providing reading practice in a one-to-one situation, playing practice games, discussing what the child finds difficult and collaborating with the teacher to support the work in hand. Parents are also often used in the library and use could be made of parents in helping with administration. The school which is determined to involve parents will find many opportunities to do this.

There are also problems. The first and most difficult problem is that of whether the school selects the parents who come in to help or takes all comers. Where parents are selected this can lead to bitterness and upset, but avoids the problem of the parent who wants to take over or the parent who is not very literate. On the other hand, it may be that the kinds of parent who are not selected are just those who would benefit most from being in the school and working with teachers. The problem of the parent who appears to want to take over may disappear if the teacher is clear what he or she wants and the problem of literacy is partly a matter of the tasks parents are asked to do. However, this too is something of a problem since there are inferences to be made from the tasks which are allocated to parents. It is also important to stress to parents helping in the school the need for confidentiality about the work of children other than their own.

In inviting parents to work in school, it will be important to discover what any individual parent can offer. A parent may have special knowledge and skills which could be used very widely in the school. It is also important to plan the work of parents and any other ancillary help in considerable detail. Bennett and Kell (1989) make the point that, in many of the classes they observed, ancillary helpers and parents were left to their own devices and in some cases were not supporting the teacher in a very satisfactory way because the teacher had not thought out how to use their services.

The non-statutory guidance in *English in the National Curriculum* (DES 1989b) suggests that bilingual parents might help by reading and tape-recording stories in the home language of children in the class and then work with them to assist in translating the story into English.

A teacher who has parents helping in the classroom needs to think out in detail what they are to do and how they should react to children. This needs discussion among the staff so that all teachers are aware of their responsibilities in involving parents in the classroom. It suggests that teachers need tactfully to give parents some training in some aspects of helping in the classroom. It may be best to ask them to undertake tasks like preparing materials in the first instance and gradually to involve them with children.

The needs of teachers in working with parents

Teachers are not trained to work with parents, and if this work is to be effective, time needs to be spent considering how best to deal with the various contacts. Work with parents could well be the topic for an in-service day, perhaps involving a number of parents during some part of the time. This might include:

- discussion about how to work with parents in the classroom and the drawing up of a policy about what should be done by way of ensuring that this help is well used.

- consideration of ways in which parents could be asked to do more to help their children with school work.
- study of the communications going to parents looking to see whether they are free from jargon and clearly and well set out. Parents might be involved in this discussion.
- work on how to set about discussions with parents, particularly where children are not doing well. Role playing may be a good way of trying out approaches to different types of parents. Parents might be involved in this, giving feedback about how they experienced the way teachers tackled the interviews.
- the preparation of questions to ask parents invited for part of the day to talk with teachers about their views. The teachers might work in small groups, each group with a different set of questions about how parents see matters. The parents then spend a short time with each group answering their questions.
- work on drawing up an overall school policy about working with parents so that there is guidance for the future.

CREATE AND MAINTAIN LINKS WITH CONTRIBUTORY AND TRANSFER SCHOOLS

Another important task is to make links with any schools or playgroups which contribute to your school and with the main secondary school(s) to which your children are likely to transfer. Continuity between stages of education is important for children and it is essential that you do everything possible to ease the transfer for children and see that the next school has the right kind of information about each child. The National Curriculum makes this easier in that there is now a curriculum in common between schools.

Links should include visits for teachers and children and there should be discussion about the children transferring both before and after transfer. Joint study groups can be helpful and it is also useful if children take with them to their next school a small selection of some typical work so that teachers in the new school have some idea of their achievement in the previous school. Such collections could form the beginning of profile records. This does presuppose that teachers in the next school or in your school will take time to look at these records and it should be a matter for agreement between the schools that such records will be passed on.

Transfer information of this kind becomes particularly important where a child has learning difficulties or is exceptionally able. It is sensible for one teacher to pass on what he or she has discovered about a child's difficulties (which is different from expressing opinions) so that the next teacher can build on from this rather than attempting to discover everything afresh.

Children need opportunities to visit the school to which they will be going and so do their parents. Some secondary schools now run two- or three-day programmes for the children who will be entering them so that they have experienced some work with their new teachers prior to transfer. Alternatively teachers from the secondary school can spend time in the primary school doing some teaching of the top year.

Parents need a good deal of information in choosing schools for their children. The primary school can be helpful in providing them with opportunities to hear from the headteachers of the various available secondary schools.

The school also needs to make links with any nursery schools or playgroups which contribute children to the school, discussing children and what they have been doing.

Most infant and first schools provide opportunities for pre-school children to visit with their mothers and spend time in school with their new teachers prior to entry. This is a particularly good time for making relationships with parents who may be nervous about their children coming to school and who may therefore be very receptive about what you have to tell them. The children need an opportunity to meet their future teacher and to begin to see school as a exciting place where there are lots of interesting things to do. It also helps at this stage if they can be reassured about problems like where the lavatories are, which can loom large in the mind of a young child. Many schools invite parents and children to visit in small numbers so that they can give new children an opportunity to join their new class on their preliminary visit and give the headteacher the opportunity to spend some time talking with individual parents.

Parents also need reassurance at this stage as well as information about matters of detail like dinner money and any school requirements. It is a good idea to explain the arrangements for keeping in touch with parents and to talk about the information you hope to give them about their children's progress. A very important part of this early meeting is listening to individual parents who have something to tell you about their children. This may not be the ideal opportunity for listening to any lengthy information, but you can at least assure them that you would like to hear about such things as early illnesses, family problems which may affect the child, such as a handicapped sibling, and anything else they feel you should know. You can then offer to meet parents at a later stage to talk about such matters in more detail and discuss how the child is settling into school.

This is also a chance to recruit for the PTA and to tell parents about opportunities for parents to help in the school.

ENCOURAGE THE USE OF THE COMMUNITY AND THE NEIGHBOURHOOD FOR LEARNING

Your school is part of the local community. You will naturally be part of community events, particularly if you are in a village or suburb where the school is central to local affairs. Your local community and environment is also a resource for children's learning, probably the most important resource you have after your teachers, since it is the source of first-hand experience for all the children. A good deal of work should start in the local area and every possibility it offers should be exploited.

Learning needs to be transferable. What children learn in school is useful only if they can apply it in situations outside the school. The world outside the school is thus not only the source of material for learning but also the end to which learning must be directed.

The local community and environment are a vital source of material for subjects such as history and geography which are partly about the development of communities and their interaction with their environment. Much material for scientific and mathematical learning is present in the local environment. It provides a basis for creative work in writing, drama, dance, art and music.

There is also a need to help children to feel a responsibility for their local environment, for improving it, trying to keep it free of pollution and vandalism, helping to make it a good place in which to be. This means developing understanding of how local government works and the ways in which people can contribute locally.

You may also have a number of people in the neighbourhood who can be persuaded to contribute to the children's learning. Every neighbourhood has professional people and skilled workers of various kinds who may be willing and able to demonstrate and talk about their work. You may also have parents with skills and knowledge which they are prepared to come and use in school. This is yet another reason why it is valuable to know your parents well.

Chapter 15

Evaluation

Evaluation and accountability are currently very much to the fore in education. Yet evaluation has been going on in schools since schools first began. Teachers have always looked at what they were doing to see whether it was successful and whether they could improve on it. What is now happening is that we are trying to make evaluation a much more systematic activity which examines the work of the school in a way which covers all the activities and not simply the work of the classroom.

Evaluation in school is an extension of the everyday task of weighing up situations and people and making assessments in order to make decisions about action. In making professional judgements we need to be more objective and to think clearly about the judgements we make. We evaluate in order to assess past action and learn from it, ready for new planning and action.

Evaluation implies a setting against values. This suggests that assessment might be regarded as a stage in evaluation where information is collected in order to compare it with standards of some kind.

EVALUATION SERVES FOUR MAIN PURPOSES IN SCHOOLS

The support of individual development

Children need to know how they are doing in order to improve. The teacher's assessment of individual pieces of work, and of work and of behaviour generally, helps children to see progress and establish internal standards so that they eventually become self-reliant adults. The general comments may be part of a profile system to which children also contribute or simply teachers' comments on individual pieces of work. There will also be statements about how children have done in SATs. These assessments are all intended to support individual development. The teacher also needs to assess where children are starting from, what is appropriate learning for them, what progress they are making, what they should do next and so on. Without this kind of continual assessment learning will not take place in any very effective way.

Teachers also need to know how they are doing in order to develop in their work especially at the early stages of their careers. This is the purpose of the appraisal system.

The management of children's learning

The teacher in the classroom assesses the stage the children have reached in order to decide what to do next. Teachers also assess in order to group children for different activities and to decide which children are able to undertake particular pieces of work and many other things

At the school level you, as headteacher, make assessments of teachers and children in order to decide which teacher should teach each class. Evaluation for managing children's learning also includes evaluating materials and developments. Teachers try something new and assess how successful it was. They assess new materials and teaching methods and decide which would best suit their purposes.

Accreditation for children and teachers

The next purpose of evaluation becomes important mainly when children are transferring to another class or school when assessment provides a form of accreditation. Here the assessment is not so much for the development of the children, although there is still an element of this, but in order to inform someone else of the stages children have reached and their current educational needs. The SATs results provide a form of accreditation and schools will also provide statements and records of achievement built up over a period for children transferring to secondary education.

Schools also provide accreditation for teachers in the form of reports upon those seeking posts elsewhere or promotion.

Accountability

Finally evaluation is concerned with demonstrating to others that the school is fulfilling its purpose adequately. Schools are accountable to parents and the community through their governors for providing for the needs of their children with the resources they are able to make available from the budget they are given. There is an increasing need to make public what a school is achieving and the introduction of four-yearly inspections and the publication of reports on these as well as the annual governors' report to parents all enable the school to be accountable. The school may need to interpret some of the information it is required to produce for parents and the community.

School also demonstrate what they are doing more informally through open days, exhibitions and collections of children's work and by inviting people into the school to see what is happening.

Although the processes of evaluation for different purposes may sometimes be similar and in some situations evaluation made for one purpose may service another, this is not always the case. For example, assessments made to help the learning of less able children needs to be positive, stressing what they can do as well as identifying the areas in which they still need to learn. It is unhelpful to such children to compare them with their more able peers. But a comparison with the peer group may be needed in order to place children in groups for learning and it will be important in this context not to discourage the less able to the extent that they give up trying. It is therefore helpful in reviewing the school's evaluation procedures to keep these four aspects of evaluation in mind.

PERFORMANCE INDICATORS

Evaluation depends upon indicators of performance. A teacher is able to make judgements about what a child knows and can do only from what that child says and does. The success of a change in organisation or of curriculum development must be evaluated on the basis of such indicators as the views expressed about it and the improvement in the children's behaviour and/or learning. Issues such as improvement in behaviour need to be defined closely so that there is agreement on what evidence demonstrates them. Some indicators such as test results or the collection of views require particular activity as part of the evaluative process, such as consideration of specific questions or the use of interviews, questionnaires or check lists.

The introduction of regular inspections does not take the place of the school's own evaluation of its activities. The process of inspection will be more valuable if the school has conducted its own review, is aware of the areas which need attention and can provide the inspection team with information about issues which are in the School Development Plan because they have arisen from the school's evaluation of its work.

Evaluation must involve consideration of what the school and the individual teachers are trying to do. Aims and objectives require formulation and it is at the planning stage of any activity that thought should be given to evaluation.

The evaluation tasks of management are to:

> Assess the current state of the school
> Establish a policy for assessment and evaluation
> Organise an evaluation system

ASSESS THE CURRENT STATE OF THE SCHOOL

It is your responsibility as headteacher to maintain an overview of all that is happening in the school. This involves seeing that there is evaluation of different aspects of the life and work of the school. You also need to see that the teachers are concerned with evaluating their work, including their teaching methods. The chart on pages 224–6 identifies the areas in which evaluation is needed. Space is left beside each item to suggest possible indicators.

It is not suggested that all the items in the list be evaluated at the same time but that a few items, probably those relevant to the School Development Plan be selected each year for evaluation so that over a period everything is covered.

It is all too easy to see evaluation as being concerned with ends. It is more difficult to assess how effective are the means by which ends are achieved. Yet much of the development of primary education over the years has been concerned with how children learn. Any evaluation of what is happening in the school needs to be concerned with process as well as outcome. You need to look at how teachers are achieving their ends, the methods being used, the extent to which children are not only learning content but in the process learning to think, to reason, to solve problems, to search out material for themselves, to weigh evidence, to discuss, to work in groups and become independent learners. You also need to consider whether children are becoming able to evaluate their own work and whether teachers are doing anything to encourage this.

One good test of the extent to which children are becoming independent learners is to give a group of children a period of time (up to a week, depending upon their age and ability) to research and produce material on a topic without any help from the teacher. However, much of your evaluation of this area will be a matter of observation of teachers and children at work and discussion with them.

ESTABLISH A POLICY FOR ASSESSMENT AND EVALUATION

The school policy for assessment and evaluation should include statements of the following:

- the aspects of school life which will be evaluated systematically and the way in which this will be done

	Assessments required	Performance indicators

Curriculum	The relationship of the curriculum philosophy to the curriculum as taught
	
	The development and progress of children
	
	The effectiveness of the learning and teaching
	
	Provision for children with special needs including the very able
	
	Continuity
	    within the school
	    with contributory schools
	    with schools to which children transfer
	
	Preparation for adult life	

Organisation	Overall organisation of the school into groups for learning
	
	The effectiveness of the management structure
	
	Staff organisation
	The use of time by
	    children
	    teachers
	    non-teaching staff
	
	The life of the school including
	    assemblies
	    lunch times
	    out of school activities
	    special events e.g. plays, concerts	

Planning	The effectiveness of the
	    planning
	    decision making patterns
	    budget management
	
	The extent and success of innovation	

Figure 15.1 Assessments and performance indicators

	Assessments required	Performance indicators
Pastoral care	Children's behaviour and discipline Record keeping Reports to parents	
Teaching staff	The recruitment of teachers Staff deployment Staff performance Professional development of teachers Staff records	

Non-teaching staff	Work of non-teaching staff including
	    office and clerical staff
	    caretaking and cleaning staff
	    kitchen and dining room staff
	    any other ancillary staff	

Parents	Relationships with parents Involvement of parents in the life of the school	

Communication	The effectiveness of communication with
	children
	    teachers
	    non-teaching staff
	    parents
	    governors
	    contributory schools
	    transfer schools	

Figure 15.1 continued

	Assessments required	Performance indicators

Relationships	Relationships
	   child/child
	   children/teachers
	   teacher/teacher
	   parents/teachers
	   teachers/governors
	   school/contributory schools
	   school/transfer schools	

Evaluation	Marking system Testing Teacher records Arrangements for school review	

Management	The personal organisation and
	effectiveness of
	   headteacher
	   senior management	

Accom/resources	Accommodation/grounds
	   physical state
	   cleanliness
	   attractiveness
	
	State of resources	

Figure 15.1 continued

- the evaluation programme
- the use to be made of children's records
- the system for assessing children's work.
- the programme for developing evaluative skills in children
- staff responsibilities for evaluation.

It is the task of management to see that evaluation policy is carried out. This means designing a system which ensures that over a period all the different aspects of the life and work of the school are evaluated.

Assessment and evaluation concern the work of all teachers since effective teaching depends upon the teacher's ability to assess the learner's needs, capacity and response. The testing of the National Curriculum makes this easier to do but there is still a need for continuous assessment of the work of children. The headteacher and senior staff need to see that teachers also evaluate their own work and keep clear records of work undertaken and learning achieved, both in order to anticipate need and to assess progress. There is a case for a staff agreeing that they will all keep a particular kind of record of their own work, so that teachers joining the staff permanently or on supply can draw on the records of their predecessors. There is also a need for evaluation of the broader aspects of school life, such as pastoral care, behaviour, parental relationships and similar aspects.

ORGANISE AN EVALUATION SYSTEM

It is self-evident that it is not possible for any school to evaluate all its work in a short period of time. A school needs to have a cycle of evaluation planned over a period of several years in which items listed are evaluated regularly, with some being dealt with more frequently according to current need. The school's own evaluation will be complemented by the four-yearly inspection programme and it may be helpful to use some of the headings from the OFSTED handbook (1993) in your own evaluation. Evaluation needs to be built into any new developments and there should be an annual programme of evaluation which asks for assessment of various aspects of the life and work of the school at different times during the year.

In making this plan it is wise to allow time for action following each aspect of work evaluated. There is little point in evaluation if it is not followed by action on the findings.

Teachers in primary schools are normally involved in the process of evaluating the work of children. They also need to be involved in self-evaluation, as teachers and in management roles – a process which appraisal should assist. Children should also be involved in the evaluation process, helping to identify the questions which might be asked, discussing their experience as learners, completing questionnaires on their views and perhaps undertaking some evaluation as part of their normal work. Older children should be able to use databases and spreadsheets to analyse some of their findings.

Samples of parents need to be involved in various aspects of the school's evaluation programme. Sometimes this will be a matter of inviting a small group of parents to discuss some aspect of school. Sometimes a questionnaire might be sent to a particular year group or area. Parent governors should also provide useful information.

Governors have an important part to play in the evaluation programme. They should be involved in drawing up the programme and in receiving reports on what has been discovered. They may also be able to provide independent views on some aspects of school life.

The processes of evaluation

These require consideration of the following points:

- There must be careful sampling.
  The evidence available for making an assessment is only a sample of what is being assessed, whether it is a consideration of what a child knows and can do, the skills of a particular teacher or the effectiveness of pastoral care in a school or anything else. The sample must be representative of what is being assessed.
- Assessments must be valid and reliable.
  Validity in making observations is increased if more than one person assesses the same material and observers come to similar conclusions. Reliability in observation is increased if observations are made of comparable situations on more than one occasion.
- Assessments need to be both formative and summative.
- An evaluator must look from different viewpoints.
  The point of the controversial inclusion of a lay person in OFSTED inspection teams is to provide a different viewpoint. Schools and teachers may feel that work is going well but parents and possibly governors may see their work very differently. There is also the problem that in observing what is happening in a school it is all too easy to see only from one's own point of view and to make inaccurate judgements about work which stem from a different viewpoint. Anyone observing teaching, for example, needs to know what the teacher intends to do if he or she is to make a judgement about the effectiveness of teaching.
- Subjectivity and objectivity should be balanced.
  The subjective view of experienced practising teachers is known to be a good predictor of children's performance. Subjective assessment has the advantage that it is faster and more comprehensive than some

assessments which are apparently more objective. Human judgement nevertheless needs occasional checking against more objective forms of assessment. Assessment is made more objective by combining the subjective judgements of more than one person.

Approaches to evaluation

A school needs to consider various ways of evaluating and choose those appropriate for the particular task. The following can be used:

- Procedures based on observation and inspection
  Teachers observe what their children do and say and question them in order to assess their progress and learning. The accuracy of judgements made in this way depends upon the skill with which the observation and questioning are carried out and the breadth of professional experience which the assessor brings to the interpretation of what is seen and heard.

  This kind of assessment is made more objective by planning observations against a form of check list or by checking one person's observations against those of another. This is not always necessary but is sometimes useful.

  Assessment by personal observation and questioning has also the advantage that a skilled and experienced observer can take into account many factors which are acknowledged to be important but which may not be easy to measure. For example, the contribution the school is making to the moral or aesthetic education of its children is probably most effectively assessed by observation.

  This kind of assessment can also take into account many factors at once, so that in watching a class at work, an observer may note that the teacher is not only covering the syllabus effectively but also teaching the children how to study and solve problems.

  In using this kind of assessment it is important to ensure that the views of children are investigated and used. This may be a matter of discussing with groups of children their reaction to the teaching they have received.

- Questionnaires
  Questionnaires to a sample of teachers, parents or children may yield useful information about various aspects of the life and work of the school. There should be some questions which are definite and can be analysed by computer as well as questions which allow for personal comment. It is always wise to pilot questionnaires with a small group in order to discover whether they produce information which is useful, whether the language is ambiguous and also to investigate the best way to analyse them. It should be remembered in using questionnaires

that the information gained will be limited by the questions asked. It is always helpful to use interviews of a sample group as a back up to questionnaires.

- Test results

All teachers devise tests for their own use and many use some form of standardised test material. SATs will also offer information.

Tests should ideally be selected according to purpose. National testing is mainly a matter of accountability but offers useful information to the teacher about children's learning. Other testing may be to discover the stage children have reached and whether they are ready for the next stage of learning or teaching. The teacher may test to discover which children have acquired the skill, knowledge or understanding required, how individual children perform relative to their peers, the difficulties individuals are experiencing and their nature, how children are best grouped for learning and the effectiveness of the teaching of a group. Testing may also reveal how children set about a task.

- Records and statistics

A school also needs records of personal achievement for children. These normally cover many aspects of school life and often involve assessments by children. They provide information for parents as well as for the next school.

There are also statistics about the school which should be on computer which yield interesting information when analysed. Attendance records of staff and attendance and truancy records of children are obvious examples.

The role of the headteacher in evaluation

Finally we need to consider the role of the headteacher in evaluation. As headteacher you must ensure that the evaluation policy and programme are in place and carried out. You are also an evaluator who is involved in identifying the problems and needs of the school community in order to do something about them. In theory you have greater opportunities for access to what is happening in all parts of the school than anyone else. In practice it is important to work at this. It can be done informally but it needs to be systematic.

You also need to sample what is happening in classrooms, seeing all staff at work from time to time, working to make this a positive activity. You also need to sample children's work, perhaps collecting in the work of a particular group or sample of individuals.

This kind of evaluation is all too easy to forget under the many pressures that headteachers find themselves under today. But if the headteacher does not do it, no one else will and important aspects of the school's life may be the poorer.

Chapter 16

Personal organisation

As headteacher you need not only to perform management tasks competently and be skilled in different aspects of the role but also be able to organise so that your personal time and energies are used to the best advantage. In today's schools this is far from easy. There have been many new demands on headteachers in recent years and no easing of previous demands to compensate. This makes the ability to manage time even more important. Being well organised is a matter of knowing yourself and having the self-discipline to maintain routines and priorities. You need to know how to get the best out of yourself.

To be well organised you must know your own strengths and weaknesses. You need to recognise the tasks you are most likely to avoid and the activities in which you most like to be involved. You need to know when you are being self-disciplined and when you are being self-indulgent. Sometimes this self-knowledge will lead you to delegate to others tasks you know you do badly. It may also affect the appointments you make, particularly where your deputy is concerned, since you may well be appointing someone who complements your own strengths.

You may be a person who likes to have everything tidy and well planned and this means you must work so that this is possible. No headteacher can afford to be disorganised so if you are untidy by nature you must work to overcome this.

THE USE OF TIME

There is a good deal of evidence to suggest that being a headteacher is a job in which it is not easy to organise time. The study by Hall *et al.* (1986) of headteachers at work and Coulson's study (1986) both look at what headteachers actually do with their time and both demonstrate the problems and show the way in which a headteacher's time is broken up by a stream of demands. This has become even more difficult since these studies were undertaken. Both bring out the need for headteachers to be single-minded about their priorities. The study of secondary school headteachers shows that while the headteachers studied demonstrated a variety of different styles of leadership, most of them gave insufficient time to staff development and to issues of curriculum planning. This is probably rather better now since the need for a School Development Plan makes demands for planning but it is probably still true to some extent in both primary and secondary schools. The primary headteacher study showed clearly the way in which the good headteacher used the opportunities which came to influence events towards a particular vision of where the school was going.

It is also a matter of knowing how you work best. Most people have a time of day when they are at their best. Some people work best early in the morning; others late at night. This knowledge has implications for the time for tackling difficult problems and work which is taxing. Some people work best in short spells; others work better when they can have a long spell of uninterrupted time. If you are unable to work when you are constantly interrupted this means that you must either make yourself unavailable occasionally or save major tasks for out of school time. If you are a full-time teacher in charge of a small school you will have to do this anyway.

None of us can increase the time we have. We can only look for better ways of using it. The meaning of the word 'better' in this context will depend upon what you are trying to do. Once aims and priorities have been established you have a yardstick for assessing the way you are actually using time. Your achievement must in the end be measured by what actually happens as a result of your actions.

There are some tasks vested in the role of the headteacher. For example, the headteacher represents the school to the outside world and time must be given to this. The headteacher is also the main point of contact for governors and the LEA. There are many occasions when the headteacher's agreement must be sought, occasions when you must function as the official leader of the school. A headteacher who opts out of any of these tasks may lose the confidence of the school community.

You also have a unique role as the ultimate authority in the school. This makes your praise and blame special and this is a part of the office which must be accepted and used for the good of the community.

You also have an important role in ensuring that there is adequate planning, development and evaluation and in seeing that the management tasks listed in the previous chapters are undertaken though not necessarily undertaking them yourself. You must be aware of what is happening in the school and be seen frequently by teachers and children. This means being out of the office and around the school for some part of the school day. You also need some time to get organised each day and time for personal refreshment. Sometimes the best way to deal with a problem is to lay it aside and seek relaxation.

Most primary headteachers, particularly headteachers of small schools, feel they are continually at everyone's beck and call and it is difficult in these circumstances to consider planning time. Yet if you analyse how you are using your time and consider how much of it you can in fact control, there is quite a surprising amount of time in this category. If you also assess how much time is used each week in dealing with events which just came up, like the desperate parents who came into school or the caller who used your time or the investigation of money stolen, you will find that there is some consistency over a period, about the amount of time used in this way. If you then write off an equivalent amount of time each week in your diary for events of this sort you are in a position to plan the use of the remaining time. This involves being firm with yourself and others about using this time in the way you plan. You will still need to interrupt this time to deal with events which occur, but you will have some planned time each week.

This is a good deal more difficult for the headteacher who also has full-time charge of a class. Tasks like seeing others teach, evaluating and influencing what is happening in the school are much more difficult. A good deal of this kind of activity must be made to come within the teaching programme so that you evaluate to some extent by exchanging classes, influence by team teaching and so on. As a teaching head you must make a special point of training your children to work independently. This is important for all children, but particularly so in this situation where you may be called upon to leave them on a number of occasions. If you are able to leave them for short periods, you are in a position to look into other classrooms and see what is happening. You may also be able to do some reorganising of the school from time to time to allow for this. Many small schools have part-time help and you need to plan its use very carefully so that you undertake the really important tasks of headship.

The starting point for improving the use of time is diary analysis. Every headteacher should take time to analyse his or her diary at regular intervals. It is also profitable to keep for a week or so a much fuller account of what happens noting the time which is spent on planned and unplanned activities, tasks undertaken which could only be undertaken by the headteacher and those that could have been delegated. Diary analysis will make clear how much time there is available for planned activity.

Another analysis which yields useful information is a study of all the interruptions which occur during the course of a day. If you keep a list of these on several occasions it may become possible to see whether the number of interruptions could be decreased or whether some of them could be confined to a particular time of day. People differ in the extent to which they can accept interruptions, so this is a matter of personal ch. It is important to be able to get uninterrupted time when it is nece

Many people find that, when they analyse their use of tin

much that they feel they should be doing but have not the time to do and very little which they feel they can give up!

This is where the priorities come in. It may be helpful to examine the following questions:

- How does the pattern of what I actually do differ from the pattern of what I think I should be doing?
  Look particularly at areas in which you are spending more time than you feel you should and see whether there is any way in which you can change things, perhaps by delegating more or deliberately not doing some things in order to have time for other more important tasks.
- Is my time being properly divided among people?
  As headteacher you must be seen to give time to each individual teacher as well as to children, ancillary staff, parents, governors, LEA staff and so on. It may be helpful to check on the actual people you are seeing over a period.
- How much of my time is planned and how much unplanned?
  A primary headteacher's day is by nature varied and changing and a good deal of time is used on events which just occur. What is important is that there is also time for planned activities. It is very easy to spend all one's time on dealing with incidents as they happen and never get round to such tasks as planning and evaluating except in an *ad hoc* way.
- What is getting interrupted?
  It is easy to use the constant demands on one's time as an excuse for not doing the tasks which you find difficult or less interesting. This can happen without your realising it and a check is helpful in avoiding this particular pitfall.

The answers to these questions create further questions about how to find more time in an already over-full programme. What must be given up? How can more time be found? The following might be examined:

Are you too accessible?

Many headteachers take pride in having an ever-open door and in being easily accessible to staff, parents and children. When teachers and others speak of the headteacher as being accessible they usually mean first of all that if they want to ask a question related to their day-to-day work the headteacher is easy to find. They also mean that the head is available and prepared to listen if they have a problem or something on which they want the headteacher's opinion. Parents also like to feel that they can just drop in and see the headteacher and most primary headteachers welcome the fact that children also like to come and talk to them.

Although this is partly a matter of people feeling that they can see you when they want to rather than when you have time to see them, it is also a matter of your attitude when people come to see you. If you are norm-ally welcoming many people will be prepared to wait a while to see you provided that they can have your undivided attention when they do see you. In fact your undivided attention tomorrow may be better than half your attention today. People have to wait to see you when you are out of the school, so there is no real reason why they should not sometimes wait to see you if you are doing something which you consider to be im-portant. You will have to make decisions about how important it is for someone to see you right away but you should sometimes be prepared to put your own work first.

If yours is a large school there may also be a case for people seeing other senior members of staff on many issues and this should limit the need for the headteacher to deal with some matters.

The other thing to remember about availability is that someone with a problem does not want time with you constantly interrupted by the door opening or the telephone ringing. You need to develop mechanisms for spending uninterrupted time with individuals. If you can do this for an individual, you can do it for your own work from time to time. The ability to ensure uninterrupted time when it is needed cannot be pursued at the same time as total accessibility. A balance is needed.

There is much to be said for setting aside time which will only be interrupted for genuine emergencies. This will provide opportunity for con-centrating on the needs of individuals and on matters such as forward planning and evaluation. If you do this regularly and everyone knows that Wednesday afternoons, for example, are sacrosanct, this will be accepted.

Extent of delegation

Diary analysis will show the extent to which you are using time on jobs which are neither specifically part of the headteacher's role nor need your personal abilities. If there are many of these perhaps too little is delegated. It is worth noting how often people come for advice or decisions which could have been given or made by somebody else. If this is happening too frequently you may be delegating too little or people may lack under-standing of where you stand on a number of issues or you have insuffici-ent policies which tell people how to act in a given situation.

Are your systems efficient?

A school needs systems for dealing with all recurring procedures which take the minimum time to implement for everyone concerned. Matters like obtaining new stationery, collecting dinner money, organising wet playtimes all need systems so that everyone knows what to do and when to do it. This saves time.

Computers make many things easy. If all the relevant information about the school is on a database, lists can easily be drawn up for any purpose. Spreadsheets make calculations easy and word processing has many applications which save time. Standard and duplicated forms of communication help to use time well since they reduce to the minimum the writing necessary and ensure that all the information needed is given.

The filing system needs to be organised so that you and anyone else who needs to use it can can find their way around it if the secretary is away and this will be particularly important for your personal filing which should include a system for bringing forward material when it is needed.

Headteachers rarely have training in office practice and the process of dictating letters takes time to learn. It is easy to waste time writing out letters in longhand to be typed, particularly if your secretary does not do shorthand. The quickest way to prepare material for typing is to use a dictation machine. This allows you to learn to dictate without anyone listening because it does not matter how long you take to think what you want to say. It also enables you to use odd moments effectively and it can be used anywhere. It is an efficient use of the secretary's time because he or she does not need to be present when you dictate and can go at a personal speed in typing back.

Drafting is even easier if you learn to use a word processor. Even if you are a very indifferent typist the ability to shift around blocks of type and change parts of what you have written make it very much easier to achieve a good result.

How do you use short periods of time?

It is very easy to waste short periods of time and they add up to a considerable period over the course of a week. It is valuable to have a number of jobs which can be undertaken in the ten minutes before a visitor arrives or the quarter of an hour before lunch.

How much time do you spend teaching?

Headteachers of primary schools are normally expected to do a reasonable amount of teaching and in many authorities are counted as part of the teaching strength of the school. Headteachers in very small schools are full-time teachers anyway. This must not divert you from the task of leading the school, although you may do some of the leading from the classroom.

The important thing to remember is that if you have a choice about how much teaching you do, the reasons for your choice of teaching particular groups at particular times are well thought out. There is so much to be done as a headteacher that you need to think carefully about any use of your time. You may, for example, decide that you want to sample classes at each stage in the school so that you get a feel for the different groups within the school. You may decide to teach some classes as part of the process of evaluating the work of the school. You may want to help staff to develop new ways of working and may choose to do this by working alongside a teacher or you may wish to complement the work of your teachers by, for example, dealing with children with reading problems or contributing a particular skill which is lacking among the staff at the present time. The actual amount of teaching that you do should be such that you have time left for all the important aspects of being a headteacher. You need time to observe other teachers, time for planning and evaluating as well as time for day-to-day chores.

One positive way of managing time is to make or add to a 'to do' list every morning, grading tasks A, B, or C or highlighting those which are urgent. You then try to concentrate on the highlighted tasks or those graded A, breaking them down into smaller tasks to make them more manageable. Another useful suggestion is that you try to handle each piece of paper which comes across your desk only once, deciding as it comes in what to do with it. It is all too easy to shuffle that paper on your desk to get it into order and feel that you have achieved something. There is also a case for keeping a clear desk so that you have room for the material on which you are currently working.

Perhaps the most pointed question you need to ask yourself on frequent occasions is 'Does what I am doing now forward the learning of the children?' There will, of course, be many things which you are required to do as headteacher which have only a tenuous connection with children's learning but it is all too easy to be drawn into doing all kinds of things which neither forward the learning of the children nor are part of the headteacher's responsibilities. It all adds up to the need for constant vigilance about the use of time.

STRESS

In chapter ten we looked at stress in relation to the staff of the school and the headteacher's need to be aware of the signs of stress in colleagues. We also need to look at stress in headteachers.

A headteacher's role is undoubtedly a stressful one. Dunham (1992) cites role conflict and role ambiguity as two of the major causes of stress in schools and this certainly affects both headteachers and other senior members of staff. Role conflict for the headteacher is the result of different people having different expectations of someone holding this office. When you first become a headteacher you are made aware that staff, parents and children all have expectations about the way headteachers should behave which may be contrary to your own views of the head-teacher's role. Different people may also hold contrary expectations of you and you quickly discover that whatever you do will please some people and displease others. This makes the first weeks in a new post particularly stressful.

There are also demands on primary headteachers on issues for which they have not been trained. Work on finance, for example, makes demands. So does the management of the school office and tasks like dictation and filing. Headteachers may also be faced with such issues as things that go wrong with the school boiler or electrical equipment – the list is endless and while in many cases there will be others, such as the caretaker and other members of staff who can advise you, the decisions about what to do are yours.

You may very well find yourself getting irritable over trivia with people, very often those at home. You may feel a sense of panic at the amount to be done and the lack of time for doing it and yet feel too tired and exhausted to get started. This is particularly true at the end of term when one often feels that another day is just too much. Or you wake up in the middle of the night worrying about how much there is to do.

A certain amount of pressure gets the adrenalin going and stimulates you, allowing you to draw on reserves of energy. Too much creates a psychological state where you find it difficult to work efficiently and also a physical state in which muscles become tense and which may eventually lead to ulcers and heart attacks.

A number of suggestions for coping with stress were given in chapter ten. It is particularly valuable to have some interests outside school especially if you live alone. Stepping outside one's professional role is not easy. Headship is an absorbing occupation and you do not stop thinking about it when you leave school. Talking about it to someone sympathetic is helpful and many husbands and wives offer this kind of support.

CONCLUSION

This book sets out to explore some of the major issues involved in running a primary school. The process is a complex one and there are many good ways of carrying out this role depending upon individual personality and individual circumstances. You can learn a good deal about it but in the end each person has to select an appropriate style for himself or herself. Your style in the first instance tends to be influenced by the headteachers you have encountered and you may copy or reject some of the ways in which they worked. Gradually you learn what works for you in your particular circumstances and develop your own style which is different from anyone else's.

Your style also needs to fit your school. Different schools may require a rather different kind of leadership and it is a mistake to go to a second headship thinking that what worked in the first will work equally well in the second. Each school needs to be studied.

The various analyses given are intended to help the reader to identify personal priorities and decide how best to work as a particular person in a given situation.

No action is isolated. Everything one does affects something and someone else. In seeking to achieve one particular development you may also help to achieve or hinder another. As headteacher you are at the centre of a complex pattern of relationships and communications so that what you do affects many others. You need a clear vision and the ability to transmit thinking and draw other people's ideas into a common vision so that the school community moves forward by a creative consensus. You also need a wider view of the local community and a sense of being part of the total process of educating young people into the way of life of our society. This requires not only professional commitment but a sense of perspective.

Most people who achieve headship have clear ideas about education but they need to go on developing and modifying ideas and extending them in the light of experience as well as absorbing the changes coming from central government. You also need to continue to read and study so that you are aware of research findings about aspects of primary education and are able to help your staff to apply any which seem relevant. A headteacher also needs to go on being a student and an enthusiast.

Leadership in a school involves liking not only children but also adults and enjoying working with them, confident in your relationships and able to use the skills of leadership developed in the process of gaining experience in senior posts. A leader needs to be a good listener, able to interpret other people's behaviour and make each person feel that he or she really matters and has something of special value to contribute. A good headteacher is skilled in helping teachers to develop their work and in guiding and counselling them.

To be a good headteacher one must be a good organiser. You must see that life in the school runs smoothly and that little time is wasted on minor matters. You need skill in identifying and tackling problems, with strategies for helping others to meet and resolve difficulties, giving them confidence that there can be a satisfactory outcome to many problems and building on growth points. A good leader is good at delegating and ready to allow the staff to take decisions, helping them to think through to a conclusion and evaluate the consequences. You need positive attitudes to change and development, even when it is unwelcome.

In all this it is important that you have good self-knowledge and are aware of your personal limitations and fallibility as well as strengths, are self-critical and use feedback from colleagues. You need to be open-minded, recognising and using ideas appropriately whatever their source.

You also need to be well organised and able both to set and to maintain priorities. A leader who has a clear sense of direction, held rationally as well as intuitively, who has a balanced view and is able to stand back from the job, will be able to withstand pressure and cope with the stresses which are inevitable in headship. You need both analytical skill and the ability to work intuitively, sensing how people feel and responding to them. It helps if you have creative ability in generating ideas to deal with new situations but you also need to be ready to recognise and use the ideas of others.

This picture of the headteacher demands a mature and balanced human being who is knowledgeable, skilled and caring and able to undertake successfully all the tasks involved. Headship is difficult and demanding. We are fortunate as a nation in having so many people who are able to do well this difficult and demanding job.

References

Adler, M., Petch, A and Tweedie, J. (1989) *Parental Choice and Educational Policy*; Edinburgh: Edinburgh University Press.

Alexander, R. (1992) *Policy and Practice in Primary Education*; London: Routledge.

Alexander, R., Rose, J. and Woodhead, C. (1992) *Curriculum Organisation and Classroom Practice in Primary Schools*; London: Department of Education and Science.

Arden, J. (1991) 'Cheques and balances'; *Times Educational Supplement Update*; October 3.

Atkin, J., Bastiani, J. and Goode, J. (1988) *Listening to Parents*; London: Croom Helm.

Audit Commission (1991) *Management within Primary Schools*; London: HMSO.

Barnes, C. (1993) *Practical Marketing for Schools*; Oxford: Blackwell.

Back, K. and Back, K. (1982) *Assertiveness at Work*; London: McGraw-Hill.

Bastiani, J. (1993) 'Parents and as partners: genuine progress or empty rhetoric?' in Munn, P. (1993) *Parents and Schools: Customers, Managers or Partners*; London: Routledge.

Beare, H.,Caldwell, B. and Millikan, R.H. (1989) *Creating an Excellent School*; London: Routledge.

Bennett, N., Desforges, C., Cockburn, A. and Wilkinson B. (1984) *The Quality of Pupil Learning Experiences*; London: Lawrence Erlbaum Associates.

Bennett, N. and Kell, J (1989) *A Good Start? Four year-olds in Infant Schools*; London: Open Books.

Bennett, N. (1992) *Managing Learning in the Primary School Classroom*; Stoke-on-Trent: ASPE/Trentham Books.

Boulton, M.J. and Underwood, K. (1992) 'Bullying/victim problems among middle school children'; *The British Journal of Educational Psychology*; February.

Brighouse, T. and Tomlinson, J. (1991) *Successful Schools* (Education and Training Paper No. 4); London: Institute for Public Policy Research.

Brown, G. and Wragg, E.C. (1993) *Questioning*; London: Routledge.

Caldwell, B. and Spinks, J.M. (1988) *The Self Managing School*; London: Falmer.

Carrington, B. and Short, G. (1989) *Race and the Primary School*; Windsor: NFER-Nelson.

Cave, E. and Demick, D. (1990) 'Marketing the school' in Cave, E. and Wilkinson, C. (eds) *Local Management of Schools: Some Practical Issues*; London: Routledge.

Cave, E. and Wilkinson, C. (eds) (1990) *Local Management of Schools: Some Practical Issues*; London: Routledge.

CIPFA/LGTB/SEO (1988) *The LMS Initiative; Local Management in Schools; A Practical Guide*; London: CIPFA/LGTB/SEO.

Coulson, A. (1986) *The Managerial Work of Primary School Headteachers*; Sheffield: Department of Management Education, Sheffield City Polytechnic.

Critchley, B. and Casey, D. (1986) 'Managing effective teams' in Mumford, A. (ed) *Handbook of Management Development*; Aldershot: Gower.

Deal, T.E. (1985) 'The symbolism of effective schools'; *The Elementary School Journal*; vol. 85. no.5; 601–20.

Dean, J. (1991) *Professional Development in School*; Milton Keynes: Open University Press.

de Bono, E. (1976) *Teaching Thinking*; London: Temple Smith.

Denham, C. and Leiberman, A. (1980) *Time to Learn*; California, USA: US Department of Education and The National Institute of Education.

Department of Education and Science (1978) *Primary Education in England*; London: HMSO.

DES (1982) *Education 5 to 9: An Illustrative Survey of 80 First Schools in England*; London: HMSO.

DES (1988) *S222 Education (Modification of Enactments Relating to Employment)*; London: DES.

DES (1989a) *Planning for School Development; Advice to Governors, Headteachers and Teachers*; London: DES.

DES (1989b) *English in the National Curriculum*; London: HMSO.

DES (1990) *Circular 7/90*; London: DES.

DES (1991a) *Development Planning – A Practical Guide*; London: DES.

DES (1991b) *The Parents' Charter: You and Your Child's Education*; London: DES.

DES (1991c) Statutory Instrument (SI 1991/1511) *Education (School Teacher Appraisal) Regulations*; London: DES.

DES (1991d) *School Teacher Appraisal*, Circular 12/91; London: DES.

Doe, B. (1992) 'How to make your school safe'; *Times Educational Supplement*; May 22.

Douglas, J.W.B. (1964) *The Home and the School*; London: MacGibbon and Kee.

Dunham, J. (1992) *Stress in Teaching (2nd ed)*; London: Routledge.

Dunne, E. and Bennett, N. (1990) *Talking and Learning in Groups*; Leverhulme Primary Project, London and Basingstoke: Macmillan.

Eckholm, M. (1976) *Social Development in School*; Goteborg, Sweden: The Institute of Education, University of Goteborg.

Elliott, J., Bridges, D., Ebbutt, D., Gibson, R., and Nias, J. (1981) *School Accountability*; London: Grant McIntyre.

Elton Report (1989) *Discipline in Schools: Report of the Committee of Enquiry*; London: DES and the Welsh Office, GBDS.

Fayol, H. (1949) *General and Industrial Management*; London: Pitman.

Fisher, R. and Ury, W (1987) *Getting to Yes (4th ed)*; London: Arrow Books.

Fletcher, M. (1991) 'In the market for understanding'; *Times Educational Supplement*; September 23.

Fullan, M. and Hargreaves, A. (1991) *What's Worth Fighting For in Your School?*; Milton Keynes and Ontario, Canada: Open University Press and Ontario Public School Teachers' Federation.

Fullan, M. and Stiegelbauer, S.(1991) *The New Meaning of Educational Change*; London: Cassell.

Galton, M. and Simon, B. (1980) *Progress and Performance in the Primary Classroom*; London: Routledge and Kegan Paul.

Galton, M., Simon, B. and Croll, P. (1980) *Inside the Primary Classroom*; London: Routledge and Kegan Paul.

Galton, M., Patrick, H., Appleyard, K., Hargreaves, L. and Berbaum, G. (1987) *Council Provision in Small Schools*; The Prisms Project, final report; Leicester: University of Leicester Mimeograph.

Galton, M. (1989) *Teaching in the Primary School*; London: David Fulton.

Galton, M. (1992) *Group Work in the Primary Classroom*; London: Routledge.

Hall, V., Morgan, C. and Mackay, H. (1986) *Headteachers at Work*; Milton Keynes: Open University Press.

Hallinger, P. and Murphy, J. (1986) 'The social context of effective schools'; *American Journal of Education*; vol 94, no. 3, 329–55.

Handy, C. (1976) *Understanding Organisations*, Harmondsworth: Penguin.

Handy, C. (1981) *Understanding Organisations* (2nd ed); London: Penguin.

Handy, C. and Aitken, R. (1986) *Understanding Schools as Organisations*; London: Penguin.

Hargreaves, D. (1984) *Improving Secondary Schools*; London: Inner London Education Authority.

Harrop, A. and McCann, C. (1983) 'Behaviour modification and reading attainment in the comprehensive school'; *Educational Research*; vol. 25, November, 191–5.

Hegarty, S. (1993) 'Home–school relations, a perspective from special education' in Munn, P. (ed) *Parents and Schools: Customers, Managers or Partners*; London: Routledge.

Herzberg, F., Mauser, B. and Snyderman B. (1959) *The Motivation to Work*; New York: Wiley.

HMSO (1974) *The Health and Safety at Work Act*; London: HMSO.

HMSO (1988) *The Education Reform Act*; London: HMSO.

HMSO (1992) *The Children's Act*; London, HMSO.

Kelly, V. (1983) 'Research in the primary curriculum' in Blenkin, G. and Kelly, V. (eds) *The Primary Curriculum in Action*; London: Harper and Row.

Kyriacou, C. (1989) 'The nature and prevalence of teacher stress' in Cole, M. and Walker, S. (eds) *Teaching and Stress*; Milton Keynes: Open University Press.

La Fontaine, J. (1990) *Bullying: the Child's View*; London: Calouste Gulbenkian Foundation.

Lawrence, J., Steed, D. and Young, P. (1984) *Disruptive Children, Disruptive Schools*; London: Routledge.

Lewis, A. (1991) *Special Needs and the National Curriculum*; London: Routledge.

Little, J.W. (1982) 'Norms of collegiality and experimentation: workplace conditions of school success'; *American Educational Research Journal*; 19, 325–40.

Macbeath, J. and Weir, D. (1991) *Attitudes to School*; Edinburgh: Jordanhill College.

Macbeth, A. (1993) 'Preconceptions about parents in education' in Munn, P.(ed) *Parents and Schools: Customers, Managers or Partners*; London: Routledge.

Makins, V. (1991) 'Five steps to peace in the classroom'; *Times Educational Supplement*; November 1.

Makins, V. (1993) 'The hard road from hope to glory'; *Times Educational Supplement Update*; January, 10.

Mancini, V., Wuest, D., Vantine, K. and Clark E. (1984) 'The case for instruction and supervision in interaction analysis on burned out teachers: its effects on teaching behaviours, level of burnout and academic learning time'; *Journal of Physical Education*; vol. 3. no. 2.

Margerison, C. (1978) *Influencing Organisational Change*; London: Institute of Personnel Management.

Marshall, C. and Mitchell, B. (1989) *Women's Careers as a Critique of the Administra-*

tive Culture; Paper presented at an American Educational Research Association Annual Meeting.

Montgomery, D. (1984) *Evaluation and Enhancement of Teaching Performance*; London: Kingston University.

Morgan, C., Hall, V. and Mackay, H. (1983) *The Selection of Secondary School Headteachers*; Milton Keynes: Open University Press.

Morgan, C. (1984) *A Handbook on Selecting Senior Staff for Schools*; Milton Keynes: Open University Press.

Mortimore, P., Simmons, P., Stoll, L., Lewis, D. and Ecob, R. (1988) *School Matters*; London: Open Books.

Munn, P. (ed) (1993) *Parents and Schools: Customers, Managers or Partners?* London: Routledge.

National Association of Governors and Managers (1988) *Building an Effective Governing Body*; London: NAGM.

National Association of Secondary School Principals (1982) *The Effective Principal*; Reston, VA, USA: NASSP.

National Curriculum Council (1989a) *A Framework for the Primary Curriculum*; *Curriculum Guidance 1*; York: NCC.

NCC (1989b) *A Curriculum for All: Special Educational Needs in the National Curriculum*; *Curriculum Guidance 2*; York: NCC.

NCC (1989c) *Planning for School Development*; York: NCC.

NCC (1990)*The Whole Curriculum*; York: NCC.

NCC (1991) *Development Planning – a Practical Guide*; York: NCC.

NCC (1993a) *Planning the National Curriculum at Key Stage 2*; York: NCC.

NCC (1993b) *Spiritual and Moral Development: A Discussion Paper*; York: NCC.

NCC (1993c) *The National Curriculum at Key Stages 1 and 2; Advice to the Secretary of State*; York: NCC.

OFSTED (1993) *Handbook for the Inspection of Schools*; London: HMSO.

Oldroyd, D. and Hall, V. (1988) *Managing Professional Development and INSET*; Bristol: National Development Centre for School Management Training.

Oxley, H. (1987) *The Principles of Public Relations*; London: Kogan Page.

Piaget, J. (1932) *The Moral Judgement of the Child*; London: Routledge and Kegan Paul.

Plowden Report (1967) *Children and Their Primary Schools 2 vols*; Report of the Central Advisory Council for Education in England; London: HMSO.

Poster, C. and Poster, D. (1991) *Teacher Appraisal: A Guide to Training*; London: Routledge.

Pugh, G. (1989) 'Parents and professionals in pre-school service: is partnership possible?' in Wolfendale, S. (ed) *Parental Involvement: Developing Networks between Home, School and Community*; London: Cassell.

Reid, K., Hopkins, D. and Holly, P. (1987) *Towards the Effective School*; Oxford: Basil Blackwell.

Reynolds, D. (ed) (1985) *Studying School Effectiveness*; London: Falmer Press.

Roberts, T. (1983) *Child Management in the Primary School*; London: George Allen and Unwin.

Rolph, S. (1990) *Budgeting and Equipment for Schools*; London: Hobson.

Rutter, M., Maughan, B., Mortimore, P., Ouston, J. and Smith, A. (1979) *Fifteen Thousand Hours*; London: Open Books.

Sallis, J. (1990) 'Working with others' in *Governing Bodies Now*; Report of the DES Conference, Stratford-upon-Avon; November; DES.

Schools Examination and Assessment Council (1990) *Assessing the National Curriculum*; London: SEAC.

Smith, D. and Tomlinson, S. (1989) *The School Effect: A Study of Multi-Racial Comprehensives*; London: Policy Studies Institute.

Strain, M. (1990) 'Resource management in schools: some conceptual and practical considerations' in Cave, E. and Wilkinson, C. (eds) *Local Management of Schools: Some Practical Issues*; London: Routledge.

Suffolk Education Department (1987) *Teacher Appraisal: A Practical Guide, Part 3*; Ipswich: SCC.

—— (1993) *Teacher and Headteacher Appraisal*; Kingston: SCC.

Tizard, B., Blatchford, D., Burker, J., Farquar, C. and Plewis I. (1988) *Young Children at School in the Inner City*; Hove and London: Lawrence Erlbaum.

Tizard, B. and Hughes, M. (1984) *Young Children Learning*; London: Fontana.

Tizard, B., Blatchford, P., Burke, J., Farquar, C. and Lewis, I. (1988) *Young Children at School in the Inner City*; Hove: Lawrence Erlbaum.

Tomlinson, S. and Hutchinson, B. (1991) *Bangladeshi Parents and Education in Tower Hamlets*; London: Advisory Centre for Education.

Tomlinson, S. (1993) 'Ethnic minorities: involved partners or problem parents?' in Munn, P. (1993) *Parents and Schools: Customers, Managers or Partners*; London: Routledge.

West Sussex Education Committee (1991) *GEN: The Governors' Newsletter*; March, Chichester: WSCC.

Wheldall, K. and Merrett, F. (1984) *Positive Teaching: the Behavioural Approach*; London: George Allen and Unwin.

Wilkins, J.A. (1990) *Restructuring Education after the Reform Act – The Role of School Governors: A Headteacher Perspective* (Occasional Paper Series no.1); Milton Keynes: Education Reform Research Group, School of Education, Open University.

Woods, P. (1989) 'Stress and the teacher role' in Cole, M. and Walker, S. (eds) *Teaching and Stress*; Milton Keynes: Open University Press.

Wragg, E.C. (1987) *Teacher Appraisal: A Practical Guide*; London: Macmillan.

Index

ability 46; grouping 38, 77
Adler, M. *et al.* 100
administration: school 105–19; tasks
  of 107–8
advice 114
age differences, effect of 76
aims 20–4
Alexander, R. 1, 87; on equal
  opportunities 43–4; on good
  practice 20, 80; on group work 49;
  on Leeds Primary Needs
  Programme 3, 38–9, 86; on
  recognising potential 76–7
Alexander, R. *et al.* 37; on mixed age
  groups 76; on subject teaching 57;
  on teaching strategies 58
analysis: of diary 134, 233; of
  management tasks 14–17; network
  30–2, 95; school 26–9; SWOT 101;
  of use of time 87
ancillary staff 24
appointments: applications for
  179–81; application forms 181;
  evaluation of 184–5; further
  particulars 180–1; job description
  179; person description 179–80;
  reports on candidates 181; short
  listing 182; staff 178–85
appraisal 137, 139, 185, 191–3;
  interviewing 192–3; observation
  192
Arden, J. 137
art 87
assessment 34; of the current state of
  the school 223; formative 228;
  objectivity of 228; reliability of 228;
  subjectivity of 228; summative 228;
  validity of 228

assertive behaviour 156
Atkin, J. *et al.* 208, 210
attitudes 19, 43–6, 72; and change 89
audit 25
Audit Commission 24
authority 3, 9

Back, K. and Back, K. 156
Barnes, C. 98, 102
Bastiani, J. 206
Beare, H. *et al.* 2; on collaboration
  and effectiveness 24
behaviour: assertive 156; children's
  120–9; staff 178–85; leadership 132;
  patterns of 122–9
Bennett, N. 38, 58; on assessment for
  diagnosis 127–8; on group work
  58; on talking about ideas 73; on
  underestimating children 45, 76
Bennett, N. and Kell, J. 216
blocked units of work 57
Boulton, M.J. and Underwood, K. 49
boundary, managing the 8–9
boys 86–7
Brighouse, T. and Tomlinson, J. 206
Brown, G. and Wragg, E.C. 39
budgeting 111–16; incremental 112;
  zero 112
buildings 116–19; maintenance of 116
bullying 49–50
burnout 143

Caldwell, B. and Spinks, J.M. 4; on
  budgeting 111–12; on conflict 142
care, philosophy of 120–1
caretaking and cleaning staff,
  responsibility for 116
Carrington, B. and Short, G. 208–9

Cave, E. and Demick, D. 101
Cave, E. and Wilkinson, C. 115
change: agent 90; consultation about
    91; defining 92; evaluating 95–7;
    identifying change needed 91–2;
    implementing 94; information
    about 91; involvement in 90–1;
    managing 89–97; preconditions for
    92–3
check lists 229
children 36–52; able 39–42, 45; their
    appearance 103; their behaviour
    120–9; their developmental needs
    36–9; with disabilities 45;
    egocentricity in 36; with learning
    difficulties 40; least able 40;
    monitoring development of 42;
    their self-images 37; their views
    about school 100
Children's Act 207
CIPFA 113, 115
citizenship 69
class: age-grouped 77; mixed age 76;
    social 45; working 45
classroom, organisation 80
clerical tasks 106
coherence of curriculum 69–72
communication 19, 162–77; with
    adults in the school 165–66, 168;
    with children 168–70; effective 173;
    evaluating 176–7; feedback from
    175; with governors 35; inferential
    172–3; oral 163; with parents 35,
    103, 210, 212–14; skills of 67;
    system 171–3; with teachers 165–7;
    written 103, 163–4
community: policy 34, 99;
    relationships 22; and school
    200–19; as a resource 219
complaint, receiving a 150–1
computer, information held on
    110–11, 236
concepts 62
conflict 142
consultancy 114
consultation 91
continuity 66; in curriculum 69–72
contributory schools 217–18
coordinators, curriculum 83–4;
    responsibility for health and safety
    119; specialist 78
Coulson, A. 231

Critchley, B. and Casey, D. 75
criteria, success 23
culture, school 8
curriculum 21, 53–72; coherence
    69–72; continuity 69–72;
    coordinators 23, 83–4; definitions
    55–6; development 72; hidden
    55–6; inferential 56; intended 55–6;
    philosophy 53–6; planning 56–69;
    progression 69–72; subject-based
    56–7

Data Protection Act 164
de Bono, E. 67
Deal, T.E. 8
Dean, J. 191–2
decision making 34; and change 90
delegation 106, 11113, 1337, 235; of
    authority 134
Denham, C. and Lieberman, A. 85
Department for Education 2
Department of Education and
    Science 5–6; on appraisal 193; on
    English in the National
    Curriculum 216; on governors'
    responsibilities 201; Parents'
    Charter 207; planning booklets 10,
    211; on school day 85–6; on school
    development plan 24–5
department head, infant or first
    school 83
deputy head 82–3; negotiating the
    role of 155; responsibilities 83; and
    stress 143
development: child 21, 36–9, 120,
    194; moral 51–2, 125–6;
    organisation 82; personal and
    social 21; professional 22, 185–99;
    programme 193–8; social 47–50;
    spiritual 47, 126; stages of 36;
    teachers' development 193–4
diagnosis, of needs 39
diary analysis 134, 233
dimensions 62, 66
discipline 34–5; policy 123; staff
    140–1
discontinuity for children 69–71
discussion 38; class 80; with parents
    211, 213–14
Doe, B. 119
Douglas, J.W.B. 206
drama 49–51

Dunham, J. 143; 237
Dunne, E. and Bennett, N. 58; on
　cooperative group work 81, 126

Eckholm, M. 37; on social
　development 48–9
education: for economic
　understanding 68; environmental
　69; European 44, 68; health 69;
　multicultural 44–5, 68; personal
　and social 68, 120–9; religious 56;
　and society 54; world 44, 68
Education Reform Act 10, 201, 212,
　215
effectiveness 3, 6–8, 18
egocentricity 36
Elliott, J. et al. 100
Elton Report 122
encouragement, importance of 6
English 86
environment, creating an attractive
　117; education for the 69, 87;
　responsibility for 116–19
equal opportunities 34, 66, 42–7;
　policy 42–3; programme 46–7
ethnic minority parents 215
evaluation 10, 32, 220–30; for
　accountability 221–2; for
　accreditation 221; approaches to
　229; by children 227–8; of
　delegated responsibilities 135–6;
　for individual development 220–1;
　for managing learning 221;
　planning 31, 66; policy 34;
　processes 228–9; purposes of
　220–2; role of headteacher in 230;
　self- 227–8; of staff development
　programme 197–8; system 227–8;
　of work of governors 205–6
expectation 8–9, 37, 45, 146
experience 38, 62; and learning 73;
　first hand 73
expressing: boredom 148;
　embarrassment 148; views of
　relative status 148; tension 148
eye contact 147

Fayol, H. 3
filing 109, 236
finance management 111
Fisher, R. and Ury, W. 155–6
Fletcher, M. 101–2

Froebel 54
Fullan, M. and Hargreaves, A. 2, 187;
　on interactive professionalism 72
Fullan, M. and Stiegelbauer, S. 1, 7,
　89–90

Galton, M. 38; on change 96–7; on
　group work 58–9, 81, 126; on
　dealing with misbehaviour 122–4
Galton, M. and Simon 49
Galton, M. et al. 58–9; on class
　discussion 80; on group work
　126–7; on intermittent workers 86
gender 43–4
girls 86–7
governors 23; role in appointments
　178–9, 183–4; involvement in
　change 95; and public relations
　99–100; relationships with 203–4;
　responsibilities of 119, 202; role of
　9, 203–4; skills and knowledge
　needed by 205; training of 204–5;
　working with 201–6
grounds, maintenance of 116
group: behaviour 194; leadership
　157–60; presenting material to
　148–9; size 80; skills 126–7; work
　49, 58, 81, 94
grouping: by ability 38, 77; by age
　77; collaborative 38; for learning
　74; mixed-age 78; vertical 78

Hall, V. et al. 231
Hallinger, P. and Murphy, J. 8
Handy, C. 6; on organisation
　activities 82; on dealing with stress
　144
Handy, C. and Aitken, R. 24; on
　appraisal 193; on group work 73
Hargreaves, D. 55
Harrop, A. and McCann, C. 124
headteacher: accessibility 234;
　personal organisation 231–40; as
　representative of the school 201;
　role 230, 232; style 238–9
health: education 69; and safety
　legislation 119
Health and Safety at Work Act 119
Hegarty, S. 212
Her Majesty's Inspectorate (HMI), on
　mixed-age groups 75–6
Herzberg, F. et al. 131

home visiting 214
hygiene factors 131

income 115
individual work 58
induction 189–90
industrial understanding 68
influence: through environment 131; through exchange 131; through force 130; through knowledge 130; through personal friendship 131; through persuasion 131; positional 131; through reward 130
information needed 164; by adults in school 165–6, 168; by children 168–71; by governors 170–1; by parents 171–2; by teachers 166–7
information technology 68, 110–11
INSET days 24
inspection 229
insurance 114, 117
interpersonal situations: common features of 146–8; effect of discomfort 147; reactions to 147–8; skills 146–61; effect of venue 146–7
interviewing: for appraisal 192–3; to criticise someone's work 151–2; an individual 149; for information 149; for problem-solving 150; to receive a complaint 150–1; to refuse a request 153; for staff selection 182–4

jargon 103; 212
job, description 179; satisfaction 131

Kelly, J. 54
knowledge 62, of learning and teaching 194; self- 231; structuring 55

La Fontaine, J. 50
language 38, 62, 86; and experience 73, 162–3
Lawrence, J. et al. 124
leadership 1–19; behaviour 132–3; characteristics 239; effectiveness 132–3; negotiating 154; qualities of 4; role 10–12; skills 12, 127; style of 5, 10–12; tasks of 5, 12–18
leading discussion
learning 74; difficulties 40; independent 19, 223; organising

73; process 223; skills 39; social 68
legislation 144–5
lettings 115
Lewis, A. 40
Little, J.W. 24; on school improvement 90; on teachers working together 175, 186
local management of schools (LMS) 106, 115, 205

Macbeth, A. 206, 210
Makins, V. 89; on classroom behaviour 123–4
management 1–19; role 11; skills 12; structure 81–4; style 10–12; tasks of 5, 12–18, 20
managing adults 13, 130–45
Mancini, V. et al. 143
manners, good 122
marketing: organising 102; the school 98–104
Marshall, C. and Mitchell, B. 10
mathematics 86
meetings 157–60; class 210; with parents 211–12; preparation for 157–8; the working session of 158–60
mixed age groups 76
monitoring: continuity 70; the development of children 42; expenditure 115–16; the School Development Programme 32
Montgomery, D. 39
Morgan, C. et al., 12, 178, 183
Mortimore, P. et al. 1, 58, 75; on collaboration and effectiveness 24; on deputy headteachers 82–3; on effective factors 7; on group work; 126 on reading and behaviour 124; on rewarding good behaviour 124; on team work 74; on whole class teaching 58
motivation 130–2
Munn, P. 207–8

National Association of Secondary School Principals (NASSP) 9–10
National Curriculum 18, 20, 40, 42, 44–5, 55–67, 70, 72, 76, 78, 83, 127–9, 178, 205, 207–8, 213–14
National Curriculum Council: on moral and spiritual development

47; on separate subject teaching 57; on units and blocks 57; on *The Whole Curriculum* 68–9
National Foundation for Educational Research (NFER) 50
National Insurance 114–15, 137
needs: assessment 196–7; diagnosis of 39; matching 40
negotiation 154–7; with governors 154–6; of leadership 154; with parents 154; principled 155–6; with teachers 154; with ancillary staff 154; with children 154; with unions 155
network analysis 30–1, 95
newly qualified teachers 190
numeracy 67

objectives 23
observation 38–9; for appraisal 192, 229
OFSTED 48–9, 51, 227–8
Oldroyd, D. and Hall, V. 186
ORACLE study 58, 80, 86
organisation 34, 73–88; classroom 80; effective 74; patterns of 77–80; principles for 74
Oxley, H. 98

parents 23–4; black 209; Charter 207; choice of school 100–1; in the classroom 215–16; as clients 211–12; communication with 207; ethnic minority 215; helping their children 41; involvement of 95–6, 206–17; meetings 103; surveying views of 99; as partners 121, 209–11; and public relations 100–1, 200; working class 209
pastoral care 34
Pay and Conditions document 114
pay, performance related 137
peer: group 37; tutoring 37
performance indicators 32; 222
personality 12–13
Piaget, J. 51
planning: curriculum 56–69; evaluation 31–2; long- and short-term 24; making and implementing the plan 30–2; policy 34
Plowden Report 54, 121

policies 32–5; appraisal 185, 188; assessment and evaluation 34, 223, 227; community relationships 34; continuity 71; curriculum 33; discipline 34, 123; equal opportunities 34, 46; organisation 33; pastoral care 34; personal and social education 126; planning and decision making 34; salary 137; staff development 34, 185–93; study skill development 67
POST project 12–13, 178
Poster, C. and Poster, D. 185
power 9
prejudice 43
problems: solving 67; personal 138; professional 138–9; relationship 141–2
process 55
professional development 178–99; evaluation of programme 197–8; modes of 186–8, organisation of 188–9; policy 188, programme 189–90, 193–8
progression, in curriculum 69–72
project work 79
public relations 98–104; objectives 101–2; responsibility for 104
Pugh, G. 209

questioning 39
questionnaires 229–30

race 44–5
racism 45
records 70, 230; of achievement 128; background 128; day-to-day 128; personal development 128, quick reference 128; staff 198–9; system 127–9; of work done 128
Reid, K. *et al.* 7; on collaboration and effectiveness 24
relationships 146; parents 23–4; secondary school 23
reliability of assessments 228
religious education 56, 61
reports 128; on teachers 165, 182; to parents 213–14
requests, refusing 153
resources 62; inventory 88
review, annual 24–5
Reynolds, D. 24

Roberts, T. 41, 121; on teacher expectation 124
role conflict 237–8
Rolph, S. 115, on selecting equipment 117–18; on security of equipment 118
Rousseau 54
Rutter, M. *et al.* 10

safety, of children 121
salaries 113–15; policy 137
sampling 228
school: administration 105–9; appearance 103; building 22, climate 123; and community 200–19; contributory 217–18; day 86; environment 22, 88; grounds 88; handbook 168; learning 88; office 106, 109–11; prospectus 103; rules 123; secretary 109; transfer 217–18
School Development Plan 10, 94, 189, 222–3, 232; costing 31; making and implementing 20–35
School Examinations and Assessment Council (SEAC) 213
science 55
secondary transfer 70
secretary, school 109
selection, staff 35, 178–85; materials and equipment 117–18
self-esteem 37–8
self-image 37–8, 68
setting 77
short listing 181–2
skills 62, 67; interpersonal 146–61; with people 146–61; study 67; social 126
space, use of 88
special needs 40–1
specialist teaching 78
staff: ancillary 24; caretaking and cleaning 119; deployment 84–5, 185–99; development 11, 22, 34, 85, 135–7; discipline 140–1; kitchen and dining room 116; motivation of 130; part-time 84; problems 137–42; records 198–9; selection 178–85
stakeholders 101
statistics 230
storage 88, 117–19
Strain, M. 112

streaming 38, 77
stress 142–44, 237
style 10; autocratic 11; collegiate 11; democratic 11
study skills 67
subjects 59
Suffolk LEA, papers on appraisal 192
superannuation 114–15, 137
supervision 121
Surrey LEA, paper on school development plan 25, 32; appraisal document 192
suspension 125
systems 235

talk, preparing and giving a 148–9; with an individual 149–154
teachers: burnout 143; class 78; deployment of 84; learning needs 185; learning opportunities 195–6, 189–90; newly qualified 190; peripatetic 114; unions 145
teaching: assistants 77; effective 76, 80; individual 80; skills 195; specialist 76–8; strategy 59; subject 57; team 78–80; time spent 236; whole class 58
team: characteristics of good team 75; teaching 78–80; work 1, 6
technology 67
testing 230
themes 62; cross curricular 66
time: managing 237; planning 59, 61–2, 233–4; priorities 234; for reflection 190; on task 85–7; use of 31, 85–7, 231–7
timetable 87
Tizard, B. *et al.* 58; on parental interest in education 207; on feedback to parents 208; on teachers' views of black parents 209; on discussion with parents 214; on use of time in infant classes 86
Tizard, B. and Hughes, M. 206
Tomlinson, S. and Hutchinson, B. 215
topic work 41, 57, 59
transfer schools 217–18
truancy 50–1

units of work 57; continuing 59; blocked 59
unions, teacher 145

validity of assessments 228
values 7, 8, 37, 51, 56; and change 89,
    96, 99, 142
vertical grouping 78
vision 2, 8, 12, 232, 239

West Sussex newsletter for

governors 205
Wheldall, K. and Merritt, F. 123
whole class teaching 58
Wilkins, J.A. 203
Woods, P. 143
world education 4
Wragg, E.C. 191